The Canadians

The Canadians

BIOGRAPHIES OF A NATION

Patrick Watson

McArthur & Company

Toronto

Canadian Cataloguing in Publication Data

Watson, Patrick, 1929 –
    Canadians: biographies of a nation

Companion volume to the television series, Canadians: biographies of
a nation.

ISBN 1-55278-170-4

1. Canada – Biography. 2. Canadians: biographies of a nation
(Television program). I. Title.

FC25.W37 2000   971'.009'9   C00-931507-1
F1005.W37 2000

Composition and Design by *Michael P. Callaghan*
Typeset at *Moons of Jupiter, Inc.* (Toronto)
Cover by Mad Dog Design Connection, Inc.
Original cover concept by Carol Powers
Printed in Canada by *Transcontinental Printing*

McArthur & Company
322 King Street West, Suite 402
Toronto, ON, M5V 1J2

ONTARIO ARTS COUNCIL
CONSEIL DES ARTS DE L'ONTARIO

10 9 8 7 6

The publisher wishes to acknowledge the financial support of
the Government of Canada through the Book Publishing Industry
Development Program (BPIDP) for our publishing activities.
The publisher further wishes to acknowledge the financial support
of the Ontario Arts Council for our publishing program.

ACKNOWLEDGMENTS

The television series *The Canadians: Biographies of a Nation*, was conceived by Patricia Phillips and Andy Thompson, and originally commissioned by Norm Bolen and Sydney Suissa at History Television, with the financial support of Charles and Andrea Bronfman's CRB Foundation and later of HISTOR!CA, the new foundation that has taken over the Heritage Project initiated by the Bronfmans. The idea of a book based on the series was the brainchild of Michael Levine and publisher Kim McArthur without whose relentless attention and entrepreneurial adroitness it would never have come to fruition.

Patricia Phillips, who not only supervised the whole television series as Executive Producer but also wrote and directed a number of episodes, has been endlessly helpful in the preparation of this book. The individual producers, writers and directors have been credited at the end of each chapter, but I add my thanks here for their patience and generosity when I needed clarification or additional information while writing the book.

Caroline Bamford edited the original manuscript and the subsequent rewrites, and has diligently and creatively done wonders in insuring clarity, relevance, and readability. I claim personal credit for the errors and omissions that remain in the text.

Patrick Watson
November 2000

Contents

◇ Introduction ◇

THE CANADIANS
BIOGRAPHIES OF A NATION

Thank God they never yielded to any vagrant impulse to do some reverently cosseted showcase on *The Great Canadians*! Four years ago, when Great North Productions' Andy Thompson and Patricia Phillips sold the as-yet-unlaunched History Television on a series of biographies, both Great North and HTV were clear from the beginning that this documentary anthology would *not* be reverent. It would traverse a wide spectrum of lives lived in Canada, ranging from scoundrel to genius. It might include a politician or two; those favourite and easy targets of the television news machine have certainly left our video archives full of political footage. But Andy Thompson told me in an early telephone conversation that he and Patricia (who would be the series' Executive Producer), did not want celebrities: the CBC had already staked out the *People Magazine* territory with its *Life and Times* and was delivering solidly within that particular mandate. Andy said that he and Patricia wanted good storytelling with characters whose lives had some texture, significance, risk and human meaning attached to them. His pilot project was Bob Duncan's life of Francis Rattenbury, the architect of the British Columbia Legislature and the Empress Hotel. That story is an astounding pastiche of murder, adultery and genius, and an effective antidote to the poisonous canard about Canadians being dull. It proved a very satisfying demonstration of the quality of program hoped for, and we are saving it for volume II of this series of books based upon the television programs.

I became involved at the beginning of the second broadcast season when HTV asked me to take over from Shelley Saywell, who was leaving for another job, as Commissioning Editor of the series, and to host it as well. It seems odd in retrospect, since the assignment has been so rewarding in many ways, but at first I hesitated. I had spent six or seven years on our 12-part series *The Struggle for Democracy*, first broadcast in January of 1989. It had been seen in some thirty countries around the world. History Television had decided to rebroadcast it. I had flirted with the idea of a comparable series on *The Idea of God*, but had set that aside. I had been working since 1988 on *Heritage Minutes* sponsored by Charles Bronfman's CRB Foundation. The satisfactions of tight, economical dramatic writing and production had me feeling that my forty years of documentaries had – besides being enormously exciting and satisfying – been a preparation for my taking the *material* of documentary storytelling and investing it with the mythic power of fiction. *Rerum factum est.* Things are what we make them. I had become fascinated with invented drama that probed into the human realities *behind* the documents.

There were, however, several factors that finally nudged me to accept the History Television assignment. The CRB Foundation, as well as generously funding the wonderfully successful *Minutes*, was also a sponsor of History Television's biographies, and I was Creative Director of that foundation. The series' first year under Shelley Saywell had broadcast work that I admired very much. There was also a kind of reverse concern, about helping the series avoid what I see as a growing threat to the documentary: the dramatic recreation. This is a device that documentary directors sometimes resort to as a solution to the challenge of visual storytelling where there is a shortage of original documents in the form of film or photographs or living witnesses, the primary *materia medica* of the documentary. The recreations are more often than not distracting; they demand that the viewer suddenly shift gears from accepting that what is being shown and told is a documented account of events that really happened, to an imagined scene that is usually not very well done. Sometimes, in contrast, where the budgets and skills are available (which is rare in television documentary) the recreations have been so well produced that they can be passed off as authentic historical footage. This was done in several NFB productions in the early 1980's. In one a police raid on the clinic of a controversial Montreal doctor was presented as footage shot by a cameraman who accompanied police on the raid. In fact it was a brilliantly produced fake. Other producers were being tempted by the excitement of these frauds – a form of pure deception or television lying that is especially reprehensible because, presented as documentary, it leads viewers to believe that what they have seen actually happened.

But more often than not, the dramatic recreation is distracting and disruptive because of its crudeness. Audiences are trained by film and television drama to expect a level of production that few documentary budgets or skills pools can provide. I believed I could help the producers and directors working on *The Canadians* to find solutions to the shortage of historical footage that would remain within the documentary form and tradition, and convey authentic and useful information.

It is our hope, all of us who plan and produce and broadcast these programs, that the stories that follow will give the reader an appetite to seek out the original documentaries, either in their video cassette release or in rebroadcast. I have appended the 2001 broadcast schedule and a note on how to find the cassettes. Many of the films have considerable value in the classroom as well as in the living rooms of that increasingly vocal part of the Canadian population who are fascinated with the stories about who we are and how we got to be the way we are.

I have written elsewhere that the first historical question is very personal, private, and local: It is "Mummy, where did I come from?" All subsequent historical questions, if they are meaningful, descend from this one. History is the process of making some kind of sense out of the world, *our* world, that is, the world as we see it from where we live. A vital part of the process is the meaningful investigation of the lives of people who share our culture and our territory, and have met the challenges and opportunities of their lives the way they do because, in large measure, they are formed by the values and the stories *and the land* that we all share.

What we have done in this volume is to select sixteen of the documentaries from the first four years of production, stories which, like the series itself, range widely across the spectrum of human activity. Each of the chapters that follow is a sort of extended review of the programs as broadcast. Something like the reviews in *The New York Review of Books,* which often give you a sufficiently comprehensive digest of the original book that you can make an informed judgment as to whether or not the book itself is something you should read. If even one of these reviews provokes enough interest in you, the reader, that you want to know more about that person and send for the video or head for the library to track down one or more of the *Additional Reading* titles I have noted at the end of chapters, then my hopes for the book will have been realized.

To order a video:

Online:
www.history.ca
click on "History Television Boutique"

By mail:
Viewerplus
90 Eglinton Avenue East
Toronto, Ontario
M4P 2Y3

By Phone: (416) 486-1227
or Fax: (416) 482-7186

VHS Copies are $29.95, plus shipping and handling.

<><Part One <>

PERCY WILLIAMS
Running Out of Time

On a grey afternoon in 1984, a frail man in dark pyjamas and bare feet walked into the bathroom of his apartment in West Vancouver. Painfully, slowly, he put first one foot then the other over the side of the empty bathtub, and stepped into it. A slight man, five-foot six, 125 pounds, moving slowly.

An old man with no family, no friends, no prospects; alone, sick, poor, out of luck, at the end of his road. In his right hand a six-shot .32 calibre revolver.

He had heard a lot of pistol shots in his life, this man. He had heard them in Vancouver, in Seattle, in Hamilton Ontario, in New York, and perhaps best of all in Amsterdam, at the Olympic games there when he was only eighteen years old. For him those pistol shots had almost always signalled the start of a race he was going to win.

Not this one. There is reason — as you will see at the end of his story — to speculate whether just at the last moment he may have felt a twinge of irony, maybe even of some dark kind of humour, if he reflected on the fact that those shots in Amsterdam had started him on two brief runs, totalling less than thirty-three seconds — two runs that would earn him the title The Fastest Man in the World. But now he was quite slow in his movements. His shoulder hurt grievously as the hand came up. This pistol shot would be the last sound he would ever hear.

He was seventy-four years old.

His name was Percy Williams. He had grown up in a Vancouver that was mad for track and field. It was also a Vancouver where people who got married were expected to stay together, and if they did not they were expected not to talk about it. Percy's mother and father were Dorothy, known as Dot, who took tickets at the Capitol theatre, a vivacious good-looker who hung out with theatre people, and Fred, an electrical engineer who did not like theatre people.

Dot used to invite actors and their friends home for elaborate supper parties that drove Fred nuts. Perhaps Percy drove Fred a little bit nuts too, with his obsessive training for the 100-yard dash. But Dot liked Percy's running, and Fred probably quarrelled with her over that as well, and after a while they broke up. When they finally divorced, Percy of course stayed with Dot. In fact, Percy Williams would end up living most of his adult life with his mother. She kept on encouraging him to run.

Perhaps he associated the running with his family's coming apart, for it seems that Percy, even as he realized he was getting to be very good at it, didn't really like running very much. This is not uncommon with athletes. In many cases it is because, having had their talent discovered by a coach or a parent, they have been put under a lot of pressure to prove themselves — not because the young athlete wanted this kind of life, but because some adult wanted to bask in the glory of the kid's success. That kind of pressure was part of Percy Williams' problem with the running, and maybe the family disputes were another part. But there was one aspect of the track that he did like: winning, and he won a lot. And so he kept on at it. Once Bob Granger saw him run in a physical education class at the high school, it almost seemed that there would be no way out of it, even if he came to hate it completely. Bob Granger was that kind of coach.

He was not, however, a professional coach, not even a physical education teacher; he was the janitor in the high school. But he was an amateur coach. He loved coaching runners. As janitor he had the run of the school and he used to hang around the PE classes when they were doing track and field; nobody minded, he was just the janitor. He would watch out for talent he thought he could apply his theories to.

He had read a lot about how great athletes develop, and he had some theories, and he was looking out for the kind of runner who would allow him to turn his theories into practice: medal-winning practice.

Granger already had a young runner named Wally Scott who was good, really good, but not good enough to stop him looking for talent, visiting those PE classes, keeping his eyes peeled. And when he first saw Percy Williams run, this slight kid with the skinny arms and legs and the big Adam's apple and the intense, slightly pouting look as he knelt into the holes you used to dig for starting from, he must have said to himself, "This is the one."

And he would be right. Bob Granger and Percy Williams became a team that would astound the world.

Granger not only knew runners, he knew what they ran on. He thought about all the conditions of the track.

Soft tracks, wet tracks. Grass, cinders, clay. Wind speed, air temperature, humidity, slopes and curves. Everything he did on the track was part of an integrated strategy. He did not work from hunches; he had strategy.

For example, the American coaches in those days were obsessed with the stopwatch, with record-setting times, because that was what made the headlines, a world's record for the 100 metres at the Olympics, say, of eleven-point-one seconds. But unlike the American coaches, Bob Granger didn't run his boys against the clock. He ran them against other runners.

He would tell his runners something like this: "You are there to beat the other men, beat them in the final. Don't try to take the lead out of the starting pits. Run beside them. Let them get tired setting the pace and worrying about you. Then put on the steam at the end and beat them in the final, on *that* day, in *those* conditions. Don't even think about the time. Let somebody else worry about the time. It's winning that counts, beating other runners, not beating the clock."

Percy Williams liked beating other runners, so he heard Bob Granger loud and clear. And they became a kind of couple. Bob Granger needed Percy to be the embodiment of his theories. And Percy Williams needed Bob Granger because Percy Williams really liked to win. There was no point running if you couldn't win. And Bob Granger was going to teach him how to win.

Granger would put him up against another very good runner, and set the other boy's starting blocks five yards ahead of Percy's, maybe even ten yards. They used yards in those days, not metres. A yard is just under a metre, .9144 metres to be exact. Percy would run races in metres a little later, in Europe, but here in Vancouver you ran in yards. So the other boy would be given a ten-yard advantage, and Bob Granger would say, "You have to be ahead of him before you hit the hundred-yard mark. Pace him at first, and learn when it is you have to pull ahead. And then you beat him in the final."

And Percy would do just that.

Bob Granger had dropped Wally Scott by then; he would keep on coaching a number of runners, "My boys," he called them. But from now on, Percy was his Prime Boy.

Bob Granger was a reclusive, difficult man, and Percy Williams was not very comfortable with other people, except his mother. He was really uncomfortable with girls. If other male athletes were partly motivated by the opportunity to impress a girl, the only female whose admiration Percy sought was Dot Williams. And Dot came through for him. But so did Bob Granger, and although the relationship was a difficult one, for neither the boy athlete nor the coach was good at relationships, in this case they recognized their need for each other.

Historians of the sport say that Percy would have stopped running after high school if it hadn't been for Bob Granger. But Granger knew he had found an authentic and maybe even unique talent. He put Percy in the Vancouver Grand Championships in 1927. Percy was just seventeen.

It is surprising, in a way, that he was running at all. They had told him when he was fifteen that he should definitely not engage in any strenuous activity. The doctors had diagnosed rheumatic fever. Anything that would strain his heart might kill him. But maybe the doctors were wrong, because under Bob Granger's demanding, constant presence, Percy just got stronger and faster, and more and more sure of himself.

That's what a coach does, more than anything else, by the way. He is present. He is a dynamic mirror in which the athlete can search for his strengths and weaknesses, and a constant source of the kind of human contact that says, often silently, "What we are doing together counts; it is meaningful; it will have consequences." Bob Granger was present, and with that presence there was always the strategy. And the object of the strategy was Percy Williams. To win. Not to place or show; to win.

Percy Williams won that Vancouver race, the 100 yards, in 10 seconds flat, uphill on a grass track, and Bob Granger was pounding his hands on the fence where he watched, pounding his hands with delight. A few weeks later it was Seattle, the prestigious Seattle championships, and the small-boned, slightly muscled boy won again, 9.9 seconds.

And now it was time for Hamilton, Ontario, a kind of pre-Olympic year meet to take a look at the coming talent. Granger entered Percy, again for the 100 yards.

With Dot's help Percy managed to scrape together the money for train fare. But Bob Granger had no money, and no Dot; so he hired himself on as a dishwasher on the CPR dining car, and that is how he got to Hamilton.

There were tryout heats, just like the Olympics. You ran against other candidates in heat after heat and the winners of each heat would be candidates for the final race, the real race. There was a group of officials who would choose, from among the candidates, whoever they thought promising enough to go on to the finals. The officials were men in straw boaters. They wore blazers, and on the blazers were always badges. So the athletes called them the Badgers. Although the track had only five lanes, the Hamilton Badgers picked six finalists, and then decided to toss a coin to see which of the six would be dropped, and they dropped Percy Williams.

He was too good a sport to quarrel with the Badgers, but he hated them from then on.

The following year, 1928, was different — the real tryouts for the Olympics. Bob Granger knew his boy would qualify. It was Hamilton again. This time there was no nonsense about the number of lanes, and this time — with no surprise to Bob Granger or the increasingly confident young runner — Percy won the trials going home, beat them in the final, and Amsterdam beckoned.

The official coach of the Canadian men's track team was an ex-soldier and high-school teacher named Cap Cornelius. There was no room for the outsider, Bob Granger. Percy and Granger both knew that they had to be together, and Granger persuaded Percy to go on ahead, he, Bob, would find a way. He hired himself onto a cattle boat shovelling manure, the worst job he had ever had, he said; but he was able to get wireless messages, with training advice, to Percy on his boat during the ten-day transatlantic crossing. Bob Granger arrived in Amsterdam a few days after Cap Cornelius had started training the Canadian boys.

Percy was so grumpy, training under a strange coach and fretting about Bob Granger, that Cap Cornelius concluded that the skinny little British Columbian couldn't possibly win anything anywhere. And so when Granger turned up and said he would take over Percy's training, Cornelius was glad to be rid of the wimp.

The American athletes stayed on a luxury liner in the harbour. The European and British athletes mostly stayed in five-star hotels, and so did the Badgers. But the Canadian boys were sent to a crummy two-star hotel. It was down in the red-light district, noisy with traffic and night voices, no place for athletes to get the good, peaceful rest that Granger believed was a key to success. Granger would harass the Amsterdam police in the streets, asking them to try to quiet the crowd down. "We've got Olympic athletes sleeping in there!" Then he would get a blanket and a pillow and bunk down on the floor outside the door of Percy's room, and shush and shoo away anyone who came on the floor making the slightest noise that might wake up his candidate.

In the morning he would waken Percy, and then after breakfast they would go back up to the room and take the mattress off the bed, and put it up against the wall as a stopper. This way Percy could practise his starts in the little room and get up to speed in three or four paces and have something soft to bump into. Thump! Thump! Thump! It echoed throughout the little hotel.

Starts had been Percy's weak point. They couldn't get time on the track to practise as much as they needed, but here in the room, between the two of them they worked out all the tiny little fine-tunings and grace notes of that crucial first second of the race, and Percy's starts became spectacular.

The heats began. The Americans were sure to win, everybody knew that. The Americans would win and the Brits would come second, or third maybe, after the Germans. The Canadians? Well, who cares, really.

Bob Granger applied some more theory. He told Percy, "You don't have to win the heat, you know. If you come in second you go on to the next heat. Just pace your guy and size him up and keep moving up the heats and you'll be okay." And Percy did that, and the Americans always tried to win and some of them tired themselves and had to drop out but Percy did not tire himself, won some heats, came second in others, moved up and up.

And qualified.

The "final" was scheduled for 4 p.m., July 30th. A hot day was forecast but it turned cold. While the other runners were down on the chilly track digging their starting pits, Granger kept Percy back in the tunnel wrapped in a thermal blanket until the very last second, then sent him down, still comfortably warm, to dig his starting pits just in time for the pistol, no shivering, warm and fit and ready to run.

There was a pistol shot, that reverberated in memory a long time.

And 10.8 seconds later — this was metres, not yards, so it was equal to almost 110 yards, 109.36132 yards to be exact — 10.8 seconds later a young unknown Canadian had astounded the stadium, his country, the world, by beating them all — the Americans, the British, even the Germans. Almost a record but not quite; that would come later. He stood up there, slight and small, beside a tall powerful black man on one side and a tall powerful white European guy on the other side, and he was the world's champion.

He wrote in his diary, "Well well well I am the world's 100-metre champion. Crushed apples, no more fun running any more."

But in fact there was a lot of fun to come.

First it was Bob Granger who, watching the race from behind the link fence, had this time pounded his hands so hard on that fence that they were bleeding. He didn't seem to notice. He suddenly decided to enter Percy in the 200-metre, 4 days later. Percy had never run the 200; he was a sprinter. Cap Cornelius was totally against it and so was the Committee.

But it is hard to say no to a coach whose boy has just won gold. So Percy began to train, and to run the qualifying heats. And a few days later, when the pistol went off, it took him exactly 21.8 seconds to beat them all again, and head for the podium to collect his second Gold Medal.

The Canadians in Amsterdam went wild. The women's team sent Percy flowers. Those women would set some records themselves that week, and the versatile Bobbie Rosenfeld (see *Part Fifteen*) would make her own gold-medalled mark as a heroine athlete. But it was Percy Williams who was the toast of Amsterdam. Even the British came over and lined up with the Canadians as the Empire against the Yanks. They all wanted to stand in the glow that radiated from The Fastest Man in the World. Then in London, Paris, Dublin, where he ran exhibition races before heading home, the crowds came to gawk and then to cheer.

And so, it seemed, did everybody in Canada. He was mobbed in Quebec City, Montreal, Toronto, Winnipeg. At last we had a national athletic hero, undisputably the best in the world. In the Vancouver Parade Dot and Bob Granger rode with him in the lead car, and even his father Fred showed up, but only in car number six.

The Vancouver sports officials knew that the young star would be wooed by American universities, which had already begun the practice of offering very substantial sports scholarships. There was no counterpart in Canada, so they pledged to raise $25,000 to send him to UBC, and even came up with a gift of $500 for Bob Granger. They also hired Granger to take Percy on the road doing exhibition meets in the States, to build the publicity they would need in order to raise that 25 grand. There was no television then, people who hadn't been to the movies when the newsreels played hadn't seen Percy's win, and the Gold Medal races had not quite been world's records so the American press had not made much of Percy. The only way to really make him famous was to arrange for people to see him "live."

It was pretty audacious, what they did. They exposed him to almost certain defeat. Granger put him up against the best college athletes across the whole United States, twenty-one races in twenty-two days. He would get up, have lunch, run a race, get on a train, sleep, get up, have lunch, run another race. All of his opponents were fresh; he was running every day. He ran on concrete, which he had never done before, and he ran on boards, also for the first time. He ran one race that was 70 yards, so he had to pace himself radically differently against a champion who always ran 70 yards, and another at 80 yards. And he won and won. Twenty-one races and he won nineteen of them.

Sports historian Bill McNulty now says that the two Percy lost were "flyers," which means that the guys who beat him made false starts, were out of the blocks before the pistol shot but were not called back by the officials, who clearly did not want the Canadian kid to win. McNulty calls it the Tour of Guts.

That had been the summer of 1929. He came home in triumph. He publicly tore up the $25,000 scholarship an American university had just sent, and enrolled at UBC. But Vancouver never did raise their $25,000, only 14,000, which was a lot of money all right, but not what had been promised. And anyway Percy found that university life was not really for him, and at the end of the first year he dropped out. He went to business school and learned how to sell insurance, and got a job doing that, and kept on running.

In August of 1930 he finally set a world's record, the 100 metres in 10.3 seconds. That record would stand for eleven years. In late 1930 he went down to the first ever British Empire games in Hamilton, and told everyone that he was in the top of his form. Perhaps he was, but this time Bob Granger was not with him, and neither was Bob Granger's thermal blanket, and the weather was cold. As he came out of the blocks Percy was still cold. Something was wrong with his left leg. He could sense it coming, and at the forty-metre mark something went snap, a muscle had pulled. It hurt like hell but he kept going. The pain was almost overwhelming but this time he had uncharacteristically pulled into the lead early in the race. He held that lead and he won the race. But something was wrong. He was hurt. He would never win another race. He was the British Empire Victor, and that was a great triumph. But it was his last.

Nobody was ready to believe it was his last, not Granger, not Percy himself, certainly not Vancouver or the Canadian Olympic Committee, and so of course off he went to Los Angeles for the brilliant, showy 1932 Olympics. Once again there was no money for Bob Granger's travel, and Granger came up with a scam, a kind of lottery, using some of his other athletes to sell the tickets. But the Olympic Committee is said to have found out about this and put the cops on him, and so he was disgraced and never made it to Los Angeles. Percy had to do without him, but even had Bob Granger been there the leg injury from the Hamilton British Empire Games was giving him so much trouble that he never even made it into the finals.

He never raced again.

Percy Williams was probably relieved to be done with it. That is what he said, anyway. He told people he was glad it was over. But not Bob Granger. Granger's nephew

Frank, now an old man himself, says that for "Uncle Robbie," it was the end of a dream.

It was also the end of the relationship. They met only once more, on a bus, by accident, in 1948. But they had nothing to do with each other, ever again. Bob Granger could not make a living coaching his boys, so he drifted from menial job to menial job, sweeping parking lots, picking up bottles, living in a little room over a barber shop.

"A beautiful person had lost touch with himself," Frank Granger says. Bob started to drink, and died alone in 1970.

When World War II broke out, Percy had joined the air force and spent much of the war in Saskatchewan training navigators. He came to love airplanes and flying, and maintained that interest for years. He took up horseback riding again, which he had learned with his father. Later he fell in love with golf.

The Vancouver sports establishment had begun to show mixed feelings about the fastest man in the world when Percy came back into civilian life after the war. In 1953 when a local newspaper wanted them to name the new stadium they were building for the Commonwealth Games "The Percy Williams Stadium," the Committee said no. The Badgers again. "He didn't give anything back to track and field," they said. Whatever that meant. So they wouldn't use his name. In the 1960's a Vancouver physician and coach, Doug Clement, put together what would become an annual track meet and got Percy to agree to call it The Percy Williams Invitational. But Percy disappointed

Dr. Clement, showed very little interest in the meet, did not show up at the dinners and press conferences and other publicity events, and generally left a bit of a sour taste all around. So the next year they dropped the name.

George Parkes, who was Percy's chief in the little insurance company where he was now working very diligently and successfully, is inclined to excuse Percy saying that he was actually a very shy person. "Unusual for an insurance salesman," says Parkes, "but he was." You can see it in the photos. The smile of triumph after a win, or in a victory parade or at an awards ceremony, is a wide, appealing smile. It transforms the small, somewhat tight face. But it is not a cocky smile. It is the smile of a man who could, indeed, be quite shy.

Perhaps that had something to do with the drinking. He had discovered golf, and gradually golf replaced flying and horses, and became something of an obsession. He was soon playing three times a week. Although he often refused to have a drink with his boss, George Parkes, saying "I don't do that," in fact he was staying late at the prestigious Capilano Golf and Country Club, where he very much valued his membership, staying late and drinking at the bar. And, worse, drinking alone at home. A lot.

He still lived with and looked after his mother, until she died in her 90's in 1978. He briefly had a girlfriend. They were together a great deal until she despaired of Percy's drinking and told him that he had to make a choice: her or the bottle. Percy chose the latter. So now he had nobody to go home to.

Before long he had no golf club to go to either. He had taken to staying very late in the lounge, and was caught, as a friend kindly put it, "imbibing other people's liquor." They took away his membership in the Capilano, perhaps the only thing that he really cherished any more, besides the drink. He was disgraced. At that point Percy Williams more or less disappeared from view.

In 1982 he had two strokes. They left him weak and in pain. He had bad arthritis in his knees, indeed in all his joints. In 1950 a Canadian Press poll had chosen him the half-century's greatest track athlete, and in 1972 that was upgraded to "Canada's all-time greatest Olympic athlete." But if that gave him comfort, it was not enough, and so he stepped into that bathtub with one of the guns from his considerable collection. He left no note. As was still occasionally a custom of kindness in the media of those times, no mention was made there of how he died. He had simply . . . died. There is a fine bronze statue of him at the Vancouver Airport. You can see it there.

There are two footnotes. One is that to celebrate his Amsterdam Gold Medals he had been presented with a symbolic pistol, which he kept all his life, in a collection of guns that in the end became quite big. The one he chose to kill himself with was the Amsterdam Gold Medal presentation pistol.

The other footnote is that he had donated those Olympic Gold Medals to the Vancouver Sports Hall of Fame, but within weeks after they went on display, they were stolen and never recovered. Bob Duncan wrote, at the end of his film biography of this great athlete, that Percy

Williams "simply shrugged off the loss, and no replacements were ever ordered."

◆ ◆ ◆

Percy Williams: Running Out of Time was written by Robert Duncan and directed by Annie O'Donaghue. Camera, John Collins, Doug Sojquist; sound, Buddy Schwadant, Lisa Kolisnyk. Editor Janice Brown. It was first broadcast on History Television on November 22, 1998, and will be rebroadcast in the spring of 2001.

◇ Part Two ◇

RUBY KEELER
The Queen of Nostalgia

Sometimes in the story of a very ordinary person who accomplishes something extraordinary, it is difficult to tell whether circumstance and accident (or "fate," as we once would say) handed that person something which lifted them, all unconscious, to extraordinary heights . . . or if there was a special strength in that person, a strength that somehow remained hidden, even after her accomplishments made her famous and thus the object of great scrutiny and the asking of questions.

In the case of Ruby Keeler, it was so common as to be expected after a while that at the end of her extraordinary life people would say, "But she was really just like everybody else, you know." Here was this kid from Dartmouth, Nova Scotia, who went through New York to Hollywood, made a string of very successful movies, had a near-disastrous marriage to the most prominent entertainer in the world, left him, found her way into a homey marriage and children with a good and uncomplicated and very private man, eventually returning to Broadway and reaching a new level of stardom when she was a sixty-year-old grandmother. Yet people kept saying, "Well, she was really, you know, *ordinary*. There was nothing that *outstanding* about her."

Audiences did not think she was ordinary. When she put on the tap-dancing shoes and came downstage and launched into one of her staccato, thundering numbers, they were rapt, enchanted. They stood and applauded and yelled for more. And yet today the tap-dancing teacher our filmmakers consulted, trying to reach some understanding of this woman's astounding success, could say that, well, compared to say Fred Astaire and Ginger Rogers, with their incredible lightness and flair and *lift*, Ruby Keeler was, well, down-to-earth; there was not that much distance between her shoes and the stage. She had facility, she was "articulate," precise, clean, her whole body was dancing, not just her feet, but measured against their almost faërie lightness and grace she was "down to the ground and earthy and loud."

She herself would say that she was not all that special as a dancer or singer or actress, did not do any of those things all that well.

But they loved her, the audiences. And perhaps it is partly because hers was the art that concealed art. Perhaps she did that thing that, like Bing Crosby's crooning, made everybody out there feel "I could do that, I could sing (dance, tap, act) like that." That must be partly what made guitar playing take off like a rocket with the advent of television in the 1940's and 50's. Suddenly millions of people saw what looked like a very easy way to make music: "I could do that," and guitar playing and, at first, the making and singing of folk songs, and then blues, and then later a genre that we used to call *rock and roll*, became something that just about everybody could do.

But if there was an aspect to the art of Ruby Keeler which demonstrated something like that seeming ease and accessibility, there was also a deep underpinning of something else we'll try to get at in this story of the long and extraordinary life of this Nova Scotian who never forgot her roots.

Like so many Canadians her Irish ancestors had actually intended to end up in the United States of America. But Ralph Hecter Keeler's mother and father had stopped off in Canada and tried to make a life here. Ralph became a butcher in Dartmouth, a successful one by all accounts, and in the early 1900's he married Elenora Nellie Lahey.

Nellie was the daughter of another Irish family, prominent in the Halifax/Dartmouth area. She was seriously Catholic, and she was stunningly beautiful. A photograph of Nellie at the time of her betrothal to Ralph is arresting in its serene grace and subtle sensuality. Ralph looks like a butcher; even in his formal photographs in a pinstriped suit with a watch chain, you can easily see him in his blood-spattered white apron, behind the counter, one hand comfortably up on the glass display case, another caressing a knife or a sharpening "steel," saying, "Sure now, Missus Callaghan, would ye be after tryin' a bit of the pork bellies today, fresh in, good as they come?" Broad shoulders, a broad man, altogether, with a broad smile, and his daughter Ethel Ruby would dote on him for the rest of her life.

Ralph and Nellie had a tiny house at 13 Oak Street, in Dartmouth, now a vacant lot. Their first child was a boy, William, and then on August 25, 1909, Ruby came along, and two years later sister Gertrude. Both Nellie and Ralph worked in a store in Halifax. It was not an easy life, with three young children. There were lots of stories of the great opportunities south of the border, the kind of legends that had brought so many Irish to these shores in the first place, and after a while Ralph and Nellie decided to give it a try.

Not surprisingly, the legend, at first, did not fit the reality. The only job Ralph could find was driving a truck. Their home was a rundown cold water tenement on the east side of Manhattan, where Bill and Ruby and Gertrude hung around in the streets, and soon were joined by Helen and then Anna May and Margie. There was never quite enough money and only barely enough to eat, and hand-me-downs for clothing. Everybody had to help out with everything, but somehow they got along.

One of the somehows was music: particularly singing and tap dancing. That old Irish love of simple music at home was part of the formation of the young Keeler family. Ruby showed such a natural feel for it, especially for rhythm, that one of the nuns who taught her at St. Catherine of Sienna's Catholic school on E. 68th street, persuaded Nellie that the girl ought to have some training. Nellie scraped together the money to get both Ruby and Bill into Jack Blue's School of Rhythm and Tap. The teaching Sister was right: Ruby did have something special, and before long Jack Blue (there really was a Jack Blue) noticed it too.

Now Jack Blue was not one of your back-room failed stage performers trying to eke out a living teaching kids how to do what he had never really succeeded in; Jack was an impresario with a wide acquaintance in the world of stage musicals. He was Dancing Master to an actor/dancer/singer/producer named George M. Cohan who was, at the time, just about the biggest name on Broadway. People who do not know the Cohan story assume that the name is a variant of Cohen and that he was Jewish. In fact, George M. Cohan was an Irishman. On a foundation of his natural talent and the street sense of a kid who had gotten himself into a lot of trouble on the pavements of Manhattan's slums, he had built an understanding of what would play to the crowd and an outstanding ability to play it himself. He was a good songwriter, too; people are still singing his "Give My Regards to Broadway." If you want to get a sense of the Cohan blend of talent and guts, see if your video store can find you a copy of the movie *Yankee Doodle Dandy* (1942). It stars James Cagney, who much earlier on would, as it happened, co-star in one of Ruby Keeler's early great successes in the movie musicals.

George M. Cohan was in production with a new musical, *The Rise of Rosie O'Grady*. Jack Blue watched the slim adolescent kid with the amazing blue eyes and the "down-to-the-ground earthy and loud" tap-dancing style, and he said to himself, I think Mr. Cohan should see this. So he told Ruby that there was an opening in the chorus line for *Rosie O'Grady*, and if she wouldn't mind lying about her age she would have a good chance at it.

George M. Cohan agreed, doubtless with some prompting from his proud Dancing Master, and within days Ruby Keeler was bringing home more than her father earned, $45.00 a week. The show opened on Broadway at the Liberty Theatre, on the 22nd of December, 1922. Ruby was thirteen years old, though her photographs at the time might give her, say, seventeen or eightteen.

Herbert Goldman, the author of *Jolson: The Legend Comes to Life*, told us that

New York in the 1920's was probably the greatest city in the history of civilization. And its nightlife scene was certainly the greatest of all time.

You had the legitimate theatre. You had vaudeville, which was still flourishing.

You had the nightlife, nightclubs, which were called "speakeasies" at the time, because of prohibition. The speakeasies played host to Broadway celebrities, politicians, sports figures and gangsters, all melded together in one big entertainment and whisky pot.

Prohibition, an absurd attempt to legislate morality by making it illegal to drink alcohol, was one of the most destructive experiments ever tried in the still relatively young American democracy. It was such a boon to criminals that it has been seriously speculated that the legislative initiative was fuelled by campaign contributions from would-be bootleggers, and perhaps even from the liquor industry. But the campaign was carried by legions of men and women, many from the Protestant and evangelical right. Quite properly appalled at the wreckage booze was causing in working-class families, they wrongly thought that instead of education and the raising of incomes they could eliminate the scourge of alcohol by forbidding it. Prohibition did not last long (1920 to 1933), but in those few years it spawned a huge criminal industry, much as the present drug laws are doing today. Prohibition also created a mythology that is still alive and well, and a legacy of story and entertainment that had much of its genesis in the very Broadway where the adolescent dancer was on her way to stardom.

In fact the speakeasies changed Ruby Keeler's life. Nils Grunland had a "speak," a pretty notorious nightclub, called The El Fey. He not only ran the club he also produced its entertainment, and when he came to see *Rosie O'Grady* there was something about the young dancer that caught his eye, so when the show closed he offered her a regular spot at the club.

One of Ruby's characteristics that struck people was an air of innocence in the midst of all this sophisticated and socially marginal life. Here was a girl — they probably assumed her to be in her late teens — a girl who *must* know the score, must know the facts of life, must have "been around" because, well, she was a showgirl after all; and yet there was a kind of *innocence* about her that struck everyone, a vestal virgin kicking up her heels in a seductive short-skirt tap-dancing routine. It is a combination that has turned many a hard male head soft, in the history of man/woman relationships. One man whose head was truly turned in this case was a gangster, "a *nice* gangster" according to Herbert Goldman, who has made an intense study of that scene, but a gangster all the same. He was an Italian named Johnny "Irish" Costello. He watched her dancing in the El Frey and was enchanted by this combination of innocence and an earthy, rough and ready knowingness. He began to suggest around town that it might be a good idea if some Broadway producers found her more roles in Broadway musicals. Producers did not like to say no to Johnny Costello, and Ruby began to get some very nice roles.

Since Johnny Costello was a kind of lieutenant for a not-very-nice gangster named Owney Madden, "Owney the Killer," you tended to pay attention to him. By the time Ruby really was 17, in 1926, it was understood all over the scene that Ruby Keeler was Johnny Costello's girl, and that if you did not want to get yourself into trouble, you would respect that fact.

Now there was a singer in the clubs and on the stages who had eclipsed the great George M. Cohan. The newcomer made his reputation by putting on black makeup and singing "minstrel songs" as a fake black man. Before he died, he was probably the most beloved and most powerful American entertainer of them all (although that kind of superlative is very hard to measure). The newcomer's name was Al Jolson.

Once again, if you want some sense of the power of this man rent a movie that hit the world like a thunderclap shortly after the end of the Second World War. It is called *The Jolson Story.* Its star is an actor who would otherwise have been forgotten, Larry Parks, lip-synching the great Jolson songs to Jolson's own recorded voice. Parks soon had a whole continent singing the songs all over again. This writer was in high school at the time; within months there was seldom a school musical in which some kid did not get up, *in blackface*, and do a Jolson song. Sometimes they lip-synched to the newly re-issued Jolson records (on hard wax 78 RPM disks then, this was pre-vinyl), and sometimes they worked at imitating the slightly hoarse, distinctive Jolson Voice, and got down on their knees holding their white-gloved hands out beseechingly and singing to their "Mammies." It was happening in just about every town and city all over the North American continent.

Twenty years earlier it had already happened when the real Al Jolson was singing. He found adoring crowds wherever he went. Here was a Jewish kid from Lithuania who had learned to sing under the cantor at his synagogue, who was now making his name disguised as a black man singing pseudo-black sentimental southern songs. "He gave every member of the audience the feeling that he was sharing a private joke with them," said his biographer Herbert Goldman. "I don't think there has ever been a performer who was able to do that to the extent that Jolson did."

He had a weakness for young girls with innocent looks. He saw Ruby Keeler in a show called *Sidewalks of New York* at the Woods Theater in Chicago, and he was smitten. Jolson was very powerful by then, very well-connected, very capable of getting good intelligence on people's comings and goings, very capable of finding out when this enchanting child would be in circumstances where he might be able to get to know her without interference from her handlers. When Ruby got off the train in Los Angeles one afternoon, where she had gone for a brief engagement, for once all on her own, there on the platform was one of the most famous men in America, calling out to her, to Ruby Keeler, "Hello Kid!"

Jolson knew he was living dangerously; this was Costello's girl. But he wanted her. He spared no expense. While Ruby was at first terrified, it is clear that if Jolson turned on the full power of his brilliantly contrived charm, he would eventually get what he wanted. Johnny Costello found out that they were secretly engaged. Apparently, instead of ordering the great man's assassination, he decided that *his* code demanded he act in Ruby's best interest. Perhaps he could understand that Ruby might really love the great entertainer. In any case, having heard that Jolson had abused a former wife, he let the singer know that his life was forfeit if he ever harmed Ruby, and that he had better make sure she was financially secure. On September 21, 1928, the couple got married and boarded a transatlantic ocean liner for their honeymoon in Europe. Costello had found out that some of his hoods were so offended they planned to take a shot at Jolson on his behalf. He threw an immense party down in Atlantic City for all of "his people," on the very night that Al and Ruby sailed from New York on the *Olympic*, and the story is that he did it to make sure they had a safe departure.

Al Jolson, as it turned out, was somewhat less chivalrous about the marriage than Costello had been. Jolson was 45, Ruby had just turned 19. Jolson was at the peak of his career. Ruby's was accelerating rapidly. Jolson seemed to adore her. But, knowing he was sterile, possibly from a venereal disease, he let her believe it was her fault that she wasn't getting pregnant. She desperately wanted children, but throughout the marriage she kept thinking it was *she* who was not fertile. In the meantime, while his career had peaked, hers kept climbing, and that added another element of stress to the relationship.

Ruby starred in Florenz Ziegfield's *Whoopee*, dancing with the young Jimmy Cagney, and choreographed by the famous Busby Berkeley. The next year there was a Gershwin musical, *Showgirls*. On opening night Jolson, in the audience, stood up and sang while she danced her star number. He came back and did it again. It might have been a publicity stunt. Audiences were entranced. Some of Ruby's friends and admirers thought he was doing it to upstage her, because he was jealous. He let on he was doing it to celebrate her, and that is credible too, as the marriage was still young and the bitter and unforgiving side of his resentment and jealousy had not become the dominant theme, not yet.

But he was a possessive, jealous man. He was embarrassed about her grief over their childlessness, but did not have the courage or the decency to tell her the truth about it. As the movies turned to sound, the clackety-clack of Ruby Keeler's down-to-earth loud tap dancing appealed to producers and before long she was a star in her first film, *42nd Street*. She played love scenes with Dick Powell. Producers were calling her all the time. Jolson hated it.

Something in her steadfast Catholic beliefs may have led her to think that a child might save the marriage, and Al agreed. They adopted Al Junior, "Sonny," in May 1935. Ruby was 25. The boy was half-Irish, half-Jewish, which seemed to fit. But the fit did not save the marriage, and Ruby turned more and more to her own private friends, and to the Church, although the Church's prohibitions against divorce did not stop her from thinking in that direction.

One night she went out to play bridge with an old friend, Madelyn Fiorito Jones. The game went on later than usual; perhaps Ruby found it easy to overlook the passage of time when the homecoming would not be something she looked forward to. But when she did get home Jolson was waiting, and he was angry, and that was the trigger. Next morning she met her friend Madelyn to go to Mass, and she said, That's it. I'm going to divorce him. Madelyn says that she asked for nothing, no support, no house, nothing but the custody of Sonny. And she took a tea set that her family had sent her as a wedding present. The divorce was made final in 1939. Ruby was 30. She decided that she was through with show business. She wanted a happy life with a man who loved her. And, miraculously, she found it.

There was one last film, *Sweethearts of the Campus*. On a blind date she met a younger man, John Homer Lowe, who had actually dated her sister Gertrude earlier. John was handsome, wealthy, a solid, unpretentious character with strong opinions and a generous disposition. Both he and Ruby were saddened by the prospect of no children, but had come to love each other deeply and went ahead with the marriage. To their great joy and surprise she was soon pregnant. Before long there were two more sisters for Sonny, and then a brother. They still lived in North Hollywood, and the movies were still an important part of their life. But they were home movies now, some black and white, some in colour. They show the still lithe, slim, lovely woman, still with that touch of innocence and the huge engaging eyes, now carrying around one or more little kids, who keep getting bigger as the home movies unwind. Now they are clowning in the swimming pool, now the whole gang out on ponies, learning to ride. Now they are taking a trip back to the Nova Scotian roots and son John Junior recalls how, when his mother had to produce her identification crossing the border into Canada, the pride with which she told them that her birthplace was "Halifax, Nova Scotia." Her son and her daughters remember her as a mother who was always there, always the number one car-pool driver, the mom in the front row at the yo-yo contest or the swimming meet. Her daughter Kathleen tells how there was one hint — only one — that there might have been something unusual in her past.

"She would occasionally do a little dance in the kitchen. We would comment on it and try it. And she was proud of the fact that she could do it and none of us could do it. Not just her children, my father as well. We all tried these little steps, from the sink to the refrigerator. That was . . . one of her moments, certainly."

But nostalgia for her time as a star of stage and screen was certainly *not* one of her moments. The children would grow up having no idea — for several years — that their mother had been a famous performer. Her daughter Theresa says,

> She would say, "Don't ever wear make-up." This is a woman who had been in showbusiness wearing lots and

lots of make-up. "Because you don't need it; you're just much too beautiful." And that's a wonderful thing, you know, to hear.

But what they didn't hear about was the showbusiness part. Theresa says,

She kept it from us because she wanted to be Mrs. John Lowe. And her stardom was not a part of her life any more. And it certainly was not a part of our lives. We did not know that she had been in the movies. And every once in a while as we were growing up she would make a television appearance, for instance on a variety show — Jackie Gleason or something like that. And honestly, we thought that probably everybody's mother did that once in a while. Isn't that remarkable?

Death began to mark her life, however. Her younger sister had died just as the marriage to Al Jolson was coming to an end, and perhaps helped precipitate the divorce. Ruby was a woman to whom family was a central value. As she became prosperous she had given everything she reasonably could to her parents and siblings, bought them houses, showered gifts and personal attention on them.

Her father died shortly after Theresa was born. Then in 1964 her mother Nellie died too. At about the same time she learned that her dear husband John had cancer. They kept the disease under control until 1969. But then she called all the children to come home, to be there at the end.

Those years in the late sixties, which so upset the moral and cultural tone of America and the world, may have been responsible for a wave of nostalgia that some cultural historians see as characteristic of America as the seventies loomed. The youth voice had become almost the loudest in the land, after the death of John F. Kennedy in 1963. There came the mounting anger at the war in Vietnam, and later the tragedy at Kent State University where American soldiers fired on and killed college students, their own neighbours, who were protesting the war.

Perhaps seeking some kind of balance to the turmoil, in Hollywood and on Broadway there was a lot of talk of revivals. They dreamed of bringing back the old light-hearted stuff that had grown up in the roaring twenties and then helped a nation make it through the dark misery of the 1930's and the worst depression ever. Producers talked among themselves about those lovely, innocent cheery musicals with Busby Berkeley and Dick Powell . . . and Ruby Keeler.

A producer named Harry Rigby dug out a 1925 musical, *No No Nanette*. He wanted his two idols, Busby Berkeley and Ruby Keeler, to get involved. Ruby at first said no, my God she was a grandmother, she was sixty years old for heaven's sake, do a tap-dance number in a Broadway Musical! Had they all completely lost their senses? But her old friend Madelyn Jones, among others, said, "Ruby, what have you got to lose?"

So she thought about it for a while. She tried a few tentative little tap routines to the fridge when she thought nobody was looking. She talked it over with Rigby. The whole family knew what a wonderful medicine it would be for the grief of losing her husband, and urged her to go for it. And so she went to New York to start rehearsals. And it went marvellously.

They did the out-of-town opening in Boston. Ruby's son, John Lowe, Jr., now a man in his fifties, was there on opening night with his sisters.

And you could hear people in the audience whispering to each other. They were trying to see if she had her tap shoes on. That's what they were looking for, "this person who couldn't tap dance very well." But the electricity in that room, and the murmur and the energy! And it all had to do with the lady who was on stage. And the feelings that were being evoked . . . And to be the son of that . . . not just part of it, but to have that be my mom, was probably the proudest thing I have ever experienced in my life.

The photographs from that musical show a fit, trim, and alert Ruby Keeler who is swinging onto the stage in her long pink pleated skirt, a skirt you just *know* will start to swirl right out horizontal once she starts into the fast turns, her eyes wide, her grin a curious combination of playfulness, serenity and excitement. And, yes, *innocence.* As if a little child had grown tall in the finding of herself, and had come out in front of the crowd to show them a great thing.

Madelyn Fiorito Jones says, in the documentary, the emotion flowing out of her, "She was beautiful."

She looked . . . twenty years old. And dancing like she did when she was twenty years old. And the audience just — when the show was over and the curtain time, and Ruby came out? The audience went wild. And of course I just sat there, I got up, and, but I was crying. And my mascara was all over my face. And I was just sobbing because of what . . . now I'm . . . and remembering it now, I'm sobbing. It was great.

The reviews were raves. After the Boston tryout and the fixes, they moved it down to New York, and it was sell-out time. Ruby Keeler, the kid from Dartmouth, had come back to New York.

Kathleen, her daughter, says she went back and back. *My heart would always pound. No matter how many times I saw it, my heart would always pound. And, because I was nervous for her, and I knew she was nervous . . . But as soon as she would start tapping, it was spectacular. She started with the soft-shoe. She came downstairs and the audience, you'd start to hear the murmurs in the audience. And then she'd start with the soft-shoe. And then everyone just relaxed. Including Mom. It was a wonderful, wonderful moment.*

She was sixty-one. She had left the stage more than thirty years earlier. She had not danced professionally for decades. She was a grandmother. She did not need to do this for money, or for self-esteem. It is certain that she knew there would be healing in doing it. But it is equally certain that she did it because there was an imperative in it, in the way all those things had come together, in America's need for that kind of gaiety just now, in the fact that Busby Berkeley was still around, and that Broadway wanted them back for what would almost certainly be a last visit. The ability to recognize that imperative, for a woman who had long ago left all that behind in order to be the mother whose role was more important than any fictive role she had ever played on the stage or before the cameras — that is not an ability that is given to everyone.

So it seems strange, now, that some of those close to her, who clearly admired her, were bewitched by her, loved her, would say that she was in any way "ordinary." An important part of the reason for their saying such an absurd thing is that here was a woman of immense strength, and talent, and determination, who apparently never needed to remind you of that strength, talent and determination. Whether or not it is true that her dancing was not especially good, part of its communicative power, the power that made people want to see and hear it over and over again, was that it seemed, not *easy*, exactly, but accessible.

She wasn't showing off something impossible; she was doin' sump'n that's neat to do.

They would say, "It made you feel that *I* could do that!" It made you feel that being up there on the stage conjuring a standing ovation from full houses night after night was something that Moms did, just as they went on Jackie Gleason and the other talk shows. And if that is what Moms do, then when we grow up we can do it too, and if we don't get around to it, well that's okay too because, hey, it's no big deal, see how ordinary she is.

And that, this writer would argue, is *really* extraordinary.

Four years after the greatest comeback in the history of the Broadway stage, visiting her family in Montana, Ruby Keeler was felled by a massive aneurism, a stroke that could have killed a person of less character. It left her unable to walk. She was determined not to let it keep her down, however. She undertook a heavy daily regime of physiotherapy, day after day, month after month. Getting out of the wheelchair was both a real and a symbolic achievement; next came the orthopaedic shoes, which she was determined to get out of too, and did. She was, her children say, still full of rhythm, as if she was about to start dancing again, even with the cane. She accepted gigs as a show host on cruise ships and TV specials. The audiences had not forgotten her.

The end came when she was eigthy-four. The children were all with her, at her Rancho Mirage in California, sleeping in her bedroom, on couches or cushions on the floor. They tell how there came a night when something woke them and they knew it was time. Then one by one they came close and said good-bye. When it was John Jr.'s turn, his sister Theresa says, he was the one who told her that it was "okay to go." And so she went.

Biographer Howard Goodman, himself a hard-boiled, savvy chronicler of the Broadway scene, and of the life of one of its most hard-boiled great characters, Al Jolson, said simply, "She was one of the most fulfilled people that anybody would ever want to meet. Ruby Keeler's life was, one would have to say, a complete success."

◆ ◆ ◆

The Queen of Nostalgia was produced by F. Whitman Tre-cartin, written and directed by Chuck Stewart, camera Bud Delaney, sound Paul Leblanc, editor Mike O'Toole. It was first broadcast on December 13, 1998, and will be rebroadcast in the spring of 2001.

ADDITIONAL READING:
  Nancy Marlow Trump: *Ruby Keeler, A Photographic Biography*

◇ Part Three ◇

BIBLE BILL
THE STORY OF WILLIAM ABERHART

The man who came out onto the platform was overweight with puffy, almost pouting lips. His thick neck strained at the stiff collar and tie. His glasses seemed too small for the massive bald head, and the suit too small for his hefty frame. Yet when he opened his mouth and began to preach, he held them spellbound. He called on them to stand firm against the Antichrist, whose evil power was spreading drought and famine across the parched, dust-blown prairie. He had that evangelical knack of reaching right into the deepest fears in the minds of his listeners. He showed them how the Gospel (his very special version of the Gospel) would save them not only from Satan and all his works, but also from the diabolical priests and ministers of the established, error-ridden churches, from the bankers, and from wicked governments.

His preaching would soon spread from the platform to the new electric medium of radio, and through that medium he would make himself powerful and famous. He left a mark on the province of Alberta that has never quite gone away, although almost every single one of his ideas has now been rejected. While his greatest fame came from his time as premier of the province, much of his influence grew out of a kind of religious cult that he founded, a sort of church that evolved from his Calgary Prophetic Bible Institute. The Institute's first graduate was Ernest C. Manning, who would also become premier of Alberta. Ernest Manning's son Preston would found and lead the Reform Party of Canada during its brief existence from 1987 to 1999, and, as its leader, would briefly be the Leader of the Opposition in the Parliament of Canada. The footprints of William Aberhart are still visible on Canadian soil.

He was born near Seaforth, Ontario, in 1887, one of the many children of a German immigrant, also named William, a remarkably progressive but alcoholic farmer. He himself would grow up detesting alcohol and all it stood for, preaching against it, and yet dying of cirrhosis of the liver, which normally affects only heavy drinkers. While his father could not read and write at all, the boy William would become a school principal as well as a Bible teacher, and an obsessive reader. He had a powerful memory, a hypnotic speaking style, and a prophetic vision that thousands rallied to. Others called him mad.

Family photographs show the father as an authoritarian, stern-looking man with a vast, spreading beard and fierce eyes. He is said to have discouraged his sons from any form of original thinking, demanding that they obey and not argue. He taught young William to plough, walking behind the team of horses and guiding the heavy blade through the stiff soil. One of the lessons that stayed with him, he would later say, was his father's instruction to keep his eyes on the tree at the end of the field, don't look down. Look up, into the distance, to your distant mark.

The young William became a solitary, isolated child when he was not obliged to work with his brothers in the fields or the cattle barns. He taught himself to play the violin, and, later, when they moved to a bigger farm, to play his mother's new piano.

Years later, as the head of a new political party he founded himself, he would win the largest majority ever registered in an election in Alberta, even though the press constantly ridiculed him, accused him of romantic nonsense and, worse, of fascism. He would propose legislation intended to bring the press completely under the control of the provincial government. One of his closest political colleagues would be sentenced to prison for counselling the murder of a number of prominent bankers. And yet when William Aberhart died in 1943 thousands of his supporters would gather to mourn the man who had briefly seemed to be saying to Alberta, and to the world, that there was a foolproof way of bringing prosperity to all. And ironically, while he never succeeded, even at the height of his power, in bringing any of his revolutionary economic theories into reality, the theoretical basis of what he proposed has never been completely rejected by economists, even though it works *only* in theory, or in a completely closed economy, a state that has no trade or commerce with other states.

The Aberhart boys had to get up at five o'clock in the morning, milk the forty or fifty cows and then load the heavy cans onto wagons and drive the horses into town to sell the milk. Sometimes his brothers would trade some of the day's production for beer, but not William. The few photographs of him in his youth and adolescence show a lean, athletic build. He became a good football player. But before long he would start to put on weight and lose his hair. The image the world has of him now is the puffy face and bulging eyes, which gave the political cartoonists so much fun later when he became premier.

While he was still in high school William went to a revival meeting and heard his first evangelical preacher, hypnotizing the crowd with passionate accounts of the Armageddon that would sweep away all the sinners and leave only the elect. William liked that idea, of being in a special group, the chosen ones whom the Lord would save at the last day. And he very much liked the role of that fire-breathing preacher who could bring the room to wide-eyed silence one moment, and then have them breathing out their ecstatic "Amens" the next. He went off in the fields, on his own, and preached to the trees and the stones. Critics would later point out that Adolf Hitler also polished his speaking skills by going alone into the countryside and speaking to the fence posts, but budding orators from the time of Demosthenes in ancient Greece have tested their skills in solitude, shouting to the sky, and are probably still doing it today.

He finished high school, got a teaching certificate and then a job in a one-room school near the farm. But within two years we find him in Brantford, Ontario, already pulsating with the life of a small but bustling town on the verge of becoming a city, even boasting a couple of these new-fangled electric tramcars, running on rails in the middle of the newly paved streets. In Brantford he falls in with a religious sect called the Plymouth Brethren. The Brethren believed that the Devil had the world under his control, and so they detested much of the world, certainly the part that *they* did not control. They were severe and exclusive, very hostile to the major churches, anti-Semitic of course, and not at all sociable.

Somehow during this period the young high-school teacher kept on playing football, and may have been something of a star on the Brantford team. The story is that it was watching him on the football field that won the heart of the lively young Jessie Flatt, who set out to win his heart in return, and did so. They were married in 1902 when the teacher was not quite twenty-three, but working hard enough to soon qualify for a principalship. This was helpful because Jessie was fond of jewellery and furs and entertaining, and not very much interested in the evangelical movement. So while they did manage to have two daughters, and it is reported that Aberhart was kind and attentive to the girls and read them Bible stories at night, it is also reported that there was not a great deal of common interest in the marriage.

He would, over the next few years, go deeper and deeper into his Bible studies. He taught Sunday School at the Presbyterian church, and began to try out his preaching skills. The Presbyterian elders became a bit nervous after a while. Aberhart's theology was pretty unconventional. He seemed to be saying that the Second Coming of Christ was just around the corner, instead of part of that Day of the Last Judgment which was, well, far enough in the future that we don't have to worry about it right now. This young evangelist seemed to be suggesting that we should do everything we could to prepare for it, here and now. And yet he wanted to stay within the comfortable family of the Presbyterians, while also spending time with the Plymouth Brethren who despised the traditional churches. Some historians, studying this increasingly strange and complex figure, have concluded that he must have had one of those "compartmentalized" minds that easily permits a person to believe several contradictory things at once, like the White Queen in *Alice in Wonderland.*

Perhaps it was criticism or even overt resistance from those elders that led Aberhart to start thinking about moving on. He had lived all his life in Ontario, but now the country was opening up to the west, and perhaps there was an opportunity there for these religious ideas that were taking over his life.

He applied for a teaching job in the newly established province of Alberta. Alberta had become part of the Canadian confederation only in 1905, and was booming as the new provincial government offered free land to attract a larger population. That population had nearly doubled by 1910 when the Aberhart family arrived from Brantford. Calgary was a boom town. There were actually houses — and even churches — built of brick and mortar instead of wood. While it did not have the elegant, quiet, tree-lined streets of Jessie's native Brantford, and she missed that, it did have some of those reassuring electric streetcars.

Jessie found the family a two-storey house that reminded her of Brantford, and an affluent church, Grace Presbyterian, where she could wear her furs to the Sunday service and feel at home. At Grace Presbyterian William became a communicant and an elder as well as a Sunday School teacher. At the same time he began to teach a Bible class down near the breweries and the stockyards in the east end, at Trinity Methodist, preaching his ideas about prophecy and the Second Coming, which would not have been very welcome at Grace Presbyterian. The Presbyterian authority was vested in the group, the elders who ran the church and determined its policies. The Methodists on the other hand responded to the authority and personal magnetism of a powerful individual, and William Aberhart liked that. He stayed on at Grace Presbyterian, officially. That was what Jessie wanted. But in 1912 the Elders had had enough of his unorthodox prophetic message, and they forced him to resign. When he moved over to Trinity Methodist, full time, a lot of his Bible class people from Grace moved over with him.

Now the Bible classes really took him away from Jessie and the girls. By 1913 his was the largest Bible class in Calgary. He led Bible studies at the YMCA and was invited to a number of different churches as guest preacher on Sunday. When war broke out in Europe it seemed to play into his prophetic hand. His sermons identified the German king, Kaiser Wilhelm, as the Anti-christ one Sunday, and another Sunday it would be Kemal Pasha of Turkey who was this incarnation of the Great Evil. Larger and larger crowds came to hear him, and it seems that they simply ate this message up.

In the social atmosphere of the time it was necessary that the Aberharts maintain at least the exterior impression of a real marriage. Although Jessie's furs and jewels were very much out of place among the cloth-coat, plain-hat congregations that the populist preacher now favoured, she came along from time to time, to maintain appearances. Aberhart kept working hard at his school job. He landed the principalship at Crescent Heights, Calgary's most important high school at the time. He moved to yet another church. Even the Methodists at Trinity had begun to dispute his right to preach those radical ideas. He learned that Westbourne Church was in financial trouble. He had not even been baptised, a sacrament central to the Baptist practice, so he arranged for that ceremony, by total immersion in the river. Then he took over Westbourne and made it his own. His prophetic message had never really fit in any of the mainstream churches. Now he was pastor of his own congregation. Aberhart had never been ordained into the ministry, but nobody seemed to mind that, certainly not the hundreds who came across with him to Westbourne, where the crowds kept growing larger and larger.

Like his father he was an authoritarian, both in his church and his school. As early as 1903 he had written a manual on the running of a school, in which he saw the principal (himself) as the general of an army, the staff and students bound in absolute obedience to his will. The attitude that underlay this was not unusual at the time. Heads of institutions were traditionally men who were expected to take total responsibility for running things, and thus had to have total authority. But William Aberhart's measure of authority went beyond the traditions of the time. He was not interested in discussion or in differences of opinion. The teachers who worked under him at Crescent Heights were made to understand that their views did not count: they were there to teach what and how he told them to teach.

He was going more and more deeply into his own mystic decoding of what a later scholar, Northrop Frye, would call "The Great Code," the cryptic messages of the Bible. His sermons became violently coloured with flames and demons who assaulted people sexually in their sleep. He sometimes seemed obsessed with the Sins of the Flesh. He banned school dances.

It is interesting to note that his immediate family paid no attention to this puritan absolutism. The photographs of the teenage girls, Ola and Khona, show a perky pair with bobbed hair (which must have outraged their father) and flirtatious grins. Now about the only congress he had with the family was the evening meal. After dinner he retired to a study he had fitted out in his garage. The garage was something new in Calgary, a mark of prosperity in a modern house as the automobile made its appearance alongside the horse and wagon, which was still the major form of transportation.

In the garage Aberhart began to develop a huge diagram of the world and the cosmos, both revealed and hidden. It looked like some mediaeval mystical chart of the hidden worlds. It was meticulously drawn with ruler and compass, a vast, layered portrayal of the world below and the world above, the past and the present and what is to come. Circles intersected circles, and the circles themselves were subdivided into sectors and segments, with carefully printed designations of the places of God and His Son, and of the Forces of Evil, the Antichrist, The Prophets, The Elect Who Will Be Saved.

Night after night, poring over the Bible, he continued his work on this great blueprint of God's intentions for the future of the human race and the vast extensions of eternity.

Does this all sound like a person who is not quite sane? He was certainly not impaired from successfully presiding over his important high school and running his church and preparing his lectures and his sermons. When the Great War was over, the troops came home and a wave of prosperity began to crest. Along with prosperity came striking changes in social behaviour. Sexually provocative dancing in public, like the Charleston, gave the evangelists, including Aberhart, a new target to deplore. Gin had become the popular drink, and as the popularity of alcohol spread and the new prosperity brought it more and more into the open, the prohibitionist movement grew in opposition. Aberhart was one of the most powerful voices against the demon drink.

But this is not a man whose evangelical obsession blinds him to how he is seen, or to what he must do to reach the sceptical. He is a calculated and knowing producer of his own communications package. The historian David Elliott told our filmmakers that, at Westbourne, he really knew how to build a show.

He puts on a good religious performance. There was lively singing. He had orchestrated music. He would give a lecture, and his voice would be a rising crescendo, and it

*would hit a sort of climax, and then there would be a kind
of cooling-off period. . . . It was interpreted by some people
as almost being a kind of emotional catharsis, even some saw
it in sexual terms. It was a kind of release.*

He began to realize that he needed a church, or something like a church, that was entirely his own; he really
had no place among the existing congregations, even the
very evangelical Baptists. But there was no money to build
the kind of place he wanted to house his great evangelical
spectacles. He kept on building his own congregation, trying hard to reach out more and more widely into the
community at large. And when the next communications
revolution arrived at his doorstep, he was ready for it.

The first public broadcast of the human voice had taken
place in 1906, when a Canadian inventor, Reginald Fess-
enden, overcame the technical obstacle that had kept
radio, until then, at the level of a wireless telegraph, able to
transmit simple sound — a tone or click that could be converted into a code composed of "dots and dashes." Fessen-
den discovered a method of modulating the simple wave
form of the radio signal so that the height or amplitude of
the waves and valleys would change according to the
pitch of the sound that was fed into the system: A.M. or
Amplitude Modulation. By the early 1920's entrepreneurs
had discovered the commercial potential of the new medium, and radio stations were springing up all over North
America. In 1925 when the new medium was just nineteen
years old and commercial radio even younger, William
Aberhart realized that it would be a powerful new way for

his preaching to reach out to the multitudes. He began to broadcast Sunday afternoon services. He was also quick to recognize that the numbers might become large enough that if he were able to persuade a fraction of his listening audience to send even a few pennies each he would be able to forget about the money problem and start a new centre to house his Bible Institute.

Radio was taking off all over the province. Muriel Manning, Preston Manning's mother, described going into some small towns and being able to hear Aberhart's voice as she walked down Main Street from one end of town to the other, because people would take their radios out onto the porches on a spring evening, to listen to what was becoming the most listened-to program in the region, "The Bible Hour." He asked his listeners for contributions, in the form of the purchase of bricks and mortar for the new Institute he was planning. You could buy a sod or a brick, or even a pew if you had a little more money, and if you could only afford 25 cents that would buy some of the sand and cement needed to bind the bricks together: a quarter's worth of mortar. By 1927, after only two years of campaigning like this, he was able to commission a $65,000 building, well over a million in today's dollars, and formally open the Calgary Prophetic Bible Institute.

Since 1923 he had been teaching night-school classes in theology in the basement of the Westbourne Baptist Church. He had been broadcasting Sunday afternoon services since 1925. Now he had his Institute. He taught many of its classes himself while still administering Westbourne, preparing and delivering his weekly broadcasts, and all the time still working as the principal of Crescent Heights High School. The energy of the man was prodigious. Now he had a school in which he could train ministers and missionaries for the furtherance of fundamentalism. With the institute flourishing he now had enough supporters to take the next logical step and found his own sect, the Bible Institute Baptist Church.

Aberhart had his detractors, of course. By 1929 even the Westbourne congregation was drifting away from his increasingly demonic theology. The diagram in the garage was getting bigger and bigger, but his hold over the Baptists was shrinking. Then in October of that same year something happened that played into his hands — the stock market came crashing down. Its collapse precipitated the worst economic crisis the modern world had yet faced: the Great Depression.

It is likely that the turbulence and fears generated by the Great War of 1914–1918 had contributed to a popular spread of uncertainty about the old establishments among people who were struggling to make their way in an Alberta that would look to us now something like a Third World country. While fortunes were being made and lost, power and prosperity were in the hands of a very few. The expectation of most people was for a short life of hard work and deprivation. But here was a message preached by a galvanizing evangelist, who told people that if only they believed in the Great Dispensations available to us through a true reading of the Bible, then there would be a paradise of rest and plenty at the end of the path. This message had a powerful resonance. It was not hard for people to believe in and to wish for the end of a world in which there was nothing but struggle and failure.

When evangelists like Aberhart can convincingly "decode" the message of the scriptures to "prove" that, "The end of the world is just around the corner and you, my friends, are going to be among the ones who are lifted into salvation while the wretched bankers and merchants will roast on the spits of hell," desperate people may listen. After all, they have little reason to desire that the present world of poverty and disappointment should be preserved as it is.

So now, when even the meagre incomes of marginal farmers and workers were taken away by this mysterious Great Depression, and the soil of overfarmed and under-irrigated prairies began to blow away in great dark clouds as an unprecedented drought dried them to dust, it was easy for many to believe that these were signs of the coming of The End. The world was being seared by "The Branding Irons of the Anti-Christ," Aberhart and his right hand man Ernest Manning wrote, in a jointly authored pamphlet. But true believers would be lifted out of all this misery, *there was no doubt of it*, while the wicked were cast into everlasting flames.

It was a time of terror. Once again, while the looming figure of the puffy-faced preacher with the little round spectacles might be seen today as the embodiment of evil, it may be that he had a streak of compassion too. Among the ideals and fantasies that streamed through his head as he pored over his blueprint of God's plan for the world and eternity, it is probable that he saw himself not only as the preacher of a paradise beyond the end of the world, but also as the hero who would bring his people up out of the dust and despair, into a new (and prosperous) Jerusalem within this present and very real physical world.

He went up to Edmonton in the summer of 1932 to mark high-school leaving exams, "The Departmentals." It is bizarre to think of this already far-overworked preacher and school principal continuing the summer work that he had begun years ago just to make a little extra money. But there he was, in that Dust Bowl prairie summer of '32, when a fellow teacher on the exam marker's board gave him a new book on economics, by a British engineer named Major C. H. Douglas. The friend suggested that Aberhart might be the man to take Major Douglas' radical ideas and save Alberta from the depression. Aberhart took the book back to his room at St. Stephen's College, read it overnight, and was converted.

Social Credit was born. Aberhart sanctified it in his broadcasts as "God's Great Economy," and began to preach it regularly. But he also began to believe that it held a practical solution to the economic miseries of Alberta, maybe of the world. And if you read it in the context of that depression, and of a provincial, not a world economy, it is possible to see how desperate people could be captured by it.

What it said was, basically, that the people providing the goods and services that were sold in the capitalist market system would never be paid as much as the goods were worth. Therefore in a free market there would always be less money going to the workers than they needed to buy those goods. It is a formula that sounds like Marxist economics of Communism, but the solution that Major Douglas proposed was in fact quite different. In-stead of the workers taking control, as Marx and the Com-munists proposed, the state would simply create enough credit for people to make up the difference between what they earned and what a reasonable supply of food, housing, clothes and other goods would cost them. Everyone would thus be able to buy everything they needed. The producers would be happy because they would sell every-thing they produced, and the people would no longer have to struggle for their basic needs.

It is a recipe for steadily mounting inflation. Govern-ment keeps putting more money into the system and the money keeps losing value, even as the markets are hum-ming along.

But if you are not tied into an external world, where other currencies are keeping their value, then in theory it will work. There is no question that Aberhart, his mind demon-strably capable of believing several contradictory things at once, saw it as some kind of miraculous solution to the poverty of his world. He developed a political platform that would become the Social Credit Party. That plat-form, within three years, would bring him to the pre-mier's office with the biggest parliamentary majority any political leader in Canada had ever had.

Although his language was careful and he never actually said he was going to give the citizens money (he called it a "credit"), in a way he had bought their votes. What they thought they heard was that as soon as he got into power every single citizen would suddenly be given $25 a month. In a world where you could put together a meagre meal for 25¢. (Milk was about 8¢ a quart, for example.) That meant that a couple would get $50 a month, enough to live on.

Paradise was at hand.

The preaching now abandoned its flaming portrait of the End of the World and began to envision a new real and present world of prosperity.

Back in Britain the inventor of the idea, Major Douglas, whom many saw as some kind of fascist, said (perhaps correctly) that only a military coup could bring about the Social Credit World that Aberhart was offering, and called Aberhart's proposals "bogus." But that did not stop his Canadian disciple. Aberhart and Ernest Manning travelled the province with a public address system mounted on cars or pickup trucks. The $25 promise swept the province like a grass fire. When the *Calgary Herald* exposed the scheme as quackery, Aberhart started his own newspaper. He told his congregations that God was backing his campaign. He made comparisons between himself and Moses leading the Israelites to the Promised Land. Bake sales and socials helped to raise funds.

Some of his people began to grumble that he was behaving like a dictator, choosing all his candidates personally and tolerating no difference of opinion. The *Calgary Herald* began to call him a fascist dictator. Mussolini had attracted world attention to the idea of fascism, and it seemed to the *Herald*'s editors to be a label they could borrow and that people would recognize. Aberhart responded simply, "We should allow none of our fellow-citizens to suffer want, and if that is what you call a dictator, then I am one, and I'll be glad to take the title." He began to use the electoral tactics of the fascist parties in Europe, as well. Social Credit goon squads began to harass gatherings of the United Farmer's party, and others opposed to social credit.

"Social Creditors would be banging on the walls outside the buildings," says historian David Elliott. "Or putting sugar in their gas tanks. And you'd have churches divided down the middle between those who were for Social Credit on one side of the Church and the non-Social Creditors on the other side. And it really was dividing the province."

Only three years after he first discovered Major Douglas and Social Credit, the 1935 vote was overwhelming. Polling stations were swamped. They ran out of ballots and they ran out of pencils. On election eve Aberhart knelt at the edge of the platform grasping hand after hand reaching up to him as though he were the Saviour himself (though never losing the expensive fedora clamped firmly on his large round head). They believed. The headlines on August 15, 1935, said,

MUSSOLINI THREATENS TO ENTER ETHIOPIA.

ALBERTA SOCIAL CREDIT SWEEPS THE POLLS.

The newspapers had seen it building, and were riveted. The major U.S. dailies sent their representatives to Edmonton. *Pravda* sent a man from Moscow. This was the most dramatic political experiment North America had ever seen. Let the Nazis take over Germany and the Fascists in Italy; this seemed far more exciting because people *believed* it, and it was happening democratically. In England the somewhat dippy and yet influential Dean of Canterbury, Hewlett Johnson, said that it was "the fulfill-ment of Christ's teaching. Here are the hungry. Let us feed them. Alberta will kindle a worldwide torch." In London an army of Social Credit supporters of Major Douglas put on their green shirts and marched in cele-bration around the Bank of England, saluting the crowd with the same straight arm salute that Adolf Hitler was turning into an icon in Germany.

Exhilarated by all this — who would not be (except, perhaps, a realist) — Aberhart turned to astrology and numerology to choose a cabinet, and took a suite for him-self and Jessie at the Macdonald Hotel. He fired off a tele-gram to Major Douglas: "Well! Victorious! When can you come?"

It would appear that Aberhart had never thought through the practical implications of what he had sold the electorate. He must just have supposed, Douglas' book having so bewitched him, that once in power all he had to do was import the genius who had invented this miraculous scheme, and simply put it into practice.

Now in power at last, Aberhart had to deliver, but he could not. He himself was living very well in his gov-ernment-paid suite in the Macdonald (which Jessie dis-liked and presently fled, going off to stay with Ola and Khona in BC). But he nonetheless had to face, on the one side, an electorate lining up for their promised $25 a month, and on the other a treasurer telling him that the province was almost bankrupt.

He went begging to Ottawa. Major Douglas, learning that Aberhart had thus "consorted with the enemy," refused to come over and put the Great Plan into effect. Aberhart pleaded for eighteen million dollars; Ottawa sent two and a half. The press lined up like tigers after the kill, and began to use the word "fraud."

Aberhart asked Ottawa for more money. A second loan arrived, but a third was refused. In April 1936 the province defaulted on its loans. Aberhart went off to Vancouver with Manning and his new wife, Muriel Preston, and a vacation on the beaches, and came back with a new scheme: they would print provincial "Prosperity Bonds" that looked quite a lot like actual currency.

He tried to pay the civil servants with what the press was quick to call "Funny Money," but nobody wanted it. A cartoon appeared in the *Herald* in which the Nazi swastika frame by frame morphed into the face of William Aberhart. Aberhart began to think seriously about muzzling the press. He was warned that the caucus was planning to oust him. His response was to throw a picnic for ten thousand people, with plenty of free food. A mix of supporters and protesters came to the picnic, but his party did not come round. When he tried to pass his next budget the caucus refused to support him.

But it was Aberhart the man they were trying to get rid of, not Social Credit. They still believed in the scheme. And so, when Aberhart refused their demand that he resign, they let him know they'd throw him out *unless he brought Major Douglas in with full power to implement Social Credit his way!* Douglas still refused to come. Instead, he sent two of his men. Aberhart's confidence was shaken. With the agreement of his caucus he turned the financial planning of the province of Alberta over to these two English fascists, who in turn were taking their orders from the Great Man, Major Douglas, in London.

"It is absolutely wild," says David Elliott. "A government is prepared to turn over its complete power to this eccentric Englishman. . . . [and] one of the first dictates he sends them is to get rid of the Mounties, put in your own Social Credit police force." They also declared they would solve the financial crisis by simply declaring that Alberta would not honour its debts.

Not surprisingly, the federal government intervened and declared the financial proposal to be *ultra vires* (beyond the powers of the provincial government). As the federal government has the responsibility of protecting civil rights across Canada, Ottawa also overturned the Accurate News and Information Act, which would have given Edmonton the power to control the press, and stopped the proposed Party police as well. Aberhart was so furious when the Lieutenant-Governor, John Bowen, refused to sign the Accurate News and Information Act into law that he evicted Bowen from the Official Residence and took away his car.

It was becoming very nasty. Late in 1937, acting on a tip from some provincial Conservative MLA's, the RCMP raided the Social Credit Party headquarters, and discovered documents proposing the assassination of certain prominent bankers. One of Major Douglas' British agents was, as a result, charged, tried, and convicted of counselling to murder. He was sent to prison with hard labour.

When the Alberta newspapers were awarded the Pulitzer Prize for their fight against Aberhart's repressive legislation, the premier fled to Jessie on the west coast, to lick his wounds. In 1939 King Edward VI and Queen Elizabeth visited, partly to build support for the war against fascism that many now feared was coming. The Lieutenant-Governor, now working from a residence he had to rent for himself, kept his premier out of sight most of the time. Aberhart was invited to only one formal welcoming ceremony, outdoors, on the steps of the legislature, where the premier made a deferential speech.

But, although he was already talking with lugubrious self-pity as though he were finished, "prepared to be cast aside like an old shoe," World War II in fact gave him a brief reprieve. His government was returned with a small majority. He joined the voices rallying against Hitler and Nazism, but at the same time kept up his anti-Semitic tirades against the international Jewish financiers. He even accused the Jews of persecuting their own people in Holocaust-ridden Germany.

He looked old now. The once fat, shining face and puffy lips became ashen in colour and his skin shrank and sagged. He, who had never taken a drink in his life, was diagnosed with cirrhosis of the liver. Visiting the family again, in Vancouver in the spring of 1943, he was hospitalized and died a month later.

But they came out to the funeral, the old supporters, thousands of them. Perhaps they still believed that his dream had held some kind of reality, if only . . . The family, however, having long ago repudiated Alberta, insisted on his being buried in BC, where he lies in a simple grave, and where Jessie joined him in 1966.

Could there be another like him? There were his counterparts at the time, notably the similarly fascistic and corrupt governor Huey Long of Louisiana, who was murdered in the lobby of the state legislature. In a society with vigorous and watchful news media, and a general population whose education is vastly greater than what it was seventy-five years ago, and where politics is almost a national sport, it seems unthinkable that such crazy ideas could be taken seriously for five minutes. But Alberta has not forgotten Bible Bill.

AN AFTERWORD: The Social Credit fantasy attracted at least one other very prominent figure, the American poet Ezra Pound. Incarcerated in Washington D.C., at Saint Elizabeth's hospital for the insane after he had made anti-American, pro-Mussolini radio broadcasts from Pisa during the Second World War, the anti-Semitic genius had also discovered and been converted by Douglas' scheme. When the present writer wrote to Ezra Pound at Saint Elizabeth's, proposing to bring a camera down to Washington for a television interview in 1957, the poet wrote back, "Elementary my dear Watson; just get Grampa out of quad and then we can talk turkey." And then he added

a whole page of notes about the great Major Douglas'
world-saving economics, the work of genius, and urged
us all to revive Social Credit.

◆　◆　◆

Bible Bill, the television biography of William Aberhart,
was written, produced and directed by Patricia Phillips,
Director of Photography James Jeffrey, sound Garrell
Clark, and editor Michelle Lalonde. It was first broadcast on History Television on January 31, 1998, and will
be rebroadcast in the spring of 2001.

ADDITIONAL READING:

David Raymond Elliot and Iris Miller: *Bible Bill: A Biography of William Aberhart*

◇ Part Four ◇

DAI VERNON
The Spirit of Magic

The figure on the screen is at first slightly obscured by watermark damage to the film, and the black and white picture is grainy and faded. There is no sound. And yet this beguiling man, who is smiling straight at us with a mixture of aristocratic generosity and mischief, is a presence, a compelling presence.

He is thirty-five years old and looks absolutely in the prime of his life. His head is perfectly formed, his features almost too handsome, his hair impeccable and his thin moustache gallant. He is doing something with his hands, very slowly.

He holds a single playing card out for us, well forward of his face, but just low enough so we can still see his devastating smile. What he is about to do with this card will be seen very clearly, but it will be perceived as totally baffling. As he turns first one hand palm out, and then the other, v-e-r-y slowly, the card vanishes. It is simply gone. There are no sleeves it could have gone up. The man rotates for us the empty palms and backs of both those hands, and then, still moving slowly, as he turns one hand back again the card is quite simply . . . *there* again. And the man is so tickled, so boyishly pleased to be showing us this . . . this *miracle* of sleight-of-hand, of deception of the eye . . . that we are totally won over. We love the guy.

As did much of the world, at that point, a few years after World War I. Dai Vernon was by 1924 the toast of High Society New York, and among professional magicians he was becoming the most sought-after master craftsman in the world. Before long they would drive across the continent or take a ship across the Atlantic for the opportunity to sit at his feet and learn. They began to call him The Professor, and they still do, almost a decade after his death. The noted contemporary magician, mentalist and historian of magic Max Maven now says that Vernon had become to magic "what [James] Joyce was to the novel and Einstein to physics: [someone who] comes along and just changes the way people approach that field."

It was a long way from Ottawa.

Dai Vernon was born in the Canadian capital city in 1894 and christened David Frederick Wingfield Verner. His father James was a successful senior civil servant, and his mother Helen something of a society *Grande Dame.* His uncle Frederick Verner was a much admired landscape artist whose work hangs in the National Gallery of Canada to this day. Young David would inherit Uncle Frederick's skill in the plastic arts. He was a gifted watercolourist as a child and, not yet in his teens, taught himself to cut superb portrait likenesses out of black paper. These silhouettes, an art that today has virtually disappeared, would be, throughout much of this really great magician's life, a reliable fallback as a source of income, and a way to flatter wealthy clients. He would leave behind arresting likenesses of society flappers and great industrialists. And of celebrities including novelist Scott Fitzgerald and dancer/actor Ray

Bolger (The Scarecrow in *Over the Rainbow)*, and of the New Deal and wartime President of the United States, Franklin D. Roosevelt. Tiny cut-outs, some of these silhouettes now command impressive prices from collectors.

Young David's father, James Verner the civil servant, dabbled in conjuring, which he had learned from *his* likeminded father, a professor at Trinity College, Dublin. James, in turn, began to show his young son a few tricks when the boy was only four or five. David was enchanted. He begged to be taught how to do it. Ottawa was an important stop on the entertainment circuits in those days, too, and while the boy loved any kind of performance, music hall, vaudeville, legitimate theatre, it was the visiting magicians who held him rapt. He haunted Ottawa's new Carnegie Library and pored over all the books on magic he could find, discovering the secrets of those travelling conjurors and teaching himself tricks to dazzle his father with. James Verner had some influence in Ottawa, and when Howard Thurston, one of the best magicians in the world came to town, young David's father got the seven-year-old backstage, where the boy confidently showed the Great Man a card trick, of his own devisal, and the Great Man said he was totally stumped.

It is perhaps not a bad idea, after all, to get a bit ahead of the story again right here, because there was another showing off to a great magician, an event that became and remains a legend among magicians, and gave Dai Vernon a label that stuck. He was in Chicago on February 6th, 1922. Harry Houdini, by then world-famous more as an escape artist than a magician, was being fêted at the Great

Northern Hotel by a gathering of magicians from all over the continent, celebrated and toasted for his lifetime contribution. The cocky Canadian was introduced to Houdini in the lobby by a mutual friend, Sam Margules. Vernon managed to persuade this Great Man to pause long enough to look at a card trick. Houdini had long boasted that he could never be fooled with a card trick if he could see it three times. Here is what Dai Vernon did, and nobody had ever seen anything like it before.

He got Houdini to put his initials, H.H., on the face of a playing card, which Vernon (he had changed his name by now, but would keep on changing back to Verner from time to time for years to follow) then inserted back into the deck underneath the top card. Then, without doing anything that anyone could see, no move, no covering the deck, nothing but softly stroking the top card for a moment, he then turned that top card over and it had become Houdini's card with Houdini's initials on it. "Again!" said Houdini. The challenge. *Show me three times and I'll know how it's done.*

So Dai Vernon did that trick not three but seven times. The Great Man admitted defeat. For the rest of his life Dai Vernon was known as The Man Who Fooled Houdini.

But we are getting ahead of our story; back up twenty years, to 1902. That year a little book appeared which would transform both gambling and card conjuring, and quite literally would also transform the life and destiny of David Verner. It was a book on how to cheat with cards. The eight-year-old boy started reading his father's copy, although James had told him it would be too difficult, too complicated and detailed for such a young mind. This proved not to be the case. He read it right through, then and there, and for the rest of his life he kept reading it, studying it, interpreting it, applying it.

In 1984 there appeared an annotated version, under the title *Revelations*. The author of this annotated version was Dai Vernon who was then ninety years old.

When it first appeared in 1902 this little volume was called *Ruse and Subterfuge at the Card Table,* with an intriguing paragraph in italics, under the title, which read:

Embracing the whole Calendar of Sleights that are employed by the Gambler and the Conjuror . . . every known expert move and stratagem of the Expert Card Handler.

The author's name was given as S.W. Erdnase. Among magicians to this day there is controversy as bitter as the arguments about Shakespeare among literary folk, as to who Erdnase really was. The book was reissued later as *The Expert at the Card Table*. It is still in print under that title, but everybody simply refers to it as *Erdnase*. It became the young David's Bible. He said he had it memorized by the age of twelve. Many others have been fascinated or even obsessed by *Erdnase*. In the spring of 2000, when *The Wall Street Journal* did a nostalgic and humorous feature story on the controversy about "The man who was Erdnase," reprints of the old text soared onto the best seller lists, ninety-eight years after being published. Very serious scholars have been taken with *Erdnase*. The Californian professor of mathematics, Persi Diaconis, lived and travelled with Vernon for a couple of years as Vernon's protégé when Vernon was about the age we first met him at the beginning of this film and Diaconis was fourteen. Much of what they did together was to track down stuff related to Erdnase.

Herb Zarrow is a gifted magician whose deceptive technique for fully shuffling a deck without changing the position of a single card bears his name, The Zarrow Shuffle. Zarrow says that when Vernon started hanging around the magic shops in New York in his late teens and early twenties he was showing card work out of Erdnase to grizzled old veteran professionals, and they were baffled. They knew Erdnase, they thought, but they didn't know *this* stuff. Vernon was on his way to becoming a legend.

Sometime between discovering Erdnase in Ottawa and those early New York days the Verner family went to Old Orchard Beach in Maine for a summer holiday. There, young David saw his first silhouette cutter working on the pier, the way charcoal artists work the sidewalks at Fifth Avenue and Central Park South, or Bloor and Yonge, today. Vernon said he went home and got a little pair of scissors and cut a couple of silhouette faces that his father praised as "better than the man on the pier." When he went back to New York a few years later he tried his luck on a pier at Coney Island, next to Larry Grey The Dizzy Wizard's little magic shop, and soon found he could make a living at it. Coney Island was a major middle-class holiday spot for New Yorkers then. Roller coasters and slides with big boats that carried a dozen passengers WHOOSH right down into the ocean, kewpie dolls and burlesque and sideshows; magic and sidewalk artists. Vernon had intended to study at the Art Students' League in New York; that was what his parents thought anyway. There is no record in the League's archives of his ever having enrolled. In fact he had by now, at the age of about 19 or 20, realized that magic was his life. Cutting silhouettes could be a livelihood to support the magic if need be. He was exactly where he wanted to be.

His personality was a contradictory blend of obsessive focus on a single subject: magic, and at the same time he was outgoing, humorous, a fine hockey player, a trained engineer and technical draftsman (skills learned at the Royal Military College at Kingston, Ontario). He was a writer and a social being. He served briefly in the Royal Flying Corps in World War One. In World War Two he went overseas with the rank of Captain in the United States Army's entertainment group as a volunteer, and gave himself to entertaining the troops with exemplary generosity.

But as a family man he often seemed to be not quite there. His son Derek now says, "As a father he was a fine magician." When Derek tells some of the details of family life when he was a boy, Dai Vernon's insensitivity to the two sons who were born in New York sounds almost incredible. He would allow his family to get evicted because he didn't get around to paying the rent. There was a bizarre afternoon once when young Derek came to him crying and bleeding from a beating he'd got from his drunken mother. She had confusedly picked up a souvenir Japanese bayonet to smack him with, and he was in desperate shape. But Vernon held up his hand to Derek for silence as he considered the move he was about to make in a chess game, called out "Check," and only then turned to attend to the boy's serious wounds.

A very strange man. And a very great magician.

There is an eccentric little magic shop tucked away in a back corridor on the fourth floor of an office building on New York's 42nd Street, Flosso's Magic Shop. The proprietor, Jackie Flosso, well into his seventies, only recently sold it after carrying on the business his father Al Flosso started early in the century. You could buy all the latest manufactured tricks there in those days, and a few books (though nothing like the thousands of magic titles you can buy now, on everything from simple card tricks to making a skyscraper disappear). But the place to be, in Al Flosso's magic shop, was the back room. And you got into the back room only if you were really good. Dai Vernon had not been long in New York before he was invited into the back room at Flosso's, which was called Martinka's when Vernon first went there. Even then, long before he was called The Professor, long before he decided that teaching and inspiring and studying were more rewarding than actually performing, even then he was showing them stuff they had never seen before.

Magicians like to say that Dai Vernon's great contribution to magic was naturalness. His son Derek says now that "it didn't look like magic, but magical things happened." What Derek means is that magic had traditionally been surrounded by, well, *hocus pocus*: much waving of hands, bizarre costumes up until the late nineteenth century (and still today, in some venues like Las Vegas), elaborate rituals with the hands, and wands, and inverted bowls and huge silk scarves. But Dai liked to keep it in close, to make things happen, as he had with the trick that fooled Houdini, in which, well, nothing actually *seemed* to happen at all.

It is not, however, true that this was Vernon's invention, not true that he was the one who brought naturalness to magic. His great predecessors, Max Malini and Nate Leipzig and others, had begun that motif. Max Malini would perform magic anywhere, with anything, and was booked by kings and emperors. He would produce a block of ice at a dinner table where he was a guest, or rip the buttons from a senator's waistcoat on the steps of the Senate Office Building and then restore them by magic. No formulas or spells or magic gestures, just natural movements and then magical things happened. Vernon admired that naturalness, and studied ways to make everything seem quite normal up to the point where the magical effect was to happen, but he didn't invent it. Perhaps his greatest contribution was to try to restore dignity and depth to magic.

Max Maven says, "The tragedy of magic in the twentieth century is that magicians have taken an art that is intrinsically profound, and trivialized it. For Vernon, magic was never trivial." He seems to have intended it to be a high art, subtle, profound, intensely refined, a matter of dignity and wonder. He would take any classic effect and refine it until he had found its quintessential centre, and then polish it until, when magicians saw *his* version of a trick, it seemed that there really could be no other way to do it. Max Maven says that Vernon set the pattern for the classic called the Cups and Balls. The Cups and Balls are often called the oldest trick in magic. There is what appears to be reference to them in Roman documents before the modern era. In at least one of the great outdoor country fair scenes of Breughel the Elder, in that gallery full of Breughels in the Kunstmuseum in Vienna, you can see a mountebank performing a version that looks almost exactly like the one this writer would perform today.

A senior British magician, Bob Read, has collected documents and drawings and etchings and paintings of hundreds of different takes on this wonderful old illusion. Any magician worth his salt has got to learn at least one version of the Cups and Balls. It was first unmistakeably described by Reginald Scot in his *The Discoverie of Witchcraft* (1584). The trick commonly uses three metal cups and three small balls the size of an olive or a grape. Some performers actually use olives or grapes. At a snap of the fingers or a wave of a wand, balls that have been clearly seen separately under each cup vanish and reappear together under one cup, or move singly from one cup to another, or vanish and reappear on command, all in the most mystifying way. Often at the end of the routine the magician asks you where you think the balls are, but whichever cup you point to you are wrong. Because now, when he lifts the cups which you have only just now seen empty, under each one there is an orange or a lemon or a tennis ball. Paul Gertner does it with three impossibly large stainless-steel ball bearings.

So Dai Vernon studied the Cups and Balls and then refined it according to his principles of naturalness. He even introduced a segment in which he actually does reveal one of the key sleight-of-hand moves that makes the illusion work, while still leaving the audience delightfully mystified. The Vernon routine, when you see it, makes you feel for a moment that, well, there really is no other way to do it. And Max Maven says that if you go anywhere in the world today and find a magician performing the Cups and the Balls, "Ninety percent of the time it will be Vernon's routine, or there will be something of Vernon's routine in it."

In the early 1920's Vernon met a gifted and beautiful sculptor; Jean Hayes. Jean had been the assistant to a great stage performer, Horace Goldin, whom Vernon had met at Coney Island. Goldin made beautiful girls rise into the air and vanish, or sawed them in half. Jean was one of the latter. Dai Vernon was enchanted. They began to go out together, and would suddenly surprise everyone by getting married one day in 1924 at Manhattan's Church of the Transfiguration, known to New Yorkers as the Little Church Around the Corner.

His New York friends probably thought that Dai Vernon had been transfigured too because, while he was hugely fond of the company of women, nobody would ever have called him the marrying type. The marriage was, in fact, turbulent. Even though Jean had worked for an extremely capable practitioner, she did not like magicians very much. She distrusted them, found them intolerably vain and self-obsessed. And yet there was something about Dai that was very special.

Their first son Teddy was born in 1926 followed by Derek in 1932. While both men now speak with a mixture of admiration and dismay about their talented parents, both developed an interest in magic. Derek kept many of his father's props, playbills, letters and photos, and only recently turned them over to the Canadian magician and historian of magic, David Ben, for cataloguing and safe-keeping.

Both of the Vernon sons have a huge catalogue of stories about their father's obsession with his art. Young Teddy, crying from his sense of neglect one day as his father characteristically practised some card sleight-of-hand over and over and over again, reported that Dai finally noticed him crying and said, "Come here, stop crying, I'll show you a card trick." Whereupon Jean intervened saying, "Stop torturing the boy! Can't you see he's had enough?"

Derek said, "If I weren't working on a magic trick or watching him work on a magic trick I don't think he knew I was there." Ted says that he entered a swimming competition once and Dai came to watch, and when the boy took third prize his father told him sternly that he must never again ask him to come and watch him race if he didn't come in first. And meant it.

It is curious, this obsession, and the way in which it kept orbiting around that one old book. Vernon's fascination and delight with Erdnase never left him. Gamblers often talked about the seemingly impossible "Centre Deal" Erdnase had referred to. It was a sleight that would make it possible for a cheat who had controlled some cards to the top of the deck as he shuffled, to imperceptibly retrieve those cards even after the other player had cut the deck so that they were now in the centre. Somehow you would deal them from the centre of the deck while it seemed you were dealing from the top in the normal way. Gamblers and magicians had long known how to deal from the bottom or to deal the second card while appearing to deal from the top, but the ability to deal from the centre seemed like a fairy tale, though a much desired fairy tale.

Some time in late 1931 Dai and a brilliant fellow-magician named Charlie Miller heard of a man in Wichita, Kansas, a farmer named Allan Kennedy, who could do this seemingly impossible feat. It is said that these two grown men immediately packed their bags and headed for Kansas. Dai Vernon is on record, on videotape (included in this documentary, by the way), saying that they searched in vain, asking everywhere, and had given up. Charlie Miller had gone back to New York, and Dai himself was about to go home too. And on the verge of heading back he passed an ice cream shop outside which a little girl was licking a cone. Vernon said that just on a mischievous impulse and not expecting an answer, he asked the little girl, "I don't suppose *you* know where a Mr. Allan Kennedy lives?" And the girl said, "Sure I do; in that house right there, up on the hill."

"I'm not a biblical scholar," Dai said later, "but I said to myself, 'And a little child shall lead them.'" It was January, 1932. He had found Kennedy. Kennedy showed him the Holy Grail, the Centre Deal, and Dai mastered it, which is something few cardmen have done since.

Visualize it. If you are watching the documentary, it is right there on the screen in front of you. The magician's hands are seen removing the four aces from the deck. The deck is cut in half. The four aces are placed on top of the lower half of the deck, and the top half is placed on top of them. The aces are clearly in the middle. The magician begins to deal four hands of poker smoothly and naturally. Each card comes off the top of the deck, as it should. At least that is certainly what it looks like, perfectly normal. Each time around he deals one card to you, one to me, one to our friend, and then one card face-up, to himself. Guess what his card is, four times in a row. It is totally deceptive. And while this writer has spent a lot of time mastering some sleight-of-hand with cards, he cannot imagine being able to perform this one.

Dai Vernon was doing all kinds of magic in those days, but cards were his first love, and cards remained his love all his life.

In 1924 he was approached by a theatrical and social-events entertainment agent named Frances Rockefeller King. While good magicians might get twenty-five or fifty dollars for an evening's entertainment in a society mansion, King guaranteed Vernon a minimum of $5,000 a month, and his minimums were soon several hundred dollars for a single evening. It was unheard-of. It was because her clients were all multi-millionaires is how he recalled it, decades later: "I only worked for the Astors and the Vanderbilts and the Schwabs. . . . 'Cause she had that kind of clientele."

For some time he had been musing about an elaborate stage presentation that would embody his ideas about the elevated art of magic. Jean, who was a gifted sculptor and designer, would do masks and costumes, and together they would create something of elegance and grace and wonder. Perhaps he thought it might rehabilitate the faltering marriage, too. They worked it up together in 1938. He shaved the trademark moustache and wore a classical Harlequin loose-fitting suit and a black widow's peak hairdo. He perfected the Symphony of the Rings, and devised a number of gracefully mysterious effects with billiard balls, rope, salt, and a version of the classic Snowstorm in China. In the intimate atmosphere of the elegant and exclusive Rainbow Room, virtually surrounded by wealthy nightclub patrons, it played brilliantly.

He had allowed himself to imagine that this same show, which for all its elegance was really an intimate thing for a relatively small and attentive audience, would play on the stage of the six-thousand seat Radio City Music Hall. It is a vast stage where people come for spectacle, for long chorus lines, brassy great orchestras and spectacular scenery. The audience simply could not see what he was doing with his hands. He was too far away from most of them, and it is pretty hard to see some of these small props from a hundred feet away. The show closed after the second night. Vernon was devastated. He began to think that maybe performing was not what he wanted to do any more.

There was one routine in the Harlequin Act that played almost as well on the big stage as it had at the Rainbow Room, Vernon's very special version of a classic known as the Chinese Linking Rings. Most published routines for this trick are based on a set of eight rings. Vernon had used twelve in the past, but for the new act he reduced the number to five. You can buy a version of the Linking Rings in any magic shop, in which one ring will have a gap in it that allows the other rings to appear to penetrate it and link to it, if you cleverly conceal the gap. Vernon's version made it patently clear to the audience that there could not possibly be a gap in *any* of his rings, and yet they mysteriously linked and separated again, musically, choreographed like a ballet.

He called it the Symphony of the Rings. This writer saw him do it on CBC television when Vernon was over eighty. He performed at Paul Soles' home-base desk on the late night show Soles was hosting then, right under Soles' nose, inches away. Soles gaped. His jaw quite literally dropped. Vernon, now a wizened and squeaky-voiced old man, didn't really appear to be doing anything at all, it was the rings that did it, gracefully and simply and mysteriously.

Performers today who use eight or five or even as few as three rings will often acknowledge that they have a debt to Vernon and the Symphony, a debt of style, or of manner. That is the Vernon effect; he left the art in a state where most performers feel they cannot do it as well as it should be done unless they take account of his way. Like physics and Einstein or hockey and Gretzky. Max Maven will go so far as to say that there is not one great performing magician anywhere whose work — of whatever genre — doesn't have some Vernon in it.

The same year he learned the Centre Deal he had published a little typewritten pamphlet, thirty pages or so just stapled together, ten card tricks. He liked writing up his discoveries and teaching them and putting them out for magicians to pick up. This modest little mimeographed manuscript sold for the unheard-of sum of $20, which is the equivalent of close to a thousand dollars today. Even at that price it sold out quickly, and Dai saw that there might be something for him to do as a teacher and an author. He still did silhouettes, too. He could go to Long Island and cut silhouettes for the Junior League convention and make a few dollars with his tiny shears and the fine black paper.

As he talked over the possible alternatives to performing, Jean began to get at him about how he had never really had a man's job. She had read that New York was at last building the East River Parkway and needed men with the engineering and drafting skills Vernon had learned at the Royal Military College. So he took an on-site job. Only days after he started he fell from a scaffolding into the East River, and broke both his arms.

A magician with broken arms is a sorry thing, and it got worse. The arms were in dreadful shape and the doctors wanted to amputate. Vernon refused, against their protestations that he might lose them anyway. Somehow they recovered, but not completely. His elbows never did function normally after that. His hands did, though, and he would continue to amaze people with those hands until shortly before he died.

For a while he worked the Caribbean cruise ships where the pay was good and the company fun. It was High Society again, which he'd gotten used to with

Frances Rockefeller King. The women were attractive and compliant. His marriage was pretty well over by now, and he could hang out with the gamblers and con men he found so fascinating.

At the same time there was this other thing in his life, the Professor thing, the teaching. Nowadays almost every good magician of repute travels and lectures to other magicians. It is a modest source of income and, if they have props or publications of their own for sale, that brings in some extra revenue too. But in the middle of the 20th century nobody had ever heard of magicians giving lectures. Vernon's first lecture, in New York in 1946, was a turning point both for him and for the profession.

Soon people were driving hundreds of miles to sit at his feet, and he liked that. He lectured in London and old magicians still talk about how the world changed that day. Ricky Jay, who the same year that Dai Vernon passed away would do a record-breaking sixteen weeks alone on the stage of a Broadway theatre with virtually nothing but cards, would later say, "Dai Vernon made happy pilgrims of us all." Ricky Jay's wonderful evening of card magic, called *Ricky Jay and His Fifty-Two Assistants*, rich in irony and often presented as a lecture rather than an entertainment, was by its very nature a kind of homage to Dai Vernon at whose feet Ricky Jay had been one of those happy pilgrims.

His friends and professional colleagues, however, worried about Vernon, because he never learned to put anything away. When he wasn't working he was often broke. People began to think about finding a kind of home for his Teaching Self, a place the Pilgrims could always find him, where he could be himself and do what he did best, study and teach and demonstrate, and occasionally perform if he felt like it. Suddenly the right place was there, staring them in the face.

The Larsen family had converted an old private mansion in Hollywood into a very special club for magicians called the Magic Castle. They invited Vernon to come and make it his home base; they would look after him. Nothing to worry about from then on.

Some of the New York magicians were dismayed. They felt that, in a way, they *owned* Dai Vernon, or that New York owned him. He belonged there. But they had nothing to propose that could compete with the Castle. The East/West rivalry became both bitter and funny. It is partly reflected in the pronunciation of the nickname, Dai, which the guys on the swimming team at Ashbury College in Ottawa had invented for him, years earlier. In New York they still pronounce it "Day." On the West Coast it sounds like "Die." When someone asked him which he preferred he said, with a twinkle, "Eether or Eyether." At Ashbury, by the way, while he was an indifferent student (if you measured by exam results), he did some fine artwork and was an outstanding athlete. In 1912, Sir Sanford Fleming, the inventor of Standard Time and an architect of the Canadian railway system, gave the school a trophy in his own name for the best track and field athlete of the year. Vernon was its first recipient, receiving the trophy from the hands of Lady Fleming just before Sir Sanford delivered the convocation address. He may very well have spent that afternoon at one of his favourite activities, playing ragtime piano, for which he had a city-wide reputation. The records of this event were discovered in the Ashbury archives by Vernon's biographer, Toronto magician David Ben, in the autumn of 2000.

The Magic Castle is still there. In a corner of the lobby, near the bar, where you first come in after whispering "Open Sesame" to a magic door, there is a table with a brass plaque on the wall behind it marking the spot where from 1963 at the age of sixty-nine almost to his death Vernon would hold court. There were three small theatres and a glass-walled conservatory on the downslope side of the second floor looking out over the city, with eight or ten little round green baize tables where magicians would sit and show each other stuff. In the trade it is called "sessions." You still have to be a member to get in, or the guest of a member. Today it feels like just another restaurant with magic theatres. But in those days, guests as well as members could sit at those green baize-topped tables and watch the sessions, and they were, well, magical.

This writer's first visit to the Castle was in 1968. I remember Vernon's performance vividly. He did the classic Three Card Monte. It was elegant and funny, and contained a Vernon invention which lifted it from the excellent scam it always was to the level of the totally baffling.

For the next twenty years he would be there to receive people who wanted to sit at his feet, to pass on what he had learned, to drink, to flirt with beautiful women. He kept on studying Erdnase. He kept on inventing and refining. The mathematician and card aficionado Professor Persi Diaconis says that Vernon's most important contribution was the bridge he built to the long and richly carpeted past of magic. While some of the masters resented the way he took their material, even when he refined it — maybe even thought him a thief of ideas and techniques — Professor Diaconis says unequivocally that if Vernon had not studied and polished and written up what these pioneers did, the world would have lost that material, and that there is a lot of magic being performed today only because Vernon preserved it.

He was often crusty and difficult. Castle regulars love to tell how he would scold young hopefuls who came to show off a new trick. He would send them away and shout after them something like: "Get out of here, go back to selling shoes, you're not a magician, that's the worst damn thing I ever saw."

But to others he was patiently generous and helpful. He left behind an impressive number of books and pamphlets, some of them dictated or "as told to" other magicians or writers. Many of the young magicians who hung out at the Castle — especially those who collaborated on the publishing projects — began to act as though they, like the New York magicians before, owned Dai Vernon, and many still seem to feel that today. But in fact he included the rights to his writings and some of his cards and coins and rings and cups and balls and other props in his estate, which his sons would inherit. After he broke his hip at the age of 96 he went to live with Ted who looked after him generously until he died there in 1992 at the age of 98.

All those years in the Castle he had been well looked after: fed and watered and adored. It would seem that the last almost quarter-century at the Castle was a golden time. A golden time for this, the most celebrated magician of the twentieth century, this graduate of Ashbury College, Ottawa, this young silhouette cutter from the piers of Coney Island. Dai Vernon. The Professor.

◆　◆　◆

Dai Vernon: The Spirit of Magic, was produced by Patricia Phillips, written by Patricia Phillips, Richard Pereschitz and Daniel Zuckerbrot, and directed by Daniel Zuckerbrot. Director of Photography Andrew Binnington, sound Ian Challis and Jack Cannon, Editor Michele Hozer. Magician David Ben was Associate Producer and magic consultant. It was first broadcast on History television on April 25, 1999, and will be rebroadcast in the spring of 2001.

This documentary has won several awards:
• Columbus International Festival (1999), Chris Statuette for Best Biography; and Honourable Mention for Writing
• New York Festival (1999), Finalist / Best Biography
• WorldFest, Flagstaff (2000), Bronze Award
• Yorkton Short Film & Video Festival, Special Jury Award

ADDITIONAL READING:
James Randi: *Conjuring.*

◇ Part Five ◇

PAULINE JOHNSON
THE MOHAWK PRINCESS WHO WAS NOT

So many Canadians are really two different people that it could almost be called a national characteristic. Nation of immigrants that we are, the experience of living more or less at ease in more than one different culture is something that the majority of us have at least observed. It is conceivable that in these early years of the 21st century the number of people in Canada who have in fact lived in two cultures may be greater than those who have not.

Tens of thousands of Canadians — from coast to coast but especially in New Brunswick, Quebec and Ontario (and particularly people in the Federal public service) work in both French and English and move easily in and out of both languages and the social and cultural environments where they predominate.

Italian Canadians have, since the end of World War II, played a major role in helping to transform Toronto from a stiff, undemonstrative Anglo-Saxon fortress into a vibrant cosmopolitan metropolis, "the third largest Italian-speaking city in the world, after Rome and Milano." Like their immigrant or first, second, or even fourth and fifth generation counterparts who came from or whose forebears came from China or Vietnam, Poland, Germany, Nigeria, Ethiopia, Haiti, Jamaica, Japan, Bosnia, Ceylon, Pakistan, India . . . they are and speak of themselves both as Canadians and as something else. Italian, Indian . . .

When most of us say the word *Indian*, we mean our First Peoples. Many of them also call themselves Indian. But other titles, such as First Nations, Aboriginal — or the actual names of the Nations themselves, Nish'nabe, Mohawk, Oneida — are becoming more and more widely known to all Canadians. Belatedly, Canada is coming to terms with injustices done in the past and with new relationships to be forged. Whereas cultural wisdom and sharing were often a mark of the European/First Nations contact from the beginning, it was grievously lost as European greed and power set out to destroy what should have been one of the great Meetings of the Nations the world has ever seen. Systematically, but grievously slow, the country seems to be trying to heal those wounds.

Six years before Confederation, a woman was born on the Six Nations Reservation in Ontario who, in a dramatic and public way, exemplified this theme of being two persons, living comfortably in two worlds at once. She used the drama of that double heritage, with all its contradictions, to turn herself into the single most famous stage performer in the country. She was the author of a body of work which became mandatory reading (and for some of us memorization) from before her death in 1913 up to the beginning of World War II in 1939.

Her name: Pauline Johnson.

And she was two people. When you see the photograph of her parents, George Johnson and Emily Howells, staring confidently out of the screen in this intriguing biographical documentary, you have to look carefully to realize that their marriage represented the coming together of two worlds. George looks not unlike a black-haired Charlton Heston, but with an intelligence and focus much stronger than the actor's. Emily is strong-jawed, dark-eyed, brimming with irony and inner strength.

George Johnson was a Mohawk. His father, Smoke Johnson, a gifted orator, had married a Clan Mother. In the Mohawk nations it is the Clan Mothers who determine much of the national policy, and whose collective decision selects the chiefs. George Johnson, the son of Smoke Johnson and his wife the Clan Mother, became a chief.

He would also apparently inherit his father's linguistic skills, and spend an important part of his life as an interpreter for the Anglican Church. Through the church connection he met Emily Howells, a young Englishwoman who was visiting her brother-in-law, the Anglican priest.

George was living in the Anglican mission at the time. There was some opposition from both families when he and Emily announced that they were in love and wished to marry. But George Johnson was not a person to be easily dissuaded, and from the strength of character that shines out of that photograph, neither was Emily. George, as a prosperous and influential chief, was able to give his English bride a fine house as a wedding gift. It is called Chiefswood, and it still stands there, on the north bank of the Grand River, a few miles from the bustling modern town of Brantford. Brantford is named for a great Mohawk chief and warrior, Joseph Brant, who was also a gifted interpreter and in his later years, living at Burlington, Ontario, would translate part of the Bible into the Mohawk language.

But more people would learn the words of Pauline Johnson than of her gifted father or of Joseph Brant, the much admired founder of the Six Nations Reserve. Growing up at Chiefswood, with a rather splendid English lady as a mother, and a father who believed strongly in the importance of education, Pauline and her three siblings would be schooled in both traditions. While she understood some Mohawk, and in her travels would pick up some phrases in other Native languages, it was in English that Pauline Johnson found her voice.

She was a journalist to begin with, and later a poet and stage performer. And her timing was very good, because it was a time when the romantic idea of the "Noble Savage," that vanishing race of wise and passionate people, was so popular that it brought Pauline Johnson huge audiences, on both sides of the Atlantic. Pauline Johnson played to those audiences, brilliantly and quite consciously, as a woman of two worlds.

Even the house she grew up in bespeaks two worlds. It had two front entrances; one on the Grand River for the Iroquois people (Mohawk is one of the Iroquois nations) who would arrive by canoe, and one on the land side for the townsfolk who would come by wagon or carriage or on horseback.

Among the visitors to Chiefswood was the inventor and speech teacher Alexander Graham Bell. The man who invented the telephone built the first working model of that instrument in his Brantford house not far from Chiefswood. George Johnson, Pauline's father, helped string telegraph wires for some of Bell's experiments. Bell had himself formally photographed wearing George Johnson's ceremonial buckskin suit.

An important part of young Pauline's education took place on the river. Her Grandfather Smoke was still alive when she was young, and they spent hours together in a canoe, as Pauline learned to handle the supple elegant little craft, and absorbed her grandfather's stories of the Mohawk people. And so she knew that she was a Mohawk. But unlike most young Mohawks she had a mother who made sure she was also raised as an inheritor of the English tradition. By the time she was twelve it is said that she had read all of the standard classics that George Johnson's well-stocked library had to offer. She began, like many young English girls of "good families," to write poetry.

Because of her father's prominence both as a Chief at Six Nations and as an agent of the Anglican Church, she met a number of distinguished people who came as guests to the house. Chiefswood was a house of hospitality. One of the visitors was the then very young Prince Arthur, Duke of Connaught, whose mother Queen Victoria thought of herself as Empress of many great nations. Some of these nations were themselves led regally by such dignitaries as George Johnson. The Great Queen sent her young son — who was later to become Canada's Governor General — to Canada to meet the chiefs — among them Smoke and George Johnson. The young Prince made the Johnsons a gift of a fine red blanket.

But a shadow was to fall over this world of privilege and distinction. Suddenly and dramatically the girl had to take another, much more practical look at the two worlds within which she had so comfortably grown up. Pauline's father, as chief, was the guardian of the Reserves resources, a role that turned out to be perilous. George Beaver, a contemporary Six Nations historian, tells it this way.

The great forests [at Six Nations] were very valuable, and white people would come and steal the wood if they could. George Johnson went about keeping an eye on things in the forests and as a result he was caught and beaten very, very badly, almost killed. A similar thing happened to him because of his opposition to selling whisky. The whisky peddlers beat him. He was actually attacked twice. And the last time he was in ill health for about ten years until he died.

His death left the family almost destitute. Emily and her daughters had to put Chiefswood up for rent, move into a small house in town, and look for work. Eva found an office job. Pauline made a little money as a freelance journalist, discovered the community theatre, studied Shakespeare and began to think about turning her early love of storytelling and verse into a life. Since childhood she had performed recitations and playlets for the family. Now she joined the Brantford Amateurs, and found that she had a gift for the emotionally extravagant melodramas that were the heart and soul of popular theatre. Her name survives on the playbills and programs of dozens of those plays. The plays themselves have not survived on the stage, but they gave the young performer a taste of that most intoxicating experience: applause.

At some point, perhaps, she began to realize that her gifts were more theatrical than truly poetic. Looking at her poetry now, readers will find themselves wondering sometimes what all the fuss was about (and there would soon be plenty of fuss), sometimes how any of this could be taken seriously. This writer was required to memorize some of it in school. The teacher, who had actually *seen* Pauline Johnson on stage when she, the teacher, was an adolescent at the turn of the century, managed to convey the idea that this was pretty wonderful stuff, the outpouring of the soul of a Mohawk Princess, after all! That there was and is no such thing as a Mohawk Princess, and that Pauline herself never actually claimed the title, did not matter. Along with probably hundreds if not thousands of other ten year olds, I had to learn lines like these:

> *. . . Swirl, swirl!*
> *How the ripples curl*
> *In many a dangerous pool awhirl!*
> *Dip, dip,*
> *While the waters flip*
> *In foam as over their breast we slip.*

It is not that much more laughable than much of the poetry of the out of doors that the era produced. But it had a greater effect than most verse of its kind, because the author was a powerful performer. Wide-eyed audiences from British Columbia to Birmingham felt that they were in the presence of a Red Indian. And that Red Indian looked comfortably just like them. Audiences were taken, swept up by the soulful beauty, the daring exposure of bare arms and ankles, the passionate declamation, the buckskin and wampum, and the famous viceregal red blanket. The poetry took on the reputation of the performer, and that reputation survived for decades.

Pauline Johnson's biographer, Professor Carol Gerson, appearing in the documentary, pointed out that when Pauline began to write poetry she was doing what any other well-brought-up Anglo-Canadian society girl would do: write poetry about graceful nature, about conventional love; imitative poems. Not poems about the Mohawk experience. Nobody else was writing about that; why should she?

But in trying to make some money as a freelance journalist she discovered that her editors at the *Brantford Examiner*, and their readers, seemed to really enjoy what she had to say about life on the Grand River, and about the traditions of the Reservation. Now those themes would begin to manifest themselves in her poems as well. An early piece about Joseph Brant (1742–1807), while it celebrated the achievements of this extraordinary Mohawk leader, sounds today like a piece of British jingoism. We do not know what Pauline's contemporaries at Six Nations thought of it; a Mohawk warrior in the present day would likely be appalled.

> *Then meet we as one common brotherhood*
> *In peace and love, with purpose understood*
> *To lift a lasting tribute to the name*
> *Of Brant, who linked his own with Britain's fame.*

She first published in about 1884 or '85, when she was twenty-three or twenty-four. She had not yet quite put together the poetic and the dramatic strands of her professional life. But the convergence had begun. In the meantime, the *Examiner* was running pieces that sounded like this:

> *Ah, who would not know it was the Grand River, with its romantic forests, its legend-thronged hills, its wide and storied flats, its tradition-fraught valleys. This was the domain of that most powerful of North American Nations: the Iroquois.*

And another, inspired by her father's death:

> *Cold had settled in all the broken places of his poor body, and he slipped away from her, a sacrifice to his fight against evil, on the altar of his Nation's good. And almost his last words were, "It must be by my mother's side," meaning his resting place. So his valiant spirit went fearlessly forth.*

It was playing well, this kind of thing. Perhaps as the young country settled into some kind of stability, and confidence and prosperity brought a time for reflection on the circumstances of its birth, some white Canadians were beginning to sense the guilt of their suppression and exploitation of the indigenous people. If that was so, here was the very comforting appearance of a voice that could accuse us of our genocidal behaviour but at the same time forgive, and even say in effect: It's really all right, because that *most powerful of all the North American Nations, the Iroquois,* is still alive and well: I am the living proof of it.

In January of 1892 a man named Frank Yeigh invited Pauline to recite her own work to a gathering of the Young Liberals club, in Toronto. This was the chance to try how far she could go. She gave them "A Cry from an Indian Wife," regrettably not one of the texts we children were urged to memorize in the 1930's.

> *They but forget we Indians owned the land*
> *From ocean unto ocean, that they stand*
> *Upon a soil that centuries a-gone*
> *Was our sole kingdom and our right alone.*
> *They never think how they would feel today*
> *If some great nation came from far away*
> *Wresting their country from the hapless braves*
> *Giving what they gave us, but wars and graves.*

Imagine the scene. Ontario Hydro was still nearly fifteen years in the future, but electric lighting was an established and popular novelty on the urban scene. In the streets of the larger towns the horse-drawn trams plying along dozens of miles of tracks were being replaced with electric trams. The electric tram had a Belgian-invented trolley in which a tiny wheel at the end of a spring-loaded pole on the roof actually brought sparking electric power down to the wheels, which in turn completed the circuit through the electrified rails beneath. People were telling scare stories about how you mustn't step on both rails at once (they were four feet apart!) or you'd fry. But that was not stopping the city folk from jumping on the trams and heading downtown to the shops and the excitement. It was a revolution in city living. For another fifty years or so the horse and the electric tram were both important parts of the transportation scene, slowly being pushed aside by the automobile. On that January evening in 1892, no cars on the scene yet, as Pauline arrived at the

Young Liberals gathering, the better-off members of her audience would be stepping out of horse-drawn carriages in their heavy fur coats, but dozens more would be arriving in the new electric trams with their little coal furnaces and uniformed motormen and conductors.

And here comes this smouldering beauty in a simple ball gown that showed off a classical figure, the dark pools of her brown eyes, the sensuous lips, a great English beauty. Then they learn that she is a Mohawk, an Indian! Who looks just like us. Who speaks to us of her pride and her anger, and yet . . . she *likes* us! She's one of us.

She was an instant hit.

Professor Gerson says,

The first performance in Toronto in January 1892 allowed Frank Yeigh to mythologize himself as the discoverer of Pauline Johnson. This shy little forest maiden who tip-toed out on stage and stood shivering before the audience and was completely taken by surprise when they applauded. Well, she was nothing of the sort. She was thirty-one years old. She'd been involved in amateur theatricals. She'd published dozens of poems in the Toronto papers. She was a known entity.

Sheila Johnston, of Brantford, has made a study of those early performances. She says:

People would go out to see jugglers juggle or bell-ringers ring bells or elocutionists speak. Pauline sweeps into town and she's got props and a costume and poetry and stories to tell. She would [first] come out on stage in an evening gown, and present herself as her mother would have wished . . . a very aristocratic, sophisticated, educated, articulate woman. *And then later on in the bill she would come out and she would be the complete opposite to that image: a Mohawk woman with her hair unbound, wearing a buckskin dress, using a few props like her father's hunting knife and a bear-claw necklace. So the audience would go away thinking, 'Well, that was worth the price of admission. I got two Paulines for the price of one.'*

And author Margaret Atwood:

Well first of all she made up the costume. That picture you see of her is not a real Indian, [not] anything a real tribe would have worn. It allowed her to write different kinds of poetry. She could write the contained, rather lady-like lyric poems, and do those first. And then she would come on in this other costume, and be another person, the Indian Princess . . . could do really blood-curdling, you know, violent poems.

> *His eyes aglow with hate and triumph as*
> *He hisses through locked teeth.*
> *An evil curse, a flash of steel, a leap,*
> *A thrust above the heart, well-aimed and deep*
> *Plunged to the very heart in blood and blade*
> *While vengeance, gloating, yells "THE DEBT IS PAID!"*

"She was a howling success," Margaret Atwood continues.

People were smitten . . . She had a very thrilling voice. And made quite an effect. She wrote in the nineteenth-century style. Possibly the biggest influence might have been Longfellow. And she wrote for performance. *So it was rhetorical, it was dramatic. And they were intended, like Charles Dickens' recitations, to make you laugh or cry.*

My hand crept up the buckskin of his belt.
His knife hilt in my burning palm I felt.
One hand caressed his cheek, the other drew
The weapon softly. "I love you, love you,"
I whispered. "Love you as my life."
And buried in his back his scalping knife.

George Beaver tells us that people would think nothing of travelling forty or fifty miles to see and hear her. The kind of publicity machinery that today manufactures celebrities overnight and by the dozens did not exist in the 1890's. And yet, within a couple of years Pauline Johnson was unquestionably a national celebrity. It would not be long before she began to think of a larger stage.

Today it is the conventional wisdom that Canadian performers and artists who want to succeed in a big way have to prove themselves in the USA. In the 1890's it was a British tour that they dreamed of. We were still in a colonial state of mind, we Canadians. And the way to demonstrate that you were as good as anyone else was to go and take London by storm. So that was Pauline Johnson's next target. She booked passage on a liner, and once again she hit the bull's eye. London was as smitten as Toronto and Montreal had been. In a sense it was easier. There was a romantic distance. Not many in London had actually seen a real Mohawk person. Londoners knew the romantic legends of the "noble savage," and had largely been spared the sight of desperate poverty and degradation of the authentic North American Indians. Pauline was a hit in the salons and on the stage. She was invited everywhere. She met the military, the aristocracy, the upper middle class, members of parliament, lords and justices. The Duke of Connaught sent to know what had happened to the famous red blanket. She pointed out that it was with her on the stage. Once again, secure in her comfortable persona, she was able to lecture them on their culpability.

Suppose we came over to England as a powerful people. Suppose you gave us welcome to English soil, worshipped us as Gods, as we worshipped you white people. And suppose we encroached upon your homeland, and drove you back and back, and then said, "We will present you with a few acres of your own dear land." What would you think of it all?

And her audiences would nod wisely and sadly, and think, Yes, we have done wrong, and isn't it comforting to see that she does not hate us for it. Because, of course, Mohawk though she may be, she is also one of us.

She was quite conscious of this. She marched into the Bodley Head, a premium imprint for poetry, and talked them into publishing her. And the collection of poems she called *White Wampum,* openly reflecting the double identity of white and Indian. She openly spoke of being two persons. It was a strength, not a weakness. It allowed her a sexuality on stage that would have been unseemly for a proper English recital artist.

As an Indian she could let her hair flow free and show bare arms and calves. When she returned to Canada she had the cachet of a British success, and now she was selling out wherever she went. It was not just the concert halls in the cities. She went to Moose Jaw and Banff. She played the mining towns and the lumber towns and gave the rough guys and the ladies of the night a taste of her own lusty and blood-drenched drama. When she walked out on stage, she owned the house.

In 1897 she moved to Winnipeg and became engaged to Charles Drayton, a banker. But it did not last, and per- haps — as is often the case in showbusiness relation- ships — what he had fallen in love with was the image, not the person, and when it became clear that his fiancée was on the road most of the time, and *certainly* not about to settle down as a Winnipeg Grand Dame, to run a home and put on shows in it for him and his friends . . . but this is speculation. They did not get married.

Soon after this her mother died. Pauline felt forsaken. Her brother Beverly was dead. Her sister Eva was far away in the States. She would soon be forty. She had been on the road for eight years. She was a success, but she was tired. There is a mannered, stilted scene in a 1933 movie called *Shadow River*. A society couple is at dinner in a fancy restaurant. She asks, "Did you ever hear of Pauline Johnson?"

"Can't say I have. Does she live in these parts?"

"My dear, Pauline Johnson was a poetess."

"Ha! That explains everything."

"You know, I think perhaps she is my favourite Can- adian writer. She died twenty years ago. She was part Indian, you know.

'Dream of tender gladness,
Of filmy sun and opal-tinted skies
And warm midsummer air that lightly lies
In mystic rings.'"

So twenty years after her death they still remembered her, the Double Person. The White Mohawk. The Indian Princess. Eighty years after her death and she is almost forgotten, but that is ironic, because the challenges that ring out from her poetry when she sounds like an authentic First Nations Poet can still be heard and admired, whereas her British jingoism simply sounds absurd.

> *Few of us have the blood of kings.*
> *Few are of courtly birth.*
> *But few are vagabonds or rogues*
> *of doubtful name and worth.*
> *And all have one credential*
> *that entitles them to brag:*
> *That we were born in Canada,*
> *beneath the British flag!*

Trite and conventional in their own time, most of us would find them silly, if not offensive now. But when she writes, "You have given us Bibles and stolen our land," her poems on genocide still ring with an authentic feeling:

> *You have killed him. But you shall not dare*
> *To touch him now he's dead.*
> *You have cursed and called him "cattle thief"*
> *Though you robbed him first of bread—*
> *Robbed him and robbed my people.*
> *Look there at that shrunken face,*
> *Starved with the hollow hunger*
> *We owe to you and your race.*
> *What have you left us of land?*
> *What have you left of game?*

What have you brought but evil
And curses since you came?

Squamish Elder Joe Mathias, great-grandson of Chief Joe Capilano who was her last close friend, says that such a voice was rare in Pauline's time. It is not that common today, either; so split personality or double identity though she undoubtedly had, in her most powerful voice Pauline Johnson may have helped set in motion some of those declarations of right and of entitlement that still importantly drive the First Nations in their ongoing search for a place in the North American sunshine even today.

By 1906 she was tired, and she had done the big work she set out to do. But she was not finished yet. Now forty-five years old, she tried Britain again. It was not quite the smash success of the earlier tour. But in London she met the Squamish chief, Joe Capilano, there to seek an audience with King Edward VI. Pauline was able to greet him in a few words of his own language. A rich friendship blossomed from this encounter. It would last the rest of her all too short life.

Back in Canada again she wrote stories for *Boys World*, and *Mother's Magazine*. She launched an exhausting tour of recitations in Canada and the USA, with her new and very loyal manager Walter McRaye. And then she had had enough. In 1909, perhaps already aware of the encroaching illness that would take her life, she just stopped. Exit. No fanfare. No farewell tour. She just stopped. She thought of Joe Capilano. She moved to Vancouver.

There would be one last great task, although she did not know that yet. Joe Capilano, according to his great grandson Joe Mathias, was a man of few words but a far-reaching intellect and had a vision of the possibilities for his people, the Squamish.

There had to be a deep spiritual connection [between them].
He was not about to share a lot of his intimate views of
the universe with [just] anybody. And, well, I think they
became such good friends that he was willing to share
these stories, these myths, these legends that come from
the Squamish people, that in a way explain who we are,
why we're here, where we come from.

Pauline wrote these stories down in her own style, and with the Chief's permission she sent a couple off to the *Vancouver Province*, which serialized them. The stories of a coastal people, until now conveyed by word of mouth, and virtually unknown outside their own circle, proved intriguing to a wide readership, soon to become wider. They were assembled in a book, *Legends of Vancouver*. The first edition sold out. A *Collected Poems* was planned. When she published it under the title *Flint and Feather*, it was, like *Legends*, an instant success. She was a popular writer again.

And she needed the money. She had been diagnosed with breast cancer. The rest of her days were spent in hospital, and much of the revenue went to pay for what was a costly business in the days before a public health care system.

There is a footnote about Prince Arthur, Duke of Connaught. He had been appointed Governor General of Canada. His first contact with the Johnson family had been at Six Nations, more than forty years earlier; then there was the message about the blanket, in London, (but no meeting).

But finally, in 1912, the Governor General came to the poet's bedside. We do not know what they said to each other. But if you look at the title page of *Flint and Feather*, you will see that it is dedicated to him.

The Mohawk from Ontario had fallen deeply in love with her new home on the Pacific Coast; the grandeur of the mountains, the easy-going friendliness of the people, the bustle of the shops. She particularly cherished Stanley Park and the long ruminative walks she took there with Joe Capilano. She asked the city to bury her ashes in the Park, overlooking the ocean. There is no other tomb in the park, that we know of. But Pauline is there. And from time to time, on her small marker, with a carved profile of the poet in stone, you will see a fresh bunch of flowers.

She died a few months after *Flint and Feather* was published. She was not yet fifty-two. Her books have been printed in many languages. There have been several biographies. Four schools are named for her, including a French Language school. She has had a commemorative postage stamp, and Chiefswood is a national historic site, open to the public. Although few Canadians now know who she is, she left a footprint. Perhaps she was ahead of her time, in her passion to both utter the passions and the stories of her native heritage, and at the same time build a bridge of understanding between the First Nations and the "Founding Nations." It is difficult to think of anyone since who has undertaken quite the same task. She represented, says biographer Carol Gerson, "a possibility in Canada that has not been reproduced."

◆ ◆ ◆

The Pauline Johnson biography was written by Simon Johnston and produced by Scott Calbeck and Morgan Earl, with line producer David Hoffert. Camera Mitchell Ness, sound Ian Challis, Eric Davies and Trent Stewart, and editing by David Hoffert. It was first broadcast by History Television on March 28, 1999, and will be broadcast again in the spring of 2001.

ADDITIONAL READING:

Pauline Johnson: *Flint and Feather*

Carol Gerson: *Pauline Johnson: Times and Text*

Veronica Strong-Boag: *Paddling Her Own Canoe*

Betty Keller: *Pauline Johnson, First Aboriginal Voice of Canada*

See the PAULINE JOHNSON ARCHIVE schoolnet site devoted to the works of E. Pauline Johnson, at :

http://www.humanities.mcmaster.ca/ ~pjohnson/mock.html

◇ Part Six ◇

ANGUS WALTERS
The Captain and the Queen

One of our coins has not one but two queens on it. Take out a dime, heads or tails. If heads comes up first you'll see the familiar face of Her Majesty Elizabeth II, as she was in her late 20's, lean and graceful and every inch a Queen. Turn it over and you'll find the image of a ship under sail, also lean and graceful. And also every inch a queen, though not yet in her 20's as depicted there in chiselled silver metal.

She is a schooner. The age of sail being long gone, for many readers nowadays the word *schooner* just means a sailboat, perhaps a little bigger than the Lasers kids learn to race on, but, hey, schooner, sailboat, same thing.

Not so.

The schooner arrives fairly late on sailing's long horizon. She is the ultimate design of that last period of the world's history in which sailing vessels went to sea to work, to carry cargo or passengers or to fish, not primarily as the computer-designed playthings of wealthy sportmen and women sailing for glory. In the late 18th century and long into the 19th, the transoceanic record-breakers were the clippers, ships of four or five masts — or even more — bearing both square sails and fore-and-aft sails, huge loads of canvas that could drive them across an ocean faster than anything that had been seen before.

The fore-and-aft sail, a triangular canvas with its luff or forward edge laced to a pole or a line, allows a vessel to sail into the wind, within about 45 degrees of head-on to it. But the big traditional square work sails of the ocean-crossers and warships of the days before steam were a great way to sail before the wind. You could not sail closer to the wind than broadside under square sails; with a straight north wind you could head up as close to the wind as straight west or east, not into the wind on a northerly course. But running before the wind you could pile on great masses of sail, acres of billowing cloth, and fairly leap over the waves.

Then marine architects began to refine the shape and distribution of sails, and to come up with patterns that somehow drew the wind over the vessel in a way that gave her more speed over the long haul than any other rig. Their great achievement was called the Schooner, a dutch word originally. The schooner's mainmast, the tallest of her two or three masts, would be the one furthest aft, the foremast the smaller. And if there were a third, the mizzen, it would be in-between in size. There was something aerodynamically effective about that big collection of sails making up a huge triangle with the longest edge the furthest back that made for speed, but also made for difficult handling. With all that wind pressure far aft, there was a tricky balance of wind and water pressures on sails, rigging, hull and rudder. You really had to know what you were about. Many a young skipper who thought he knew sail would find himself in trouble the first time he took a schooner into a serious bit of wind.

Not Angus Walters. If you look at photographs of the Newfoundland and Nova Scotia fishing fleets going off after the cod towards the end of the 1800's and the beginning of the 1900's, bit by bit you see more of those tall mainmasts aft, the shorter foremast, bit by bit three masts reduce to two and the square sails vanish, bit by bit, until by the time Angus Walters was ready to take command of a vessel, his first command, at the age of twenty-three, *Captain* Angus Walters, there was little doubt in the minds of serious fishermen that the schooner was the rig. Angus Walters could really not remember much of a life before he went to sea, and when he went there it was in schooners, and their little dories in which the men went off for the cod and brought it back to the schooner for salting and packing.

Cod is a cold water species, found mostly in the North Atlantic. Now, in the 21st century, stocks are grievously low. But when early explorers first entered our waters, they found so many that the myth was you could throw a basket over the side with a line on it and haul up the crew's dinner. Some even claimed that the fish on the surface were so thick they slowed the vessel down. When the Italian Giovanni Caboto reported back to the King of England who had commissioned him in 1495, he confidently reported that the waters off the New Found Land were so rich in fish that Europe could be fed for the rest of time.

Cod would become a prize for which nations went to war. For centuries conflicts between France, Britain, the Scandinavian countries, and finally Canada and the United States, over cod, were in many ways as important, if not as bloody, as the conflicts over sovereignty and land. They are not over yet.

Angus Walters was born in Lunenburg, Nova Scotia, on June 9th, 1881, one of twelve children born to a sea captain and his wife. Many a Nova Scotian kid would be off to the cod at the age of eight or nine, especially if his dad had been lost at sea and the kid was suddenly the man of the house. But Angus' dad wanted to make sure his kids got a good schooling, and Angus did not turn up working the cod, a "throater" cutting the heads off as the fish were gaffed up over the side of the schooner, from the dories, until he was thirteen. By the age of fifteen he was out in the dories himself, a doryman under the tutelage of an experienced fisherman, the dory skipper.

His first time out was almost his last. A thick fog came down on them, they could neither see nor hear the mother ship, night fell, the older man feared that their fate would be that of hundreds, maybe thousands of Nova Scotian men who went out in the dory into storms or fog and never came back. They were lucky that night. The fog lifted. In the distance the boy and the man could see lights, a red light and a green light, their schooner, and they rowed and yelled and rowed and yelled, and made it back safely.

A few years later, still in his teens, Angus was on deck one night with the captain, who was his older brother John. The sea was running very high, just the two brothers on deck, everyone else below. A wave washed right over the deck. Angus heard a cry from his brother, and when he could get the water out of his eyes, the young skipper was gone, washed overboard. It was fairly easy to get washed overboard. The rails were built low to permit the fish to be easily gaffed from above or thrown from below when the dories came back with their catch; the sea often washed over the deck. Men sometimes lashed themselves in place at the wheel but John wasn't tied on that night, and he was gone. Young Angus showed his natural flair for command, took over the ship, yelled for some men, and ordered a dory lowered over the side. Almost miraculously John caught a line hanging from the dory, and was saved. Angus had had his first taste of command.

It came to him not long after, with a vessel called the *Minnie M. Cook*. Although he was but twenty-three years old, he was already known as a veteran of the Atlantic cod fishery. Young Captain Angus Walters. He is still remembered as extraordinary by those who sailed with him.

His son Spike says, "He might have been small, but he was mighty. All you had to do was sail with him on a fishing trip . . . and you'd know that he had fight in him. If you fooled around he'd just as much say, 'We'll throw *you* overboard.'"

Sailors were a bit afraid of him. Authority then was taken seriously in every field and was often fearsome. But Angus' sailors loved him, and the survivors still do; you can hear it in the warm burr of their Nova Scotia voices. Clem Hilz sailed with him for years, and says, "There was no fear in him. And you didn't have too many men saying anything back to him or you know, that wasn't in the books. When he said 'We'll do such,' that Such — whatever it was — was done."

They remember him, even from those early days, as a "sail-dragger," a skipper who liked to pile on the sail and push the vessel as hard as she could be pushed. But not beyond reason. He impressed them even then, in his young twenties, as a captain who knew very well that he had the lives of his men in his hands. But he loved to push a vessel, to make her lift, to get the last one percent of a knot out of her.

The cod fishery had a strong racing tradition. It was not just racing for sport: the fastest vessels would be first in with a catch and would command the market. Nonetheless, whenever a pair of ships were on the last leg home, or even outward bound for the Grand Banks empty and fresh, and came within hailing distance, chances are one skipper or the other would pull up alongside the other man's ship and haul out a megaphone and cry "Let's have a Hook!" And that meant, let's see who'll be first at the fish, or first back in port. And then it would be pile on the sail and all hands on deck, and cheering and yelling taunts back and forth. They sailed dangerously close to each other, learning their vessel's quirks and quiddities, and looking for that tiny bit of added speed that would not seem very much from minute to minute, but overnight, say, or through a long day, could bring one skipper home to port a minute or two or even an hour or more ahead of the other.

So racing was a great sport and also a way to improve your profit margins.

When he was twenty-six Angus Walters fell in love with and married Maggie Tanner. Sons Gilbert and Spike and Stewart arrived over the next seven years, although their dad was at sea at least as much as he was home, building a reputation as a Highline skipper who brought home huge catches. He would take his new vessel the

Muriel B. Walters (named after his mother) to the same grounds as another man, and come home with twice the catch. Substantial profits for his shareholders, and a comfortable income for his young family.

And a hell of a reputation whenever they went for a Hook, outbound or homebound.

You can see his picture from the high days of the schooner trade, on the 37-cent Canadian stamp issued in 1981. It is a lean-boned tidy face, with eyes that are always scanning the horizon and the weather and the set of the sails. The mouth usually had just a hint of an ironic pout, a turnup at the middle of the outer lip that made you wonder if he wasn't thinking of some stunt or some technique for making her sail just a bit faster. It was a face that would become famous. It is seldom seen, that calculating face, under a formal captain's peaked cap with an anchor, or over gold-braided shoulders. It's more often an old cloth cap like an Irish farmer's, and a tweed jacket, or oilskins. The old cloth cap is what he wore at the wheel, and almost everywhere else. It is hard to think of him without it.

In 1920 someone got the bright idea of turning the Hook into a formal international race. Many of the skippers from Lunenburg had gone up against their counterparts from Gloucester, Massachusetts, and other New England fishing ports, and there was a kind of international rivalry that was friendly and respectful but intense at the same time. So they put together the plans for a series, the International Fishermen's race. This wasn't something for well-off sportsmen. The vessel in competition had to be a working fishing vessel, and the men sailing her had to be fishermen. The first race would be in September, and so Angus took the *Muriel B.* out against fellow Lunenburger Tom Himmelman in command of the *Delawanna*, in the qualifier off Halifax. And Angus piled on the sail — too much, as it turned out, for the *Muriel B.* He should not have done it. It was not necessary. He was well in the lead. But now he was carrying nine thousand square feet of sail five miles short of the finish line, and the *Muriel B.* couldn't take it. The foremast snapped, and the foredeck was a mess of splintered spruce, broken lines and tangled canvas. The *Delawanna* pulled ahead and crossed the line six minutes ahead of Angus and the *Muriel B.*

As if that wasn't bad enough, the *Esperanto* out of Gloucester, up against Tom Himmelman and the *Delawanna* in the finals, simply walked away with it. The *Esperanto*'s skipper Marty Welch sailed home with the $4,000 prize, the equivalent of $100,000 or more in today's money, dollars that the Nova Scotians had put up, confident that *their* man would win. But he didn't. It was shameful.

Nova Scotia Curator of Education Ralph Getson says he believes it was then that Angus began to think of building the greatest schooner ever, a vessel that would win that cup back from the New Englanders, the ship that would be the *Bluenose.* He stewed all winter about the strain it would put on his family life, with the three young boys and a wife whose health was not the best, but he knew it had to be done and sensed that he was the Lunenburger who could restore honour to the port. He talked it up with politicians and businessmen. The money was raised. They sought out a naval architect named

William Roue and told him he had to build them a schooner that would beat the Gloucestermen.

There was never any question as to who would command her. Ralph Getson says that Angus "had a track record. He had proven he could handle a vessel. . . . They were still fishing. He was a fish killer. He could find a trip of fish. . . . Also he could handle a crowd of men."

He was passionately committed to the new project. Obsessed is probably the better word. He was down at the yards most days that winter. He even began to interfere with the design. That made for some hard feelings, for a while, with William Roue, according to Ralph Getson.

The tradition in designing accommodations for fishermen was that the men's needs did not matter as much as the design of the hull for cargo and speed. But Angus Walters was a sailors' skipper. He said, "My men are not midgets. They need more room in the fo'c'sle [forecastle]." The fo'c'sle is where the sailors sleep. Angus wanted his crew well-rested. If you look at the photographs of the hull you can see what they call a "knuckle" at the bow, where they raised the deck above the forecastle, an eighteen inch add-on that Bill Roue always said slowed her down. Roue kept on saying it long after Bluenose *became the fastest sailing ship in the world.*

"No!" said Angus Walters, in an interview with J. Frank Willis, this writer's old colleague, a gravel-voiced CBC announcer and TV host who had sailed with Walters on her last great race, sending the race out live by radio.

"It didn't slow her down. He [Bill Roue] thinks that by raising her up, when you 'haul by,' . . . that there was much more wood higher up in the air. But on the other hand, when you were off [sailing before the wind], there was that much more wind up higher in the air in that. So I don't think it affected her one way or the other. . . . Raising her up forward still made her a drier boat. In bad weather or . . . a fairly good breeze. . . . If it had been down eighteen inches lower, more water was going to come over, and more come over it had to go back off the deck and run off of her. . . . (And) you never want water on deck when you are racing if you can help it!"

Ships in the Nova Scotia fleet often carried the name of a woman, the wife of an owner or master often as not. But this time the schooner that was going to be the pride of Nova Scotia and of Canada, a symbol of maritime pride known around the world, for twenty-one years the fastest of her kind afloat, would be named for her people, the Nova Scotians, the Bluenoses. She was launched from the Lunenburg yards on March 26th, 1921. Her skipper was thirty-nine years old. He was at the height of his powers.

Clem Hilz says that Angus talked to her as if she were a person.

Honest to God. He always talked to that ship. . . . He could do more with that ship than he could do with any …I don't believe he could have done it with another ship. That ship and him were just like bosom pals. Wonderful!

He could go up and take the wind out of the sails (of the competition) and sail by them. . . . "Luffing" they used to call it. Luffing. Get up windward of a guy and his sails would be going this way, and the Bluenose *would be going right along you know. Smooth sailing. Oh yes. Tricks in*

all trades. And he had 'em. . . . That's the beauty of it. And
he knew he had a ship that could do the tricks if he put it
to it. And he used to put it to it!

Luffing works like this. You are slightly behind the other vessel, sailing just a bit upwind of her. That is, if the wind is coming from the starboard, your right hand, the other vessel is a few metres ahead of you and to port, to your left. It is desirable to be upwind of the other vessel. Presently you will have to make a turn in that direction to tack onto the next leg, and if you are upwind that means you are ahead as you turn. But there is this luffing trick that allows you to make it even better.

If you pull her too hard into the wind, trying to "haul" as Angus said, to get even further upwind, you will lose a little speed. You have this trade-off between getting a little more speed by falling off a little to port, just off the wind, or holding up into the wind, keeping upwind but a little slower.

Here is what Angus Walters (and generations of racing sailors after him, including this writer) would do. He would suddenly turn slightly to port, falling off the wind, picking up speed substantially but crossing right behind the other vessel where, for a moment, he would be blanketed by her sails as he pulled ahead but slightly downwind of her. It seems, the first time you try it, as though you have lost position, in relationship to the wind. But you are really fast now, and that momentary blanketing effect is so brief it hardly affects your speed at all. And so the next thing you know you are pulling ahead of the other guy, but slightly downwind. And there is a curious effect that takes place if you judge the positions of the two vessels very precisely. There is a backflow coming off your sails that disturbs the flow of air over the sails of the ship upwind of your starboard. You are "covering" her. And before he knows it the other skipper, who has everything set for this close-hauled course, close into the wind, is losing his wind, luffing, slowing down grievously.

He is in a kind of trap. He can't come much off the wind towards you to recover or he'll hit you. If you play it just right (and it *is* a high-risk manoeuvre, requiring a *very* nice judgment) you begin to pull ahead. Then you can position him dead behind you, the luffing gets worse in your slipstream, you pull away ahead and he never recovers.

Angus pulled that in the two qualifiers, and then sailed *Bluenose* down to Gloucester for the International, and of course brought home the cup and the money and the glory, to Lunenburg, where it belonged. And the next year he did it again.

Clem Hilz says, "They could build boats forever and a day over in Gloucester, they'd never build one to beat that *Bluenose*. In calm waters, yes, *maybe*. But you give her 25 knots of wind and the devil in hell couldn't catch her!"

Bluenose will never be forgotten. There will be a *Bluenose II*, we'll come to that. She'll be skippered by Angus Walters' grandson Wayne Walters. But even Wayne, proud as he was of *Bluenose II*, still speaks of the original and her skipper with a sense of wonder.

He knew how far to push it. . . . He knew the vessel. The
vessel was part of him. He knew every inch of canvas and
wood, and he knew the breaking point of everything, and
I think he must have had that extra sense of being able to
tell when there was going to be a slight change in the
wind, or where the best position would be to take advan-
tage of . . . ah . . . of "covering" the other vessel, so to
speak.

Before long, Angus Walters, of Lunenburg, Nova Scotia, a town few west of New Brunswick could even find
on the map, became not just a hometown hero, but a
national hero. His schooner was now officially the fastest
sailing vessel in the whole, wide, windy world. This
seemed not to go to his head. He kept perspective. Work
was what it was all about. Work to do as well as the other
fellow, perhaps a little better. Work was best if you had a
vessel you could talk to, who could listen to you. But
there was a lot of luck that went with the work, and you
depended critically upon the skills and support of the
crew, all able sailors, each one knowing what he had to
do at every moment.

Angus Walters radiated a quiet pride now (how could
he not?) but he didn't wear it like medals or a flag. He
was firm but soft spoken, apparently not interested in
personal glory; just in doing the best that could be done.
That is how they remember him.

There was another well-respected Atlantic coast cod
fisherman. His name was Ben Pine. He fished out of Gloucester, Massachusetts. Now the Gloucestermen looked at
Ben Pine, and they looked at *Bluenose,* and they said *Blue-*

nose was the ship to beat and Ben Pine was the man to beat her.

But they didn't have a ship. So they decided to do exactly what the Lunenburgers had done; they would build one. They hired the best marine architects they could find. Money was no object. They knew that the Lunenburg yards had produced something the world had never seen before. But maybe it was a fluke, and they had the science and the resources to do better than those fishermen in Nova Scotia; they were Americans, after all. And so they gathered it all together and got to work.

The result, the following year, was the *Columbia*; sleek, some secrets about the hull they wouldn't let anyone even look at, the latest in materials and fittings, the best craftsmen New England could provide. She was a beauty. Ben Pine looked on the *Columbia*, and saw that she was good. He hand picked a crew. Every member of that crew was himself a Captain. The skipper and his captains set out for Halifax, for the next running of the International Fishermen's. The world was watching. The first race began. It was very close for a while. At one point the ships got too close to each other and as she came about for the next tack *Bluenose*'s boom raked the *Columbia* and caused some damage. Angus Walters said, "As soon as we got clear of him, it was just the same as saying goodbye to the *Columbia*, because from there in we still crossed the line between two and three minutes ahead of her . . . well, we come in . . . it's officially announced . . . *Bluenose* won, everybody felt happy, and no more about it."

But there *was* more about it. *Columbia* won the second race, and then the race committee changed the rules. *Bluenose* won the third race, but the committee declared that under the new rules, which had not been discussed with the competing captains, Bluenose had rounded a buoy the wrong way. So they awarded the race — and the cup — to Ben Pine and the *Columbia*.

Angus Walters said that he went to the chairman to protest, and said, "Can you give us a reason? Oh yes, he said, a protest entered and you did this and you did that. . . . Well, I said, we got our rules, I said, before the race started. And you and no other committee can do anything out of those rules without the consent of the two sailing masters."

And then one of those extraordinary events happened that gives grace to the world of high competition between people of character and integrity. The Gloucestermen heard of it. And Ben Pine and his crew of captains said to each other, Angus is right. And they told the committee they would not accept the prize under that unheard-of piece of flim-flammery where the rules had been changed without the captains' agreement. The committee had to find some way to save face. And the only way they could think of was to hold another race.

Pine and his captains agreed to this, but Angus Walters said, "No, not unless you put up another trophy and raise some more money. We're due to sail for Lunenburg in the morning." And that was the end of it. Bitterness all round. Ben Pine and the *Columbia* crew felt the same: too many rules, too much bureaucracy. The spirit had gone out of the thing. The International would not be held again for eight years.

As far as the world and the fishermen were concerned *Bluenose* was still undefeated and Angus Walters was simply one of the best skippers on the whole Atlantic coast. All his life at sea, and skipper of the world's fastest sailing vessel. And still fishing her, and still able to get a trip of fish where other men were just "fish peddlers," coming in with a skimpy catch while *Bluenose*'s holds were full.

There was a close call one night in August of 1926, when they were hit by a storm that most of the men at sea could not recall the likes of. Fifty Lunenburg sailors drowned that night. And while it may have been luck in part, there is no doubt that Angus Walters' extraordinary knowledge of his ship, of the sea and its weather, and of his men, were the main reasons why they all came through. Clem Hilz said they all prayed, and they said to each other if she went over they would all get up on the high side and hold hands and jump in the water together. If they had to go, they would go together.

Angus was anchored off Sable Island, "The Graveyard of the Atlantic." When the barometer dropped and the wind began to make up he was trapped right in the middle of one of the storms of the century. He put on just enough sail, all forward, to keep his beloved vessel ahead of the wind, stern to the towering seas but moving enough so she wouldn't be "pooped," that is, drowned by a following wave pouring over the ship from astern. Then he made sure he was going to steer her out of it.

Clem Hilz, who lived through it, said,

And you talk about blow! I never saw nothing like that in my
life and never want to. . . . Heisted up what sail we could get
on her, was the double reef foresail and a double reef jib and
jumbo. That's all you could use. And he got lashed to the
wheel. He stayed there for eight hours. Now you talk about a
brave and courageous man. That he stood there knowing in
his own mind and saying in his own words, "We'll never see
Lunenburg again." But, good ship that she was, and brave
. . . and capable man that he was, we sailed out of it and next
morning we was out in plenty water.

In 1931 the International was held for one last time. Once again *Bluenose* sailed home well ahead of the competition. But it was almost over now. The age of the schooner was effectively gone. Diesel engines and steel hulls and factory ships with refrigerated hulls were moving in. *Bluenose* was only sixteen years old, but it began to look as though she was a museum piece. Angus considered retiring. Maggie had died. He was tired and dismayed as he saw the end of his era like a cloud blowing in from the east. There would be one more go at the International Fishermen's, against the Gloucestermen, and this time in their waters, off the coast of Massachusetts. It was 1938. *Bluenose* lost her mizzen topsail half-way through the final race, but Angus got the lads working together as well as ever they had worked, and got a line on her, and cleared the mess, and won the race.

In the *Heritage Minute* that celebrates that last race you can hear Angus Walters (and the actor who played him was at the actual wheel of the real *Bluenose*, brought into a movie studio for the making of the *Minute*), you can hear him whispering to his beloved schooner, "Just one more time Old Girl and then you can rest." That was a scriptwriter's invention, of course; we don't know what he actually said. But we do know that Angus talked to his great love, the ship he loved more than he loved his house. He would have saved his ship before his house if they both burned at once, the sailors said. So he *could* have said exactly that.

And we do know that she was going to her rest.

At least that was what Angus Walters hoped for her. They had put diesels in her for a while, but it wasn't the same. The old Skipper tried to get Nova Scotia to draw her up on land and make her a museum. He would stay with her and tell visitors the stories of her glory days. But the money didn't come, and Angus was broke. And so in 1942, when a couple of guys from the States offered him $25,000 cash for her, he had no where else to turn.

She was gone. Many of them said Angus was gone too, from that moment on. Oh, he married again. He started a dairy business. His grandson, who would skipper *Bluenose II* years later, remembers Angus rousing him at four a.m. when he worked for a summer on the milk truck. Angus Walters was eighty years old that summer, and hoisting sixty-five pound cans of milk, one in each hand, onto the truck, maybe a hundred of them in a morning's round.

The last chapter in the book of the great schooner *Bluenose* was ugly. They took the masts off her and used her as a barge in the Caribbean, under tow. In January 1946 the old barge, with still a few marks of paint on her bow that once said *Bluenose, Lunenburg,* struck a reef off Haiti, and began to go down. The skipper of the tug said to hell with it and cut the line and let her sink.

Wayne Walters was at the curling rink with his grandfather when they got the news. "You might as well have put a knife in his heart," Wayne said.

But, curiously, just when it seemed that the story was over, the myth began to grow. People came to Lunenburg to seek out Angus Walters, to hear his stories of the *Bluenose*. The Lunenburg yards had built a replica of the *Bounty* for the MGM movie; so people said If we can build a *Bounty* we can build another *Bluenose*. This time, the money was found and the keel was laid. In February of 1963 Angus Walters, *Captain* Angus Walters, drove the first spike for the laying of that keel. A replica of his Queen, and his own grandson to skipper her.

He died on August 12th, 1969, at eighty-seven. But his story did not die. Take a look at your dime again.

◆ ◆ ◆

The Captain and the Queen was written by Ian MacLeod and Chuck Stewart, and directed by Chuck Stewart. Produced by F. Whitman Trecartin; Director of Photography Pat Kennedy sound Andy McKay; editor Mike O'Toole. It was first broadcast on History Television on April 13th, 1998, and will be rebroadcast in the spring of 2001.

There is an ANGUS WALTERS web site at:

www.schoolnet.ca/collections/
wayfarers/bluenose.htm

◇ Part Seven ◇

JUDITH JASMIN
TELEVISING THE REVOLUTION

Now in the early years of the 21st century, when the Province of Quebec is noted for its advanced social legislation in education, justice, health and welfare, and for its vigorous popular culture and professional and commercial sophistication, it is easy to forget that early in the 20th century it was comparatively poor and backward. Its French-speaking population was looked upon by official Canada as a source of cheap labour. Its educational standards were abysmal. Its politics and social standards were dominated by the Roman Catholic Church.

It is almost always wrong to ascribe important social changes to any single cause. But in the case of Quebec the arrival of Radio-Canada's first French-language television station in 1952 was swiftly followed by a torrent of social and cultural change. It would be difficult to argue that there was not a cause-and-effect relationship, however simplistic that might seem to some sociologists. The era had the marks of a genuine social revolution. It would bring to an end the Church's domination and the officially sanctioned suppression of the population's self-fulfillment in its own cultural terms.

The growth of an astonishingly widely viewed entertainment industry, with brilliantly produced variety shows, comedy, sports, and extended soap operas called *téléromans*, gave this French side of the CBC an early and powerful success that outstripped (and still does) the impact of CBC's English-language television. Home-grown television along with other forms of popular entertainment was, and remains, a vital element of modern Quebec's pride in its own culture. But at the beginning it was, above all, the journalists who brought to Quebecers a portrait of themselves as a special people of distinct character but with unacknowledged rights and unfulfilled potential. That portrait would contribute substantially to the rejection of old values, of the old compliance in the face of authority. Out of those changes grew the new Quebec: vocal, demanding, confident, different, troublesome, rich, energetic, ambitious.

One of the most famous of the television journalists who helped transform Quebec was a gifted woman named Judith Jasmin. She was to take the standards of investigative journalism to heights not yet achieved anywhere in Canada. Jasmin was a woman of profound convictions about justice and humanity. She would be accused by some of allowing those convictions to colour her reporting and analysis, at a time when "objectivity" was supposed to be the watchword for journalists. It was an accusation she acknowledged with good humour, insisting that fairness and completeness were what really made for good journalism, and that it was simply unrealistic to pretend that a journalist's work should not be influenced by her values. When she began in television the medium was completely dominated by men, and the conservative and machismo management at Radio-Canada must have been surprised to find themselves, giving this . . . this *wo-man*! . . . such prominence.

But they couldn't refuse her; she was just that good.

Talented, brilliant, determined, energetic, wise in the ways of the world, Judith Jasmin had, however, a turbulent and often disastrous personal life. Somehow the men she loved — and there were many of them — could not give to her what she yearned for. And when late in her life she would say that it was her career that had prevented her from marrying and having children, you could sense a deep, melancholic wistfulness behind the radiant, resolute, confident, and (to Quebecers) comfortingly familiar strong eyes and knowing mouth.

Thirty years after her death, with a park named after her, as well as a building at the University of Montreal where students are taught to be journalists, few of those students know anything about this once most famous of Quebec women. Asked about the name on their building, present-day students will say, "Well, there is a journalistic prize in her name." A rare respondent will know that she was a broadcaster, and a few more know that there was some connection with René Lévesque.

But the old broadcasters know. Pierre Nadeau, now in his late sixties and in many ways the surviving dean of the television newsmen, remembers Judith Jasmin as "a fabulous reporter, a great journalist, a great human being, and a very joyful person." But that is partly, as he admits, what he wants to remember; it leaves out the melancholy side.

She was born in 1916 into an unusual family. Her mother was an ardent and premature feminist, with a huge laugh, a strong, country kind of face, and great energy. She learned to drive a car at the age of seventy, in a Quebec where women were still, on the whole, expected to stay in the kitchen and bear a child a year until they collapsed.

Judith's father Amédée was a socialist, which was unusual in Quebec then, and — even more unusual — a feminist like his wife Rosaria. Often he was the only man present at the meetings of the small pioneering group of feminists in the province. Women were not allowed to vote in provincial elections in Quebec until 1948, thirty years after they had received that right in federal elections.

In 1921, when Judith was five, the family moved to Paris. Monsieur Jasmin wanted to study co-operative work projects and expose his two little girls to an atmosphere richer in the oxygen of the human imagination than what he could find for them in the convent schools of Quebec.

Paris, in the 1920's! The booming, illusory prosperity of those post-war years, before the Great Crash of 1929, had turned Paris into a favoured destination for people from all over the globe who were seeking intellectual, artistic, and physical pleasures. The bookstalls along the river Seine, the presence of art and design almost everywhere you looked, the turbulence of the night life, the debates about life and meaning that overflowed the walls of the universities and penetrated the streets — all these had attracted people who would leave an indelible mark on the way in which the modern world looks at itself.

Picasso, James Joyce, Gertrude Stein, before long Ernest Hemingway, musicians, philosophers . . . the vitality was breathtaking. And when Jasmin Père decided eight years later to take his adolescent girls back to Montreal where there seemed to be an irreversible surge of prosperity at last, he had on his hands a very rebellious thirteen-year-old named Judith.

You can see it in the family photographs, of which many survive. The confident tilt of the head, the frank gaze, comfortable with the camera. There are people in the world whom the camera loves. Judith Jasmin was one of them. That has a lot to do with why she became such an influence as a television journalist years later. And you can see it in the youthful photos and the odd moments of home movies that have come down to us. The relationship with the camera was one she seems to have trusted all her life.

She stuck it out in Montreal for two years in the convent schools and the stultifying role-determined world where girls were scarcely considered to be people, but rather instruments for the propagation of the race and of the Faith. After the stock market crash of October 1929 had generated the worst global economic depression ever, only months after their return, the spirited teenager suddenly realized that she was poor.

"For the past two years we have lived frugally," she wrote, in her clear angular hand in a diary she had begun to fill with youthful outpourings of inspiration and desire. "Maman does all the chores and totally deprives herself. Papa too. [Me], I don't want . . . a life of poverty."

Somehow — it is not clear where the money came from — she managed to get two more years of school in Paris. And then it was back to Montreal and a college for girls, where she completed a degree and helped support her family by working in a bookstore.

In the bookstore there was time to listen to the radio. Judith Jasmin began to think that there might be a world out there that she could thrive in. She joined a theatre group and began to act. She discovered that she had a natural gift for the stage. Her reviews were glowing. A little more money coming in. And then, one day in 1937, her world shifted once again, when she auditioned for a role in a radio drama series, the forerunner of the television *téléromans* that would later bring Radio-Canada TV its most numerous and most loyal viewers. The series was called *La Pension Veldor.* They gave her a starring role. Before long her photograph was in all the papers. She and the series were a big hit. She fell in love with a theatrical impresario named Paul Maugé, and moved in with him. Maugé was popular with the stars he booked into Montreal, partly because he was a great host. Night after night there was champagne and caviar. Maugé's little apartment would be packed with glittering people, artists from Russia and France and America. It became the glittering world of Judith Jasmin.

She stayed with Maugé for about twelve years, but her friends and admirers say now that she was not really all that happy. Maugé was separated but still legally married. To be with a married man was a genuine scandal in Quebec at that time, but he refused to get divorced, which at that time in Quebec required an official Act of the Senate of Canada, and was a long, difficult and expensive process. Restless, she tried a job as a radio producer, at first not thinking that it was a vocation, just something to do. Radio exposed her to a new world. She began to think about reporting, getting out in the world, bringing stories home to her people.

Judith would say later, in a television interview when she was fifty, that the theatre had never been her real craft. She had fallen into it by accident. She felt that there must be something else more meaningful. When she took her first steps as a radio reporter, she knew she had found that something.

But it is possible that she was at least partly wrong about the "accidental" attraction of the theatre, and that she had undervalued the importance of her theatrical ability. While she cut her journalistic teeth in radio, and there met and was encouraged and trained by another young and ambitious reporter named René Lévesque, it was in television that she would come into her own. The really strong television journalists have always had a strong sense of theatre, of using the body, the voice, gesture, the measured or dramatic rise and fall of the narration, to compel attention and convey meaning and a sense of importance. Think of the Canadian reporter Morley Safer in Vietnam, and the cigarette lighter sending the thatched roof of a suspected Vietcong village family up in flames. Think of Walter Cronkite and the persona of reliable Uncle Walt that he carefully cultivated. Jasmin knew what it was like to be in front of an audience, how to use that dancer's body, the light flick of the eyes or the tiny curl of the corner of the mouth. She understood the power of dropping the voice at the crucial moment, the moment when a non-theatre person might go loud to gain attention whereas Jasmin knew you went soft.

Whatever the relationship between theatre and television journalism (and this writer believes it to be very close), Jasmin's years in radio, in harness with the seasoned reporter that Lévesque already was, turned her into a shrewd field reporter, a populist with a sense of the streets. She and Lévesque are credited now with having effectively invented broadcast street journalism for Quebec, going out with equipment that was new to them but seems so primitive to us, such as wire recorders, and talking to ordinary people instead of officials and authorities.

The wire recorder preceded the tape recorder and changed journalism radically. Before the portable recording system, recordings could be made in the studio on huge machines that physically cut sonic grooves in huge wax discs. Reporters came back from the field with notes, wrote up their stories, and read them on the air live. Lévesque and Jasmin changed that and took the microphone into the streets. What they were doing is normal now; then it was a breakthrough.

Judith Jasmin and Lévesque moved over to television in 1952, and she realized she could go around the world with the 16mm film camera and bring that world back to her audience. The cameras were primitive, by today's standards. The sound was recorded on an optical track right on the film, and the quality was not very good.

Equipment was cumbersome. But it was a heady time; journalists were at last able to bring back to their audiences a vivid, moving visual representation of the experiences they had formerly been able only to speak or write about. Some of them were becoming stars.

Judith Jasmin's name became a household word. In the view of some of her surviving colleagues such as Pierre Nadeau and Jasmin's biographer Collette Beauchamps, she became one of the most significant contributors to Quebec's new awakening to the world, and to Quebec's place in that world. Algeria, Israel, France, India, Haiti — there now came pouring out of our screens an ongoing visit with parts of the world that we had only dimly heard of before. And if we lived in Quebec and spoke French, Judith Jasmin would be there, night after night, making sense out of the chaos of poverty, revolution and global transformation.

When she went off to New York, as she did in 1967 to cover the Women's March on City Hall, it was undoubtedly part of her strategy to be conveying to the women of Quebec the news that there was something afoot in the world. There were changes in outlook and values, and possibilities; things that they ought to be part of. As a woman she was a pioneer, out there in the field with a cameraman and her wits and her courage. In those early days at Radio-Canada TV there were women with Ph.D.s working in the news department and the best they could get was a research job clipping newspapers. But Jasmin was reporting social change in Manhattan and social paralysis in Latin America, and everyone in Quebec was listening.

Her partner René Lévesque was another journalist who had quickly made a distinctive mark for himself in the television era. Later to be the first leader of the independence party known as Le Parti Québécois, and for nine dramatic years the premier of the province, Lévesque had honed his journalistic skills as a war correspondent in Europe during World War II. Now, with the advent of television, he started a television series, in which he simply lectured, with a blackboard, like a schoolteacher. Working without a script, he talked to his audience, not with the lofty, condescending attitude that was characteristic of many of his colleagues in the news business, but treating them as equals and as fellow citizens. He told them what was going on in the new post-war world, with a particular focus on issues of social justice, education, and politics. The program was *Point de Mire,* which means focal point, and it made Lévesque into a kind of journalistic hero.

René Lévesque and Judith Jasmin became one of the most powerful journalistic teams in the history of Canadian television. René Lévesque was more experienced than Judith Jasmin, though younger. He had been married shortly before they began to work together. Although the personal chemistry between them was an important element in the professional relationship, that relationship remained strictly professional until about a year and a half after the partnership began. They were in mining country in northern Quebec. They were looking for a location to film, and had stopped for a rest. And suddenly he grasped her in his arms and kissed her. She wrote later: "It was as if we had loved each other in another life."

So now she was travelling the world with the man she loved, doing the work she loved more than anything, and doing it better and better. They were in some respects an odd team. She was deliberate, thoughtful, careful, a demon for preparation and study and careful planning and scripting. Lévesque was an improviser. The veteran reporter, newscaster and news executive Knowlton Nash remembers Lévesque from much later, during the democratic presidential convention in Chicago in 1968. Nash himself would be in the studio for a good half-hour, polishing his report before reading live at airtime. Lévesque would come in fifteen seconds before airtime, his pockets bulging with notes, no script, and just stand there and tell it to his viewers, occasionally digging out a crumpled note to refresh his memory. Judith's style was to take time, think everything out methodically in advance, and deliver her reports with an air of authority and seriousness that was in marked contrast to Lévesque's playful improvisations.

But they were a team, professionally and personally, until that mysterious day four years later when he just left. One day he was there, the next day gone. Collette Beauchamps says, "It happened just like that. He stopped and he went to somebody else. Without any explanation or anything."

Judith Jasmin's life was shattered. In 1954 she pulled up stakes and left the country. She had reported from India and had sensed the intensely spiritual quality of life on that subcontinent, as so many visitors do. Although she was a thoughtful atheist, she was in anguish and in deep need and hoped she might find some kind of insight, and heal some wounds if she went back to India to stay for a while this time. She told her diary, "This trip is necessary to dissolve my last illusions. They will be washed away little by little by silence, by distance. It is as though I am under the effect of a drug that allows me to escape from myself. I am prepared for solitude."

When she came back to Montreal, in 1955, Lévesque still haunted her. She addressed him in that same diary: "I want to forget you, but I am more connected to you than ever. Six years of silently loving an unattainable man. . . . the thought of suicide has subtly been taking shape . . ."

But she was a survivor. With the help of a therapist she fought off those thoughts of suicide. Like many professionals she found healing in her work. And then she fell in love again.

The torn, oppressive poverty-stricken Caribbean nation of Haiti had been one of her first foreign assignments as a television reporter. Now, back in that country on assignment, she met a tall, handsome black economist named Jo Chatelain, and would later say that he was her greatest love after René Lévesque. Chatelain was unmarried, a free man. Perhaps he wanted to keep it that way, because while they were together off and on for seven years, he lived in Washington or Paris and she in Montreal, and they met when they could. She decided Paris would be a better base: she would see more of Jo. So she decided to take her chances on the freelance life and return to the City of Light that had so enchanted her adolescence. It was tough. Unknown to the French-broadcasting community she found only a little work there. She made a meager living by sending pieces back, as a freelancer, to Radio-Canada, who paid her a disgraceful pittance, sustenance pay, a fraction of what staff reporters were making back home.

But she was free, working in Europe and North Africa, keeping that distinct voice and figure in front of her own people, bringing them an international perspective on her favourite issues of justice and liberty.

And those two themes were what would draw her back to Quebec as the long simmering independence movement brought the so called *Révolution Tranquille*, the Quiet Revolution, into louder and clearer focus, month by month as the 1960's began. It was a time when the rousing and energetic new culture of Quebec led more and more intellectuals and artists and young people of all backgrounds to interpret the liberal Premier Jean Lesage's slogan, *Maîtres chez nous*, Masters in our Own House, more and more literally.

And so back she came, once again. She had earlier been vice-president of a movement promoting secular schools. That had nearly cost her her job at Radio-Canada in those days, but now the mood was changing. There were even a few clergy whose view of the Christian message gave pride of place to justice and liberty, and Judith made sure that her work helped get that message out. She brought the most outspoken and famous of those young priests before an astonished television audience on *Premier Plan* ("Foreground"): he was Father Jean-Paul Desbiens. He had anonymously published *Les Insolences,* a book on Quebec and the Church, whose stance was so outrageous he had prudently signed it only "Frère Untel," Brother So-and-So. His superiors found out who "Frère Untel" really was and told Father Desbiens to shut up. But there was another radical priest, Paul-Émile Cardinal Léger. Léger would later renounce his own princely title and go to live among and serve the lepers and handicapped children in Cameroon. At the time of the Frère Untel controversy, Léger intervened as the principal Roman Catholic authority in Quebec, and allowed Desbiens to go on television. Judith Jasmin jumped at the chance, subduing her usual hard-edged questioning, and encouraging him to promote his cause.

"The cause . . . was dear to her heart," he would say later. "And she had no intention of putting that cause at risk by being too aggressive [with me]."

Some of her fellow journalists were scandalized at her apparent public support for a cause while she was supposed to be doing objective journalism. Some would say that even today you could not get away with it. They are probably wrong. If you review Jasmin's archived interview with Desbiens, while it seemed unusual at the time, that was likely because a conventional interview back then would have reflected some hostilty towards a seemingly rebellious priest — hardly an objective stance.

Long after she had been recognized as one of the truly great journalists, she would be challenged publicly on this issue. Interviewer Wilfred Lemoine asked, in 1966, "Being involved in certain social causes . . . doesn't it damage your credibility [as a journalist]?"

Jasmin's answer was that if you are doing your professional work with sincerity and good faith, the fact of your having personal views and commitments doesn't have to weaken your credibility. It is a valid answer, but the issue is one that still occupies journalists today, some still maintaining that you should try not to have opinions and if you have them, conceal them. Judith Jasmin would probably have thought that naïve and unreal.

"Reporting means sticking to the facts," she said. "And even if a journalist has private opinions, that's not important if he reports the facts."

She did support the independence of Quebec. Then, as now, it was not uncommon for journalists at Radio-Canada to hold separatist feelings. It is a tribute to their professionalism and to the policies, standards and management of that news service that those opinions have seldom contaminated the highly professional news service. Inquiry after official inquiry, especially after election campaigns, has consistently exonerated Radio-Canada journalists from charges of letting their biases distort their work.

In 1963 she wrote a letter to the editors of *Le Devoir*, a newspaper that was often sympathetic to the separatist cause. Some shadowy rebels calling themselves the FLQ (*Front de Liberation de Québec*) had blown up a couple of mailboxes. They would later kidnap a British diplomat, James Cross, and viciously murder a Quebec cabinet minister, Pierre Laporte. There really was no FLQ, no genuine movement as such, only a few isolated cells of romantic misfits. And Jasmin's public letter probably reflects the opinions of the majority of even the most dedicated separatists of the time.

She wrote it from Algeria, where she was on assignment:

> *Here, in this land bathed in the blood of a million victims of the war of liberation, I think about those of you who have adopted some of the combat methods employed by Algerian patriots. At the core, both are issues of independence. But the context here is very different. In the history of the conquest of Algeria in the 19th century there are countless pillages, rapes, massacres. What exists in our Quebec rebellion to compare in scale with the martyrs of Algeria? Aspiring heroes of Quebec's independence, lay down your arsenal of violence. The work we must accomplish at home is more difficult than you imagine.*

It would be interesting to know how the proponents of journalistic "objectivity" would view that letter now.

Judith Jasmin's career as a television reporter would take her into the heart of some of the great stories of the era. She was in Dallas within hours after President John F. Kennedy was shot. Remembering that the alleged assassin's mother was born in Canada she used her "Radio-Canada" status to attract the bereaved woman's attention, and managed to get an interview with Mrs. Oswald, not long after Lee Harvey Oswald was shot dead. Jasmin seemed at ease in hot-spots. She was jailed at a demonstration against racism in New York. Pierre Nadeau had to go down from Montreal and bail her out. At home the press loved it, but in Washington, where she was then Radio-Canada's official correspondent, things were different. It had already been especially difficult for her as a woman, since women were not then admitted to the National Press Club, where much of the real information passed between politicians and the press. Now, as a result of her having been jailed in New York, the White House took away her permanent pass, and she had to apply for a day pass each time there was a press conference. Knowlton Nash, the CBC correspondent who worked out of the same office and had come to have enormous admiration for Jasmin, laughingly says, "I presume the security people felt [the President] would be better protected if they didn't give her [the] pass!"

She could laugh at those little hardships; the big ones were still, as always, the pain of loneliness and the loss of love. She would rationalize her childlessness by pointing to her career. But she felt the lack, and took on the role of surrogate mother to her sister's son Christian, sometimes even taking him with her on her foreign assignments. Christian is a man who now has a profound love of and admiration for his late aunt and substitute mother.

And then there was the loss of a breast. Diagnosed with cancer, she had a radical mastectomy. She told her close colleague Jean LeTarte, who had been her cameraman in some of the toughest hot-spots and still says that she was always much more courageous than he was, that she was "no longer the woman I used to be."

All this time her reportorial style got stronger and stronger. At Radio-Canada headquarters in Montreal the management decreed that she was not to do live reports or commentary any more. It was too risky. Record her stuff and then if she was too outspoken something could be cut. And yet those journalism students at the University of Montreal, the same ones who couldn't tell us exactly who Judith Jasmin was and what she did, once they had been shown some of her work and told the main outlines of her life expressed envy for the way it was, back then, for this pioneering reporter.

But more importantly, for these young journalists who are just starting out but are already very critical of if not skeptical about contemporary television news with its fads and formulas and ten-second sound bites, the work that Judith Jasmin was able to turn out seems almost like paradise. Yes, she was a pioneer: the first woman to be made official foreign correspondent. She broadcast long thoughtful reports. She had time to prepare them thoroughly, to think about them, to edit with care. She had room to add interpretive tags, to make her reports mean more than just a quick flash with a few pictures of people yelling or being beaten or a cliché background shot of a landmark like the Eiffel Tower or the White House. Journalism has changed, since Jasmin. She was there when television news editors expected meaningful stories, not just entertainment in the form of a few hits of random information or the faces and flavours of the month.

All that time the cancer that had cost her a breast was still lurking. When she came home in 1968, just fifty-two years old, it had spread to her bones. Old friends gathered around. René Lévesque was close and affectionate and more supportive than he had been since those early days working together. But her old employers at Radio-Canada were not so kind. Where once she had been their first choice to interview world leaders, now that she was not able to fly off to the danger spots she was assigned to local stories about fires and fashion shows. Her friend Francine Bastien, still bitter, says, "Even her, who had been such an outstanding person . . . who brought so much quality to what CBC was about, and put CBC on the map so to speak . . . was treated very shabbily towards the end of her life. She was very ill, and not much attention was paid to try to treat her decently or with respect."

For some, having put up with insults and injuries from such an employer all her life, it might have been possible to just accept that as one of the ironies with which one lived. Not so for Judith Jasmin. "[It] hurt her a lot," her nephew Christian says now; "I remember her crying about that."

She needed Jo Chatelain then, badly. But Jo seldom came; he was all over the world. Her mother was still alive, and would visit her in the hospital, and bring her flowers, and say, "Oh, these are from Jo. Jo sent you these lovely flowers." But she knew.

Her old cameraman comrade, Jean LeTarte, would come and sit by her bedside. He remembers one phone call, when he said he was on his way over, but Judith said, "No, don't come any more. I'm not the Judith you knew. Let's keep on speaking only on the telephone."

She died on October 20, 1972. She was fifty-six. As a young television producer in Toronto, helping to start *Close-Up*, in 1957, the first Sunday Night Current Affairs Magazine program in English-Canadian television, I had heard a lot about Judith Jasmin and her program *Premier Plan*, which was the counterpart to ours, though we seldom got to see it as there was no French television in Toronto then. Jasmin was already a legend in 1957. Her reputation would grow steadily. The men and women who helped bring Quebec into the modern age in those decades now give her credit for a major contribution to that amazingly peaceful revolution.

In one of her last interviews, asked what her life as a reporter had meant to her, she said, with feeling and humour, "It was marvelous; it was the kind of life you'd expect to pay for the privilege of having."

◆ ◆ ◆

The biography of Judith Jasmin was written by Maureen Marovitch and directed by Maureen Marovitch and David Finch. Carrie Madue was line producer. The Director of Photography was Richard Burman, with additional camera by David Finch, who also did sound. The editor was Lewis Cohen. The program was first telecast on March 8, 2000, and will be seen again in the spring of 2001 on History Television.

◇ Part Eight ◇

THE RELUCTANT WARRIOR
THE STORY OF BEN DUNKELMAN

One of the well-entrenched ideas that Canadians seem to have about the character of the nation is that we are a peaceable people whose armed forces are primarily intended to be sent to trouble spots around the world in order to help keep the peace. But this is a relatively recent image. Canada became Canada out of warfare. Its capital is placed in a totally unlikely part of the country to keep it safe from invasion. Soldiers from Canada marched on Washington and set fire to the presidential residence, whereupon it was painted white to cover the scorch marks and remains the White House still. An Iroquois unit under the command of the great Tecumseh crossed the river from Windsor during the War of 1812 and conquered Fort Detroit. Canada sent soldiers to the Boer War in Africa at the turn of the century. In World War I the per-capita (of the national population) of Canadian soldiers killed far exceeded that of our American neighbour. In World War II Canadian troops conducted the almost suicidal dress rehearsal for the invasion of France, on a blood-soaked beach called Dieppe, and later, when the real thing happened in June 1944, successfully captured and held their assigned Normandy beaches.

Anyone who lived through that last World War, here in Canada, remembers vividly the way in which the country pulled together around the war effort. The words "we" and "us," that have long since been dropped by our political leaders as they try to win the country with tax cuts or spending, resonated then with a passionate, cohesive power as millions of us collected scrap metal, put our savings into War Bonds, hand-knit socks and toques for soldiers and sailors and airmen, and lined up at recruiting depots faster than we could be enlisted.

War divided us, too: French Canadians in Quebec found it difficult to believe that they had a responsibility to help Britain with a war that nobody really wanted, both in 1914 and again in 1939. The conscriptive solutions arrived at by governments who, themselves, had been pretty equivocal about going to war, left scars that are not yet healed.

So we have had our experience of the costs of war, and of its glories, if that is still a valid word. And some historians believe that we have been too ready to forget the sacrifices and the courage that our men and women have shown in battle and behind the scenes of battle, despite the war memorials in the civic squares of big cities and of little towns. And we are perhaps too ready to forget some of the outstanding individuals who fought in those battles.

One of them was vividly remembered in episode number 39 of *The Canadians*. His name was Ben Dunkelman, a big, broad-shouldered, soft-spoken man whom this writer met just a few months before his death in 1997. We were planning a film on his extraordinary life and exploits and hoping to find a way to do it while he was still able to participate.

We called this episode "The Reluctant Warrior," not because Ben Dunkelman was in any way slow to offer himself for duty when the country went to war, but because he really saw himself as a peaceable guy who joined up because that is what you did when your people needed you. But when his spectacular ability as a battlefront soldier and commanding officer brought him an offer to take command of the entire armed forces of a small but powerful nation, he refused: it was time to get back home and do what he was supposed to do in the beginning, namely run the family business.

That was quite a business. If you lived in Toronto in the 1930's and after, you could not fail to be impressed by a big building down on Front Street, just west of the old Maple Leaf Baseball stadium at the corner of Bathurst Street, with a tall sign at roof level: TIP TOP TAILORS. Ben's father David had arrived as a penniless immigrant from Poland. He started this mass-produced men's clothing business soon after, and made a huge success of it. By the time Ben was born in 1913 the family was very well off. The present Sunnybrook Medical Centre on Bayview Avenue, just north of Eglinton in what was at the time deep countryside, was originally the Dunkelman family estate, Sunnybrook Farm. Ben grew up in an atmosphere of luxury and play. He had his own sailboat from the time he was in his teens, and was a prominent figure at the Queen City Yacht Club. Jews were not allowed in the Royal Canadian Yacht Club at that time, but Ben always said that while he knew there was an anti-Semitic substratum in Toronto in those days, he was not really aware of it, it didn't affect his life. He had a naturally sunny disposition that went with his imposing stature and prodigious natural athletic capacity, and perhaps if anyone ever felt like putting him down for being Jewish, any such notion vanished upon actual contact. From the time of his adolescence his was a big, winning, even commanding presence.

Another permanent reminder, however, of the extent to which Ontario's Jews were excluded from the mainstream is Balfour Beach on Lake Simcoe, a forty-minute drive north of Toronto. A cottage culture had bloomed on Lake Simcoe early in the century (and has left most of its shores now almost saturated with summer dwellings), but it was difficult for Jews to buy a cottage in the developed areas. Ben's mother Rose simply saw to it that the family bought up thirty acres of excellent shorefront and turned it into a club where Jews and only Jews were welcome. She named it for Sir Arthur Balfour, the British politician whose Balfour Declaration had paved the way for the creation of the State of Israel. A street in Balfour Beach is named after The Czarina, as they called her, but misspelled as Dunkleman.

Israel did not exist when Ben Dunkelman was a boy, but hundreds of young Jews from other parts of the world were already building towards it by wresting productive farmland out of the stony desert on collective or communitarian farms called *kibbutzim*. Young Ben would hear tales of the *kibbutzim* from the Zionist leaders whom his mother often entertained at Sunnybrook or at their Balfour Beach house. He said that he often sat staring into the flames of the cottage fireplace, dreaming about taking part in the building of the New Israel. He had passed an adolescence of parties and sailing and girlfriends, and now he was beginning to think about the *why* of it all, and that *why* kept coming up Israel. On his seventeenth birthday his parents gave him passage to Palestine and five hundred dollars in cash, and off he went. He said that he found it intoxicating, a kind of homecoming, and decided to stay and work on a *kibbutz* at Tel Asher, a tiny settlement surrounded by not very friendly Arab villages. It was a long way from Sunnybrook Farm, Ben wrote later.

That experience changed his life. Sometimes he referred to it as a "trial by *turiya,*" the Hebrew word for the hoe with which he was assigned to try to cultivate the parched stony fields of the *kibbutz.* He confessed to having been overweight and soft when he arrived. Before long the fat was gone, the muscles were hardening, and the adolescent was turning into a tough and idealistic young man. He said that it was an early short-wave broadcast from Germany that alerted him to the alarming new phenomenon in Germany called the Nazi party, and that it chilled him. But he went back to Toronto in 1932, to work unhappily at Tip Top Tailors. Those were not good years. He drank too much bootleg liquor, but would clear his head and find some solace afloat on his much loved sailboat. It was a schooner whose design he had commissioned from a celebrated naval architect named Hand, built by Cecil Schramm, in Port Dover, and sailed on Georgian Bay, out of Midland. He called her *The Dinny.*

Seven years went by like this.

When Ben Dunkelman was five years old he had stood in the streets of downtown Toronto waving a Union Jack and cheering the return of soldiers from the Great War. He said that the experience marked him with a sense of patriotism and of the nobility of soldiering. So when the Second World War broke out in the autumn of 1939, he not only saw it as a way of escaping what then seemed the vacuous routines of the men's clothing business, but also a way to demonstrate his pride in his country, and to do something about that horror he had first learned about on the short-wave radio in Palestine.

He wanted the Navy. Later he would say that it may have been his Jewishness that got him rejected, but in fact the Navy was not accepting recruits in those first months of the war: the government was trying to steer young men into the infantry. Ben found himself in the Second Battalion of the Queen's Own Rifles. Perhaps because of connections and a good education, but certainly aided by his stature and presence and natural gift for leadership, he was soon commissioned as an officer and headed overseas.

Ben Dunkelman knew how to party, and his first months in England saw plenty of drinking and brawls and rowdiness. But he discovered that he was a natural soldier, and he found that a stubby little weapon called the mortar was right up his alley. The World War I mortar was a huge, squat, heavy kind of cannon firing an explosive shell on a high trajectory. By the time Ben was training, it had shrunk to a small tube about five centimetres in diameter (the calibre) and less than half a metre long, propped up by two small legs (the bipod) and aiming into the sky at an angle of about sixty to eighty degrees. At the bottom of this smooth-bore tube was a central firing pin, really just a hard little knob that would strike the cap of a cartridge that was dropped on it. You dropped a small bomb in the mouth of the tube and got your hand out of the way in a hurry. The bomb was shaped like an elongated pear, with fins on the narrow end, and in a tube at the centre of the fins was a shell that looked exactly like a shotgun shell. When that shell hit the pin it was exactly as if you had pulled the trigger on the shotgun. The shell had enough cordite in it to propel the bomb high into the air, over the heads of your own forward troops if necessary, and down into your target. You could use it against tanks or a fortified position, but the target was often enemy troops, perhaps out of sight of your riflemen but vulnerable to something looping down out of the sky.

Ben Dunkelman seems to have rapidly mastered the mortar. If you could concentrate the fire of several of these tubes on a target, and get a trained group of mortarmen working together so that you could have a lot of bombs in the air at the same time, the effect on your enemy would be terrifying and devastating.

The Canadians, Americans, British, Free French, Free Polish, Australian, New Zealand and South African troops mustered in England all knew that sooner or later there would be an invasion of Europe; that was what they were there for. It was a long wait. A lot of beer was drunk and a lot of hangovers slept off. Many English girls became pregnant and some even got married. Rumours were all over the camps. Some of the rumours foresaw a Nazi invasion of Britain. But bit by bit the strategists were putting together a plan that Prime Minister Winston Churchill called *Operation Overlord*, and then, early in June 1944 the orders came to move out. D-Day was on them. Seasick men tumbled out of their landing craft on the beaches of Normandy at dawn the next morning, and waded ashore with their weapons held high over their heads to keep them dry. Lieutenant Ben Dunkelman of the Queen's Own was in the second wave. He was thirty-one years old.

Hundreds of our men were cut down by machine-gun fire as they came ashore. Ben saw a close friend's body crumpled on the sand as he ran dripping up the beach. But the first wave had cleared the closest German positions with astounding success, and Ben's career as a mortar specialist began in earnest. The big guy from Toronto, with the easy smile and the confident manner, soon attracted the attention of the war correspondents:

The Toronto Star. With the Canadian Army. December 14th, 1944. Big Benny Dunkelman of the Canadian Army is a mortar man. In fact he is Mr. Mortar of the Canadian Army. Ever since D-Day Benny has been making music with those mortars of his . . . using his observation post as a sort of podium to direct his fire, like an embattled Toscanini. He likes to pull out all the stops and make big music. He is not happy until each mortar crew has 22 bombs in the air [all at once].

One of the most decisive battles was in the 30-km zone from Caen to Falaise. The Canadians ran into some still very strong Panzer and SS divisions of the German army, and a badly planned opening assault led to a terrible casualty rate among the Canadians. It would have been even worse, according to the Queen's Own official history, "had not Lt. Dunkelman detected German tanks hidden in the haystacks" around the target. His mortar unit went to work. Dozens of bombs were in the air, all at once. The Germans were pinned down and the Allied retreat well protected. Ben was blown off his jeep by an exploding shell and his seatmate killed outright. His steel helmet was snapped down on his head by the explosion and he lost consciousness momentarily. When he came around he threw away the helmet and refused to wear one from then on. It was called *Operation Totalize*. While Ben would later blame the Americans for not properly closing the Allied pincer movement, and allowing a considerable German retreat through the famous gap, nonetheless the operation killed or wounded an astounding four hundred thousand of the enemy. "We crushed a whole damn army," he wrote.

1945 found him in the mud of the Scheldt estuary, trying to clear the way into the crucial Belgian port of Antwerp. Mud and the stench of death. Ben now was Acting Major. A young war artist from Amherst Nova Scotia, Lieutenant Alex Colville, was on that campaign and recorded its horrors in some powerful paintings.

A reporter wrote, "The bitter five-day fighting in the Hochwald ended Sunday when Toronto soldiers drove the last of the Germans out. Though the Germans were still mortaring and machine-gunning the area, Canadian troops, unshaven and dirty, enjoyed their first rest in four days. The enemy was stubborn, but Major Ben Dunkelman confirmed that they surrendered readily when hemmed in."

Ben wrote later, in his autobiography, the single modest line, "For my part in the Hochwald action, I was awarded the Distinguished Service Order." A newspaper put it this way:

The Distinguished Service Order goes to Major Ben Dunkelman of 53 Russell Hill Road, Toronto. Under murderous fire, the Major picked up a gun whose crew had been killed. He then rushed forward killing ten Germans with his pistol and bare hands. All the time shouting to his men to press forward and the enemy to come out and fight.

Ben Dunkelman was not an especially modest man, but his friends did not hear him talk about that episode afterwards. There was nothing in his account of himself to suggest that he took any pleasure from the killing. He seems to have been a soldier because that is what you were expected to do. He didn't wear or show off the medal. His friend Barney Danson, who fought in the same war and would become Minister of National Defence years later, said, "I recall seeing it only once when we had a special ceremony up at Meaford and Ben was the guest speaker, which he didn't want to be, he hated to be. Everybody else had beautifully polished and mounted medals, and Ben's looked as if he had fished it out of some bottom drawer somewhere, where it had been lying since the war."

When he came home after it was all over, after *three hundred* days of combat from the beaches of Normandy to the banks of the Rhine, he had had it. They offered him the command of the Queen's Own. He was thrilled at the honour but he turned it down, and went back to the family business. The post-war prosperity was dazzling, but Ben was soon preoccupied with the struggle for Israel. "He was a super Zionist," Barney Danson says. "And before I knew it he was gone, and over there fighting again."

And soon the Canadian Press was reporting (June 2, 1948):

A distinguished officer with The Queen's Own Rifles overseas in the Second World War, Major Ben Dunkelman, is reported to have gone to Palestine to be second-in-command of the Jewish army in their fight against the Arabs.

Shimon Peres, who later became prime minister of Israel, knew Ben in those early days.

[David] Ben-Gurion (Israel's first president) was very anxious to have a group of professional soldiers in an organization that was more of a movement than a disciplined army. Now Ben came in. You know he was a very imposing person. Tall and heavy and talkative and charismatic. And he brought this authority of experience, of a commander. . . . I would like to have him as my friend, not my opponent, if I have a choice, and secondly, my second impression, would be that beyond his toughness he was a very soft person. As much as he put on the air of a great commander, he was a very emotional man, I believe.

Ben developed a close relationship with Ben-Gurion, whom he came to respect enormously. He tried to organize an all-Canadian unit in the Mahal, the technical elite of the Israeli forces. But Ben-Gurion assigned him to the Palmach, an assault group for *Operation Nachson*, to open up the Jerusalem road. Ben was struck by the quiet personal power of the twenty-six-year-old commander, the young, blond, Yitzakh Rabin (later to be assassinated when he was Labour prime minister); a youth with the fate of a hundred thousand people in his hands.

That was the big tactical challenge, the road from the coast to Jerusalem, cut off since the beginning of hostilities, depriving the Holy City of water and food as well as military supplies. Tackling the relief of that siege put Ben back in the line of fire. They assembled a motley collection of trucks and cars, rigged with metal plates that they hoped would be some protection against the fire they knew would come. You can see the remains of those vehicles now, on that road. They have been mounted up on the hills as a monument to the battle that soon came. Ben later said it looked to him like a kind of mass Armada, a mass suicide. At one point he switched places to take over as driver of a second car. The man he switched with was shot dead with a bullet through the head. The situation looked dreadful, but somehow they turned it around, and later carved out a permanent, protected route that Ben-Gurion would eventually name the Road of Valour.

The new State of Israel was proclaimed on May 14th. The fighting went on. An Arab stronghold at Latrun was a key strategic target. They brought in new immigrants, scarcely trained but passionate for the defence of the new state. "That is our secret weapon," Rabin said. "They have nowhere else to go."

They took Latrun. Ben was put in command of the Seventh Brigade, the Latrun Veterans, and was ordered to move north. He took Tel Kissam, then Shafa Amir, where Ben found an undefended "back door" that could be taken by night if you kept your nerve, and they took Shafa by night. Again and again he deployed the surprise attack by night. The Israelis were outnumbered and out-gunned, at least in theory. But at night the enemy could not see how little force was actually coming against them. The Israelis kept on winning.

And now it was the biggest target of all: Nazareth, both symbolically and strategically of enormous impor-tance. Most of the Nazarenes were Arabs, and its reli-gious significance was more Christian and Muslim than Jewish. But Ben said he fell in love with Nazareth. He said its rocky, pine-covered slopes reminded him of home, of the Canadian Shield, of granite and pine. Militarily it was delicate: harming the alleged birthplace of Christ would alienate a lot of friends whom Israel needed, especially in the United States, which had been quick to recognize the fledgling state, and was now watching the war with intense scrutiny. Ben-Gurion signalled, "I would just like you to remember that Nazareth is a holy place for the Christians, and don't hurt any holy Christian place, nor Muslim holy place." Ben could respect that order, but Professor David Bercuson says that there was another order that he disobeyed.

"Nazareth was a place where Dunkelman was defi-nitely given the order to drive out the Arab population, and refused to do it. He was going to fight a clean war, as far as he was concerned. But he was not going to fight a war against civilians."

And at eight-forty, local time, the morning of December 17th, he sent Ben-Gurion a simple two-word signal: NAZARETH CAPTURED.

The war had been an exhilarating series of unexpected successes. But Ben was tired now, and racked with malaria. He had to rest. During a lull he met a young female corporal named Yael Lifshitz. He was short-tempered with his illness and fatigue, and would later ruefully recall how rude he had been to her at first. But a relationship was forming. The delicately beautiful young soldier was not as delicate as she perhaps looked at first. She had a fine sense of humour and a strong intelligence. As the days went by the initial rough spots were worn smooth, and before long they decided to get married, with the Seventh Brigade standing by. The marriage would last until his death, in 1997.

Ben Dunkelman could have stayed in Israel for the rest of his life. By the end of that war he had built a solid reputation for courage, inventiveness, tactics and strategy. But he had gone out there to do a definable job, to help get the struggling young nation on its feet. He was not a soldier by vocation. He spoke of himself as a reluctant warrior. When this writer sat with him over dinner, a year and a half before his death, his warm voice and expressive hands could still conjure up vivid pictures of some of the adventures he had lived through, and he was proud of his contribution. But he said that he was always eager to get home. Toronto and the family and the business were his real responsibility. The government of Israel was prepared to offer him a position of high command for as long as he wanted it. A professional soldier would not have hesitated to accept: Ben did not hesitate to turn it down and call it a day, for his career as a soldier.

There is a tradition in the Canadian military of the vital role of the non-professional soldiers. Our standing army has always been small. When there has been a war it has been fought primarily by volunteers like Ben Dunkelman. Many of them joined up not because they saw themselves as soldiers, not for a career, but just because the country needed help in a crisis, and they hoped it would be over soon. Sir Arthur Currie, the brilliant commanding officer of the Canadian Expeditionary Forces in World War I, was an "amateur" whose successful strategies, some historians argue, were made possible precisely because he was not saddled with the traditions of the professional army, whose officers always seemed to be fighting the previous war rather than this one.

Ironically, for many, those war experiences turned out to be the most meaningful time of their lives, and they talked about them wistfully for the rest of their lives. We were planning a different kind of television biography with Ben; one in which he would take an active part. He could summon enthusiasm for the stories, but they were the stories of a man whose heart had always tugged him homewards. He died before we could bring together the resources to make that documentary, but Yael and his family and friends were generously helpful in the making of this one, and I cannot finish this section without a word of thanks to them, and to Ben himself, the reluctant warrior.

◆　◆　◆

The Reluctant Warrior was written and directed by Bruce Yaccato, with Carrie Madu as line producer. The Director of Photography was Paul Freer, sound Rami Nechemia, and editor Robert Hossack Kew. It was first broadcast on History television on March 22, 2000, and will be rebroadcast in the spring of 2001.

ADDITIONAL READING:

Ben Dunkelman: *Dual Allegiance*

◇ Part Nine ◇

BEHIND THE RED DOOR
The Story of Elizabeth Arden

The door to a handsome if modest brown-brick building at 691 Fifth Avenue, New York City, corner of 54th Street, is enamelled a bright red. During business hours, which last till well into the evening, a uniformed doorman swings the red door open with a flourish when customers arrive. The customers are mostly women. The dignified stone lettering across the façade of the building proclaims: ELIZABETH ARDEN INC., for this is the headquarters and principal salon of the world-famous cosmetics company founded in this city more than 70 years ago.

Elizabeth Arden is a name known throughout the western world, and still epitomizes high-quality cosmetics despite a growing number of competitors. Unlike Betty Crocker and many other brands based on a fictitious person, there was a real Elizabeth Arden, and in the 1930's and 1940's she was a North American celebrity. It was not, however, her real name, and she was not an American.

She was a Canadian woman from Woodbridge, Ontario, where she was born in 1878, on her father's precarious "truck farm," the common phrase at the time for a market garden farm. She was christened Florence Nightingale Graham, because, it is thought, her mother was dismayed at her own descent from an upper middle-class British family to what her daughter Flo would call a "farm drudge" by the time this fourth child was born. Susan

Graham, née Tadd, Flo's mother, feared that without a little extra help the new girl child would suffer the same fate as most working-class or farm girls: drudgery, invisibility, toil, exhausting non-stop child-bearing, and something more like servitude than a free and creative life. The most famous female "doer" in the British Empire at that time was the heroine of the Crimean War, the nurse Florence Nightingale. Susan Tadd Graham is said to have hoped something of that energy and determination and maybe even fame and accomplishment would come to her own little Florence Nightingale along with the name. Whatever the influence of the name itself, the young namesake would, after her first three decades of relatively undistinguished endeavour, suddenly find what it is she was meant to do in life, and would indeed demonstrate the energy, determination and accomplishment, that Susan Tadd Graham had hoped for her. But Susan never knew it; by that time she was long dead, at thirty-nine, from tuberculosis, which was so common at the time that it was assumed, when someone died young, that TB was probably the cause.

Flo was only six when her mother died. She had to take on farm chores *and* the care of her younger sister Gladys. That relationship would remain central, one of mutual love amounting almost to adoration, for the rest of their lives. The other task they gave the young Flo, just as soon as she could manage it, was the care of the horses.

In the year 2001 the chances of a child seeing a horse on the streets of Woodbridge, Ontario, are pretty slim, and in downtown Toronto next to nil except for those rare moments when the Police Department sends out one or two of its fine mounts for ceremonial occasions. The horse at the beginning of the 21st century is an animal associated with leisure and prosperity. Fairly well-off people in Ontario, if they retire to a country, often take up riding, but it is a costly sport. The wealthy raise horses, some for racing, although horse racing going into the 21st century was losing its fans so rapidly that the desperate race-track operators started installing slot machines at the track, thinking somehow that might stanch the haemorrhage.

But in the 1880's, when her father Willie sent her to work in the stable, horses were the principal form of transportation. They pulled carriages with people in them and wagons carrying goods. There were no automobiles and in a village the size of Woodbridge the electric tram, making its first appearance in the larger centres, was still unknown. Horses were a necessity, and caring for them an art. And the little girl seemed to have inherited something else from her famous namesake: healing hands. Horses need to be rubbed down and when their legs get sore, as they often do, a good horse person will spend a great deal of time on her knees rubbing the horse's knees. Flo was good at that, and liked it.

A lifelong connection with horses was started, which would, in a completely unexpected way, have a lot to do with rubbing their knees, too, even after Flo Graham had become the rich and famous Elizabeth Arden.

Willie, her father, wasted a lot of money buying horses that he hoped would win at the races, which they seldom did. His real business was selling vegetables at the market in town, and Flo had to help out there as well. It is possible that some of her early ideas about the role of women were formed in that Woodbridge marketplace. It was a time when women were coming out in public more than they had in the earlier part of the Victorian era. Some had a little disposable income, as we would say now, and were spending it on clothes that would give them a modest elegance. Some of them — probably in secret — were applying substances to their skin to make them look younger, more attractive, more . . . *distinct*.

The writer Alfred Allen Lewis, author of *Miss Elizabeth Arden: An Unretouched Portrait*, is a biographer who, as he appears in this television documentary account of Elizabeth Arden/Flo Graham's life, demonstrates a more than academic curiosity about his subject; his warm (and sometimes magisterial) observations about her life and her personality are always coloured by a sense of affection. And at this point in her life he sees her as soaking up the experiences that would lead her on to the amazing success that *seemed* to come upon her so rapidly, more than a decade later. He says that those days in the market place, watching the newly elegant women, were important to her.

All of her life Elizabeth Arden was a sponge. She was a quick study. She saw things, and she absorbed them, acquired them . . . She would pick up their manner of speech . . . she obviously could not pick up the clothes, but she would take on their airs and graces.

Not very admiring of Willie Graham, the father, biographer Lewis says that he spoke flirtatiously with those women as he tried to interest them in buying his vegetables, and that young Flo disliked that; and especially disliked the way he became deferential to them, subservient, lowering himself. But, Lewis suggests, what remained with the now nearly adult girl was a sense that she would rather be the woman who induced that deference, and that perhaps the idea began to form right there in the Woodbridge market.

She began to think that money was the secret to life. It was money that allowed those women to humiliate her deplorable father. She is said to have answered, when asked what she would be when she grew up, "The richest little girl in the world."

It certainly seems likely, in light of what happened later, that she was studying the faces of those market-going women, as well as their clothes and their voices. Women had been painting their faces for centuries. From what we can tell of the ancient Egyptians in the great treasures of sculptured and painted portraiture that survive, they appear to have used makeup in a highly formalized way, especially around the eyes. Shakespeare talks about makeup: "Let her paint an inch thick, she must come to this." Queen Elizabeth the First, powerfully played by Cate Blanchett in the 1998 film about that monarch, established a chalk-white face with a startling red mouth as a sort of icon with the power to summon a sense of her power and her brilliance. In the eighteenth century there was a torrent of satire against the extravagant painting and coifing and gowning of women. But in the Victorian era makeup had become something unseemly. Painting your face meant falsehood, and cosmetics, if they were to be applied at all, tended to be done in secret. It was an injustice against women. The conventions of the time still meant that it was the pretty woman with the smooth complexion who was likeliest to marry well and thus live well. However, if she were known to have done anything artful in order to *achieve* that complexion, she risked the rejection of those same male arbitrators upon whose approval she depended. We are told that women began to use "secret ingredients," ranging from the healthy use of lemon, through slightly more risky whiteners such as hydrogen peroxide, to creams compounded with lead, which could be deadly. The aim was to appear to have a "natural complexion" in the achievement of which there had been no artifice.

But then towards the end of the 1800's there seems to have come — along with the prosperity and bustle of the times, with the bicycle (which women were riding with abandon) and the tramcar and the softening of the old Victorian disapproval of being seen in public — a new commercial venture, the Beauty Culturist. This began in the form of small, discreet, commercial hair salons.

In the meantime, since Willie Graham could not afford to keep his girls in school (Flo never finished high school), and the life of a stable hand and a weekend vegetable stand attendant were clearly not leading her anywhere, Flo went to Toronto and enrolled in nursing school. Perhaps her healing hands would find a more dignified employment there. But she did not feel the same sense of calling as her famous namesake, and in fact she did not like nursing at all. The squalor and smell of the hospital and the indignity of illness offended her. The filth and the blood were as bad as the dirt of the stables, no, worse: because they came from human beings. She thought of her mother's tragic illness. She found illness ugly.

There is a lovely photograph of her at about this time, and she was strikingly beautiful. Photographs of her throughout her long life appear in this television biography. This one of the eighteen or twenty year old shows her contemplating the camera in a slightly challenging way, as if to say, "Guess what I am thinking!" And it is conceivable that she was thinking about cosmetics. During her brief spell at nursing school she worked for a while with a hospital chemist who was experimenting with skin-healing creams. She thought perhaps it could help make the skin look better. She quit nursing school and went home to Woodbridge and tried cooking up some kind of cosmetic "cream" on the kitchen stove, with rendered fat and lemon juice, rosewater from the drugstore, a little lye and perhaps some lanolin, and herbs from the vegetable garden. We know only that she made a stink, and that her father was furious. Soon after, she had had her fill of him and of Woodbridge, and, for the time, of concocting creams. So back she went to Toronto.

She knocked around at this and that for several years — shopgirl, secretary, whatever she could get, nothing permanent, nothing productive, nothing interesting. One of the few amusements was the Nickelodeon, "High Class Motion Picture Theatre: Admission Five Cents." A bit later she would be seeing the early pictures of another

Toronto girl, Gladys Smith, who was out in California making three or four short dramatic pictures a week, and already known by her movie name Mary Pickford. The new phenomenon of the Movie Star was just around the corner. Already, at these "High Class Motion Picture Theatres," Florence Nightingale Graham, nearing thirty, no prospects, no way she was going back to Woodbridge though she missed her sister Gladys a lot, was seeing painted women in positions of power. Fictions, perhaps. But they suggested something to her, and part of what they suggested was that she had better get out of Toronto and get herself a lot closer to where, it seemed, women were at least within arms reach of something like power. As luck would have it, her brother Bill had gone to New York. He was doing well as a salesman. She got on a train and changed her life suddenly and dramatically.

Later she would say that after she stepped out of Grand Central Station and began to walk along Fifth Avenue, she just *knew* that it was going to be her street. Shops of undreamed-of luxury and elegance, "a flow," as biographer Allan Lewis says, a whole area downtown called Women's Mile. There was a salon for women, something more advanced than the early Beauty Culturists, but grown from the same root. Flo began to think about cosmetic creams again, and took her healing hands to a Beauty Culturist salon called the Adair, moderately famous at the time. She studied a facial procedure called the Strapping Treatment, and learned massage. She learned how to gently rub creams into the sagging skins of the wives of wealthy New Yorkers. Allan Lewis says that not long afterwards Flo "met a woman named Elizabeth Hubbard. . . . [who] had a better cream than [what they used at] Adair. But she had no gift for massage. Florence had no cream and a great gift for massage. And so they got together and they opened a little salon on Fifth Avenue near 42nd Street.

The nerve of it! Here she was, only months into her new life as a New Yorker, and she takes the long chance and opens a business. Her brother Bill was an important anchor for her, he had a bit of money, and could borrow more, and he admired and encouraged Flo to "go for it." When he heard that she wanted to borrow $6,000, which is more like a hundred thousand in today's money, he balked for a moment. But she said firmly, "You have to spend money to make money," and Bill believed that too, so he came up with the cash.

And it was at this time that she hit on the idea of the brilliant red door, which is still the Elizabeth Arden Salon signature, and gave its name to this episode of *The Canadians*.

Wherever it came from, Florence Nightingale Graham had brought to New York an extraordinary confidence, a readiness to take a chance, and an almost uncanny sense of what was waiting for her out there in the great marketplace. The colour red was prophetic: red, in lipstick especially, would be more than just a colour for her for the rest of her life; it would be a symbol and a confirmation of her power and her skill. She loved red; she would experiment with hundreds, maybe thousands of different reds, and invent names to make each one of them special in the eyes of the women for whom she was going to make going out in public an adventure where they would win.

And that was explicitly another component of the many complex forces that were converging in this woman: the drive to make women strong. It does not matter a great deal, and in any case is impossible to determine, whether this concern was generous or cynical. Most likely it was both, as in the good works of most of us. But she certainly knew that what she was setting out to do would grow in the way she wanted it to grow only if her creams and other cosmetics gave something like her own confidence to other women. She joined the suffragette movement. That fit the motif, and it also brought her directly into contact with a lot of women who had time and money and who were very much interested in how they looked when they appeared in public.

She needed a name. The image of the wartime nurse, Florence Nightingale, going through the tents of the wounded with a storm lantern did not quite fit. She took the Elizabeth from her former colleague (the partnership with Ms. Hubbard did not last long). Elizabeth was nice; she would use that. At the time she was reading a classic by Alfred Lord Tennyson, *Enoch Arden*, and the Arden had a ring to it. How to test it? Was it a marketable name? Who had a better sense of the market than she herself? She had to see it in print, or something like that. In a frame. In a formal, official kind of presentation. So she wrote herself a letter, addressed to Elizabeth Arden at her Fifth Avenue address. It looked pretty good on the envelope, better with a stamp on it, but it would be still better when the postman handed it in and it had a post-mark on it, making it an official kind of a thing. So she mailed it. And there was something fine about the look of it when it came back in the next day's mail. She said, "That's it." And from then on, when she was doing business she was Elizabeth Arden. Among those who watched her reinvent herself over the next few years there is some speculation that Flo never really went away from her interior life (how could she?). But officially, Elizabeth Arden was here to stay.

She was still trying to come up with a cream that would outsell the others. She put on a white lab coat at night and experimented. Elizabeth Hubbard accused her of stealing the Hubbard formula, but in fact almost all the creams that the salons used were made of the same basic ingredients; it was the scent, the name, and the packaging that made the real difference then and still does today. Elizabeth Hubbard had called her concoctions Grecian Creams. Arden decided that Venetian Cream sounded better and would lead women to think they were buying something substantially different from what Elizabeth Hubbard was selling.

That was the beginning of the Elizabeth Arden Line. The now omnipresent craft of packaging was in its infancy in those years before the First World War, but Flo — or perhaps we should refer to her by her professional name, because she is firmly established in that new life now — Elizabeth Arden was one of the packaging pioneers. Her eye-catching containers had to work in the elegant department stores, not just in the Fifth Avenue salon. She had to get them out across the United States, and she knew already that her real market was the world.

By 1914 makeup was establishing itself as a norm for the modern woman. The historian Kathy Peiss has written a whole book about it, *Hope in a Jar*. She says, in the documentary, "They [women] needed to create a social image of themselves. And they do that in part through the use of makeup. Makeup implies putting on products to help you realize who you are. You make up for a show. You make up for a public performance . . . that is the modern connotation of makeup."

Robert Goldman, who has also written on the sociology of makeup, said that this woman had seen her lovely, almost aristocratic mother descend into drudgery and fatigue and ultimately death because, as Arden saw it, the woman who had been Susan Tadd allowed herself to fall into a role instead of taking control. Elizabeth Arden was obsessed with control. Goldman says of her, "She became very much aware of the nuance of *action* in everyday life. From observing the women in the [Woodbridge] market, and how they could use their beauty to gain control, to her recognition of what she could do in a male world to wrestle control away . . . just by putting on a particular outfit or by putting on a particular face."

Arden was now mixing her own colours to help women achieve this kind of control. Her colours were brilliant, not subdued. She understood them as a way of making a statement about yourself. Her clients began to recognize that when you went to the Arden salon, you entered with one face and left with another, and they liked the other. They told their friends. The old taboos about the unseemliness of makeup were evaporating, and Arden was doing her best to accelerate the process. The business prospered.

While pioneering in the concoction and marketing of cosmetics, she was also fastidious about the safety of her ingredients. There was a history of women poisoning themselves with cosmetics. Kathy Peiss told us, "Women who worked as ballet dancers, or secretaries, [had used] lead-based powders [and developed] symptoms of lead poisoning. . . . The doctor keeps asking them, Are you using lead powders because I can't understand where you are getting the lead from . . . They are keeping it a secret because they are ashamed [of using makeup]. They don't want their cosmetic use to be known."

By 1914 that attitude would be waning. That was the year when *Vogue* magazine, THE authoritative voice of fashion, would declare in favour of makeup ". . . a discreet application of colour will enhance a woman's appearance." That was still a couple of years ahead, but Arden was preparing the way for it, and with colours that were not all that discreet. She wore the white lab coat in the salon now, to emphasize the scientific care she took in developing her materials, and her own complexion was still miraculously childlike. At thirty-five she looked twenty-five. She was her own best advertisement. She was selling *control*, and, as she knew very well, she was selling desire.

But Florence Graham, according to biographer Allen Lewis, was still there inside the aggressive, confident Elizabeth Arden, and Florence Graham was not yielding to her own desires; they were too dangerous. Eloping with a handsome young ne'er-do-well had meant that her mother's desire led to a kind of imprisonment that she, Flo, wearing her Arden mask, was determined to avoid. Sex was dangerous; it could kill you. "Elizabeth Arden wanted to be the safest woman in the world, and there was only one way to be safe if you were a woman," said Allen Lewis, "and that was to be independently wealthy."

But men were smitten by her, all the same. And one of them, a banker named Thomas Jenkins Lewis, authorized a substantial loan for the expansion of the Arden business, and let it be known that he was very, very interested in her as a woman. Elizabeth Arden was courteous but cool. She held him at bay but he kept calling. She went to Paris. She wanted to see what the French women were putting on their faces. She was struck by the eye makeup she saw in the fashionable cafés. There and then she started experimenting, enlisting the hotel maids as subjects for her experiments. She went from salon to salon, buying samples of creams and colours and perfumes to take back to New York, and analyse, and improve upon. She had to cut the visit short. War was imminent. She crossed to England, and boarded the *Lusitania* for New York.

The *Lusitania* had been built to challenge what was then the German mastery of the seas, in terms of fast transatlantic crossings. The great ship *Kaiser Wilhelm der Grosse* had won the Blue Riband in 1897 and Germany had held on to it ever since. The Cunard Lines, with massive financial support from the British treasury, had built the

Lusitania and her sister ship the *Mauritania* to win that mastery back from Germany. At 31,500 tons and almost 800 feet long, the *Lusitania* was a winner. She had won the Riband back with her second crossing, in October of 1907, completing the westbound voyage in just under 116 hours. Arden did not know that her banker admirer, Tommy Lewis, would be on board. She was annoyed at first, but accepted his invitation to join his party for dinner, and learned that there were advantages to having a male companion during a sea voyage; she would be right in the middle of the first-class passenger society. These were people who could be useful to her. Tommy Lewis may have misinterpreted her enthusiasm, and on the voyage he proposed marriage. She was 36 but looked 26, and he was, by now, totally enchanted.

But Elizabeth was not, and she let him know that while she would like to see him from time to time, she was not interested in a relationship; business drove her life. Back in New York she threw herself into the work, moved to a larger building, hired a chemist to analyse the samples from Paris and develop lighter creams and stronger colours. She moved to a much bigger apartment. If there was a Flo inside her, a Flo who wanted relationships and comfort and affection, that person would have to wait. She was on the crest of a wave. She coined a new slogan for the salon: "Where everything is so refreshingly different and the spirit of youth is so pervading that you cannot leave without catching some of it." If that seems long-winded today, it worked then. Her profits kept going up.

But now, in an oblique way, the *Lusitania* came into her life again. On May 1st, 1915, the great ship cast off from New York, bound for London with nearly two thousand people on board. None of the passengers knew that she was also carrying tons of munitions, bound for Britain. But German spies, prowling the New York docks, did know, and that may have had something to do with the submarine U-2's intercepting the *Lusitania* off the coast of Ireland a few days later, and sinking her with a single torpedo. She went down in 20 minutes, and nearly 1200 people died. The controversy about that sinking is still debated today, with one faction claiming that she was callously used as a way of bringing America into the war, that Winston Churchill, then First Lord of the Admiralty, had arranged that it would go into waters where the German submarines were known to be on patrol, and others arguing that it was purely an accident.

The sinking of a passenger ship shocked the world. For Tommy Lewis the banker it was also a reminder of his relationship with Elizabeth Arden, and he sought her out and proposed again, and for reasons that are not clear she accepted. They were married soon after, and the moment the ceremony was over she went back to work. Tommy joined the army and went off to war. Elizabeth acted as though she scarcely noticed, but in fact she was lonely, and asked Gladys to come down from Toronto to work with her. She had her own war to fight, the cosmetics war. Helena Rubinstein had opened a competing business and set her sights on the wealthy and glamorous movie stars. The competition between Arden and Rubinstein was ruthless. Arden staked out the high-society market. While she talked about the democratizing effects of makeup ("Beauty is every woman's right"), her prices were aimed at the elite class.

"She threw around her products an aura of exclusivity," Kathy Peiss says, "so that any woman who bought an Arden product would know . . . that ordinary women could not have purchased it."

Tommy Lewis came back from the war, and Arden gave him a job in the company. Before long he began to see other women. Arden would put up with that as long as he was discreet about it. Her biographers say that she seemed not to have wanted a sex life, at least not with him. Whatever the truth of that, it is clear that she didn't want anyone to see any cracks in her domestic life. She kept Tommy intensely involved in the business, perhaps hoping that this would keep him faithful.

Within a few years the giant companies Ponds and Colgate became stiff competition to Elizabeth Arden and Helena Rubinstein, mass-marketing cheap cosmetics of reasonable quality and high safety standards, and Arden was tempted to compete with them on their own ground. But Gladys and Tommy, who had become close colleagues in the business, persuaded her to stay on the elite upscale exclusive side of the marketplace. They would sell less but they would charge a lot more. They opened a salon in London and then one in Paris. Instant success. Soon there were forty salons. Profits kept rising.

Despite the success, Elizabeth Arden seemed to be very unhappy. She would fly into rages at employees, screaming at people in front of both customers and staff, then later regretting her outbursts and sending huge bouquets of conciliatory flowers to the offending, or offended, employee. Perhaps it was because she knew that her husband was sleeping around, but had no idea how to deal with that profound insult to her person. Her biographer, Alfred Allen Lewis says that it had something to do with a sense of frustration at the fact that with all this wealth she still was not accepted as an equal among those New York High Society women whom she pampered and creamed and coloured, and admired and envied but could not join.

This was about to change. She met Elizabeth Marbury. Bessie Marbury was Old New York, Old Money, and a prominent member of what they called the Sapphic Circle, a homosexual circle of wealthy New Yorkers in the arts and society crowd. She was a successful theatrical agent and producer. She was friends with the Morgans and the Vanderbilts, and her friendship with Elizabeth Arden, which may or may not have had a sexual side to it, as Bessie was certainly a lesbian, was a spectacular display of contrasts.

Bessie Marbury, in one photograph, looks something like a sumo wrestler, massive, an almost Asian lift to the corner of her eyes as she confronts the camera aggressively, glowering under the upswept hair that is also in the sumo style. Muscle and heft and confidence. Beside the slim, graceful, almost petite and certainly not visibly aggressive Arden, she loomed like a fortress.

They became inseparable. Elizabeth went up to Bessie's farm at Lakeside, Maine, and soon built her own house there, which Bessie named Maine Chance. They bought horses. She would leave Tommy in charge of the business in New York and go off for days to Maine with Bessie. She looked great. She was fifty-one in 1929 when the depression hit, but she looked thirty-eight and said that was her real age. The depression did not much hurt the business; women still needed lipstick, perhaps more than ever as the gloom of the Great Crash spread around the world; while a lipstick still cost 75 cents, and that was a lot of money for ordinary folk, people kept buying. In 1930 Elizabeth refused an offer of 15 million dollars for the company, something in the order of 200 million in today's money. By now her husband's infidelities were more than she could bear, and when she found out that her brother Bill was covering for Tommy's adventures, she fired both of them. Bill died not long after. Biographer Alfred Allen Lewis says that, bitter and unforgiving, she acted as though she scarcely noticed.

"Her only statement . . . was, 'My sister's brother died today. It's going to be a hard day at the office.'"

Through Bessie's connections she had joined the racing set and now had a new hobby, buying and breeding thoroughbreds. But then Bessie died. In her grief Arden turned Maine Chance into a kind of shrine in memory of the only really close friend she had ever had. The house became the first real beauty spa in America, according to Lewis:

> *The food was excellent but it was diet food. Women dressed for dinner. There were exercises, there was swimming, there were parties. It was a woman's world but a*

*very upper class woman's world. . . She developed what
many called the greatest treatment cream ever devised
. . . It was Elizabeth Arden's Eight Hour Cream. What
had first been thought the whimsical dream of this crazy
woman from the cosmetics business became a part of
treating horses all through the late thirties. Everybody
was using her eight hour cream on their horses as well
as their faces.*

Her motto became: "Treat a horse like a lady, and a
lady like a horse." She would go out to the stables herself, and get down on her knees as she had in her father's
stable back in Woodbridge, and rub a horse's sore legs
with her own cream.

Sister Gladys had moved to Paris and married a
wealthy French count. Now it was 1939 and another World
War had broken out. When Paris was occupied, Gladys
courageously helped allied troops to escape. She was
caught by the Nazis, and her aristocratic husband revealed
himself to be a collaborator, did nothing to help her, and
allowed her to be sent off to a concentration camp. Arden
was devastated, but there was nothing she could do. She
began to use the business as a contribution to the War
Effort, devising a "Victory Red" lipstick, and featuring
women in uniform in her advertising. She met a powerful
Hearst Corporation executive, another Tom, Tom White.
Inexplicably she seems to have fallen in love, but he was
married, Catholic, and very correct. She could not have
him. On the rebound, she married an exiled Russian
Prince, Evlanoff, seventeen years younger than she. It was
a disaster. When she found out that he was homosexual

and insisted on travelling with a male lover, she divorced him.

In 1944 Gladys was released from prison, but not long after that Elizabeth's relief over her sister's rescue was scarred by the loss of a number of her favourite horses when a fire destroyed her stables at Arlington. Then, in a way, horse racing came to her rescue. She became the first woman in history to win the famous Kentucky Derby, with a thoroughbred called Jet Pilot. Her still youthful face appeared on the cover of *Time* magazine. Her business was better than ever. But, according to A.A. Lewis, this preoccupation with age was building within her a serious level of stress. She would say, "Father Time, you don't bother me and I won't bother you." But in fact they were bothering each other. Lewis said, "As Florence Graham aged, Elizabeth Arden was remaining young. She was Dorian Grey."

There is an ironic touch about those last days. She was a friend of the designer Oscar de la Renta, and he made an extraordinary gold lamé gown for her, but she never wore it. De la Renta appears in the documentary, talking about that dress. "I said, Miss Arden, I made a tea gown for you. It took me a lot of time to do. It cost me a lot of money. And you never wear it. She would always say, 'No, No, I am saving it for a special occasion.'"

That special occasion was Elizabeth Arden's funeral. She died in 1966. She was 89, and even she could no longer avoid seeing that she was really old. No tape or cream or puffs or colours could hide the drying skin, the sad eyes, the wasting figure. She was heard to say to the mirror, "I am old. I am really old. I will not be here much longer."

The rich and famous came to say goodbye, as she lay in her casket. Oscar de la Renta was shocked, he said, when he saw that at last she was wearing the tea gown.

Feminist, suffragette, industrial pioneer, innovative marketer and manager, Elizabeth Arden had built a business that at her death was worth millions. She may not have been "the richest little girl in the world," but she was able to leave legacies of eleven million dollars. Four million went to Gladys, one million to John, two million to her niece Patricia Young, and four million to the employees of her company. She had not protected the business, though, and it was the subject of ongoing wrangles. Millions were spent in legal fees before the company finally ended up in the hands of Eli Lilly and Company, who soon set about to make things more efficient, less exclusive, more profitable.

But she had achieved her ambition. She had conceived the idea of a revolutionary business, brought it into existence, made herself rich, and left the world with a name that still stands for elegance, beauty and power.

She also left a mischievous a poem.

> *DAUGHTERS OF EVE*
> *You don't really wish to start*
> *A seven years war*
> *But*
> *It's nice to know that*
> *You've got that kind*
> *Of face.*

you don't really wish
men
to break their hearts
for love of you
but it's nice to know they feel
that way.
you don't really wish
to twist
monarchs
round your little finger
but its nice to know
you could.
you don't really wish
other women to envy
the beauty that
Elizabeth Arden gave you
but it's nice to know
they do.
Elizabeth doesn't wish you to be
a menace
you don't wish to be
a menace
but it's nice to know
you are!

◆　◆　◆

Behind The Red Door was written and directed by Patricia Phillips, with Carrie Madu as line producer, Dwayne Dorland as Director of Photography, and sound by Ivo

Hanak, Larry Macdonald and Todd Johnson. The editor was Doug Forbes. It was first broadcast on April 12, 2000, and will be seen again on History Television in the spring of 2001.

This program won Honourable Mention at the 48th Columbus International Film & Video Festival (2000).

ADDITIONAL READING:

Alfred Allan Lewis and Constance Woodworth: *Miss Elizabeth Arden: An Unretouched Portrait*

◇ Part Ten ◇

NORTHROP FRYE
A LOVE STORY

Northrop Frye
What a guy
Read more books
Than you or I.

Some time in the mid 1970's, a hearing of the Canadian Radio-television and Telecommunications Commission was receiving submissions from a citizens' group concerned about violence on television. Among the commissioners was a small man in his early sixties, a man with a huge mop of unruly waved hair that had once been a spectacular yellow colour but was now grizzled. He was a famous scholar, a university professor who served on this government body because he felt it was his duty to undertake a public responsibility when asked.

His expression suggested puzzlement and amusement at the same time. The slight humour of his characteristically pursed lips was more than balanced by a narrowing of the eyes — almost to invisibility sometimes — which people often interpreted as more sinister than it really was.

On the floor, an intervenor was expressing earnest outrage at what she characterized as an almost uninterrupted flow of violence on our home screens. When she said that this violence was worse than anything the world had ever seen, or something to that effect, the quizzical professor signalled to the chairman of the meeting that he would like to comment.

He said, "Madame, have you read the *Old Testament*?"

This was Northrop Frye, who had read the *Old Testament* more carefully than most of us. At the time of his death early in 1991, if it had been suggested that a documentary film on his life should be subtitled "A Love Story," most Canadians who knew the name would have been puzzled. With a million copies of his books having been sold around the world, he is indisputably the widest-read Canadian scholar, well ahead of Marshall McLuhan and Harold Innis. Scholarship and literary criticism were the fields that made Frye famous. His achievement in the understanding of the eighteenth-century genius William Blake initiated a whole new era in the study of literature. As a teacher he had the capacity to send students reeling from his lectures, almost overwhelmed with the power of his ideas and of the questions he raised.

Frye had other personae, among them the broadcast regulator, a commissioner on the CRTC, helping decide on television licence applications and even on the rates the Telephone Company can charge. He was also an administrator, principal and later Chancellor of Victoria University in the University of Toronto; and he was a clergyman, an ordained minister in the United Church of Canada.

So why did we call his television biography "A Love Story"?

A few years after his death his letters and notebooks began to be published. Columnist Robert Fulford, in the

Toronto *Globe and Mail,* reported with apparent delight that this prim-looking scholar we had gotten to know over the years was prepared to write to his wife such surprising sentences as "We are fucked and far from home." But what these papers revealed more importantly was a passionate, lyrical, playful (and sometimes wittily obscene) spirit. Frye honoured — at the very centre of his being — the primacy of sexual love as "the gateway through which most of us enter the life of the creative imagination." He said that religion, love, poetry, music and indeed all art, are intimately involved with each other, perhaps even aspects of the same human gift. When he spoke of love he very often meant love between the sexes, a passion that at its best lifts the human experience to the highest realms.

Herman Northrop Frye said he felt he had come close to something that teases and seduces every single human being who ever stops to reflect on life: its meaning. During his lifetime he would experience several sudden, clarifying moments. Taking decades to work out the language with which he felt he could express what those revelations had contained, he began to feel that he had uncovered the secret to some of the most profound and puzzling questions. He wrote about the nature of sex, of God, of beauty, truth, science, art, politics and society. Reading Frye, we sometimes feel that if he had lived long enough he would have written about every single thing in life that is worth thinking about, and that he would have had something disturbing and fresh to say about each one of them.

When the actors Don Harron and his wife Catherine McKinnon began to read those letters, between Northrop Frye and his wife Helen Kemp, they almost immediately saw them as the text for a stage presentation. Daniel Zuckerbrot, the writer/director of this episode of *The Canadians*, chose to begin the documentary at one of those readings with:

Saturday night, Spring, 1932. I would have given anything to come to you. I wanted to spend about a day lying on the floor in front of you, with my arms around your ankles and my head on your feet. But of course I didn't do anything as silly, or even try to. I had my institutional dignity to think of! What would the English and History course say if they saw their Norrie Frye making a fool of himself in front of a female?

It's one o'clock. You're sleeping now. My lips have brushed your forehead and my hand has smoothed down your hair.

But you don't know that.

You're asleep.

Frye himself said he thought his life had not been very interesting. On his sixtieth birthday, in one of the tens of thousands of journal entries that scholars are now poring over, searching for what is ultimately close to a mystery embedded in the huge range of this man's mind, Frye wrote:

I notice that at the age of sixty I have arranged my life so that nothing has ever happened to me, and no biographer could possibly have taken the smallest interest in me.

But this is simply not true, as the documentary quickly set out to demonstrate. The camera moves along a set of corridors, descending into the lower regions of a climate-controlled section of the Pratt Library at the University of Toronto. It is a long walk to the Frye collection, which is kept in a locked section accessible only to qualified scholars. Men and women sit in their tiny cubicles a few buildings away, transferring and indexing material from pages and pages of handwritten words in that collection. They are sorting through thousands of journal entries and letters, cataloguing and analysing the vast outpouring of ideas and speculations about everything from God to the motor car. It is becoming clear to the Frye scholars (who come together from time to time, to international conventions where men and women from all the continents meet to discuss his work) that at the heart of that work is a series of sudden flashes of what seemed to Frye to be profound and intricate insights that would require a vast amount of rigorous thinking to explore and to make comprehensible both to himself and to others.

They had begun when he was still in his teens. Like many adolescents he was struggling to make sense out of a world that was dominated by a version of Christianity that seemed to him to deny his own sexuality, his liberty, his imagination, in short: his humanity. This was a fifteen-year-old boy from New Brunswick, the son of a travelling hardware salesman, who one day on his way home from school was struck by a sort of spiritual and intellectual searchlight beam. He said that he had known at the time it would take him years to find out what the sudden clarity meant, but he also knew right then and there that it would change his life.

"Just then suddenly," he wrote later, "that whole shitty and smelly garment of fundamentalist teaching I'd had all my life dropped off into the sewers and stayed there."

That does not sound like a boy who will in a few years be ordained as a minister in the United Church. But it is the opening chapter in a series of spectacular and sudden insights that will lead him to see the whole of human life — that part of our life, that is distinctly human, is different from all other creatures — as being shaped by the combined forces of love, the imagination, and the divine. In the end these three powers, in the mind of Northrop Frye, seem to be different expressions of what is really one distinctly human power or capacity.

Herman Northrop Frye was born in Sherbrooke, Quebec on Bastille Day, July 14th, 1912. His grandfather was a Methodist preacher. Methodism, which had begun as a humanizing protest against the politics and theology of the Church of England, had by then become a rather severe fundamentalist movement, and Frye's mother Catherine was a serious Methodist. For Catherine and Herman Frye life had seemed a solid, reliable path along which we are clearly guided by the precepts of the faith. Then this illusion of assurance and safety was shaken up badly in 1918, when young Norrie was six; first by the death of his brother Howard, a soldier overseas in the Great War, and then by the failure of the family business. Herman took the family to Moncton, New Brunswick, and Frye grew up there, shy, somewhat solitary, an intense student of the

piano at which he himself said he was "infernally precocious," and of literature.

"I read all of [George Bernard] Shaw at fifteen," he
would say later, "and he turned me from a precocious
child into an adolescent fool."

There would be very few besides Frye himself who
would ever refer to him as a fool.

A couple of years later, the agile fingers that were already flashing prodigy-like up and down the piano key-
board turned out to be what was needed to get him out of
Moncton and into a world where his powerful imagination and eccentric personality would be an asset, rather
than a reason for him to hide away at home: he learned to
type. He became very good at it. There was a national
typing competition. Frye won the local playoffs, and that
got him a railway ticket to Toronto for the grand championships. Somehow that led to his taking a look at the university, and deciding to enroll in what was then called
Victoria College (now Victoria University). There he met
another young man who was destined for the ministry,
Kingsley Joblin. They would remain friends for life, and
Joblin says that he vividly remembers an early demonstration of an unexpected talent.

*He was pale in complexion. He was slight in build. He had
this mop of yellow hair. He had been all through high school
what the kids would call a nerd. . . . In those days of initia-
tion he and I were walking through [the famous Vic arch-
way on Charles Street] and we were met by three sophomores. You remember that great mop of yellow hair. The
first said, "Good morning Butter-cup." And the second*

said, "Does your mommy know you're out?" Well Frye let
loose a stream of profanity that curled their toes and mine
too. Nobody ever called him that to his face again.

But one student would give him a nickname based
on that yellow mop, and get away with it. She was Helen
Kemp, also a gifted pianist and a fine artist. They met at
the Drama Club. Out of that love those hundreds of pages
of letters would flourish, along with a marriage that lasted
more than fifty years.

At the University he was finally among people who
found him fascinating. The apparently shy exterior mixed
with a dazzling intellect and plenty of raw personal courage was daunting but intriguing. It was a world where
brilliance was recognized and respected. That was new to
Frye. Soon he was editing the college literary magazine
and making his mark on the debating team.

Helen wrote to him while he was visiting the family in
the summer break, "Having decided that I will not improve my mind or do anything the least uplifting or educational this summer, I shall be very interested in seeing
how *your* muse develops, Feathertop."

Apparently pleased, and not at all offended, he replied,

You ask about my muse. It's still stubborn. I have a good
idea but no technique. I have a conception for a really good
poem, I am pretty sure. But what I put down is flat and dry
as the Great Sahara. I guess I'm essentially prosaic. I can
work myself up into a state of maudlin sentimentality, put
down about ten lines of the most villainous doggerel imag-
inable, and then kick myself and tear the filthy stuff up.

However, I got a book of twentieth-century American
poetry at the library, and that cheered me up. There are
bigger fools in the world!

Before very long Frye's teachers at Victoria College
realized that among that small group of very bright young
people who stayed after the lecture to ask the questions
there didn't seem to be time for during class, who could
be found in the library late at night and early in the
morning, and who were turning in witty and perceptive
essays, this Frye was really something special. One day
his Romantics professor, a well-known academic named
Pelham Edgar, told him, "I think you're the guy to write
on Blake in this class."

Blake is a poet who has baffled both scholars and
lovers of poetry. He has created some of the most durable
and powerful images in the history of English literature.
All serious readers of English — and thousands not so
serious — have read or heard:

> *Tyger, Tyger, burning bright*
> *In the forests of the night*
> *What immortal hand or eye*
> *Could frame thy fearful symmetry.*

Perhaps not quite so many, but still enormous numbers, have felt the delight of the apparently simple lines:

> *To see a world in a grain of sand*
> *And a heaven in a wild flower*
> *Hold infinity in the palm of your hand*
> *And eternity in an hour.*

In churches and on choral concert stages all over the
English-speaking world, the great hymn "Jerusalem," set

to music by Charles H. Parry, is Blake's preface to his epic poem *Milton*. It begins,

> *And did those feet in ancient times*
> *Walk upon England's mountains green?*

And continues,

> *Bring me my bow of burning gold*
> *Bring me my arrows of desire*

And ends,

> *I will not cease from Mental Fight*
> *Nor will my sword sleep in my hand*
> *Till we have built Jerusalem*
> *In England's green and pleasant land.*

It is not hard to see the young scholar being swept away by those resonant lines. However, very few, none but serious scholars these days, have ventured into Blake's long, complicated mythic epics about the origins of the world and the titanic struggle of huge mythic figures with names such as Orc and Urizen. But all who read Blake are struck by two things at once: the power of the words, and the sense that they convey something far more profound than you would expect from their seemingly simple form.

What happened to Frye when he tackled Blake for the first time went far beyond the sense of delight and even mystery that many feel when they first encounter this daunting writer. Like many students he had put off writing the essay until the last possible moment, in this case the night before it was due. He had to work late into that night. Suddenly he had another vision:

> *Around about three in the morning the universe broke open, and I've never been, as they say, the same man since.*

It was just a feeling of enormous numbers of things mak-
ing sense that never did before; a vision of coherence.
Things began to form patterns and make sense. It was a
mythological frame taking hold. I've had two or three
nights where I've had sudden visions like that. They were
visions of what I might be able to do.

What would those things turn out to be? Professor
Michael Dolzani, who spent years in close association with
Frye as his research assistant, said that Frye envisioned a
coherent single body of work, composed of eight great
separate but related pieces:

. . . a set, an interlocking set that he called The Ogdoad:
sort of an old word for a set of eight gods. These were not
even necessarily to be books. They were going to be . . .
eight great symphonies or something. They were to be . . .
the eight elements of the total vision that he had come into
the world to say. It was only towards the end of this life
that the notebooks start to say, "I'm coming to see that
this vision, this ogdoad total pattern, is not only some-
thing to see, let alone something to write: it is something
to see by. Like a lens, rather than something that is pro-
jected out into the world."

And central to this projection was the *act* of literature. "He calls literature a power of meditation," says professor Dolzani. "And it's available to anybody. You don't
have to do drugs. You don't have to get into arcane things.
Literature itself can be . . . an expansion of consciousness."

Much later in his life, Northrop Frye would write
two very provocative books about the Bible: *The Great*

Code, and *Words With Power*. These books, of which the subtitled theme is "The Bible and Literature" (*not* "The Bible *As* Literature"), examine the Bible as the Western world's prime source of all of the great stories that we use to make sense out of our lives. Frye shows how those stories keep turning up: in Shakespeare, in movies, even in comic strips. One of the striking things about these two books is that, while they are focussed on the Bible, they discover reflections of its myths and legends in just about every aspect of modern life. One of the contributors to this film biography, Phillip Marchand, the literary critic of the *Toronto Star*, even finds the role of the umpire in a baseball game embedded in the same set of ancient myths about the Scapegoat that Frye said was the soil from which grew the story of Christ.

This was a view of the Bible very different from the one that Frye felt he had been saddled with, and an uncomfortable saddle at that, in his Methodist upbringing. That Bible was a set of rules and threats of punishment for those who broke the rules. The Bible that suddenly broke free of those rules, as Frye plunged into the strange and powerful poetry of William Blake, was a radical document. It was not an authoritarian prescription for a way of life that would get you into some creamy place up in the sky if you did what you were told. It was in fact a revolutionary call to arms, spiritual arms.

Frye said, "The Bible to Blake was really the *Magna Carta* of the human imagination. It was a book that told man he had the power to create and imagine. And the power to create and imagine *was ultimately the divine in man."* For the rest of his life he would condemn the way in which the traditional churches had allowed themselves to be used throughout history as a political instrument to keep people in their places so that the powerful could rule in comfort. This was a form of tyranny, he said baldly. It contradicted the real message of the Bible, which was God is everywhere, including inside each one of us. The creative imagination is an expression of the divine in man, he said. Its purpose is not to keep us in line but to free us so that we can realize our divinity, escape the tyranny of rulers and of our own blindness. Religion is about love and liberty, not about doing what you're supposed to do so that you'll get into some place called Heaven — where there is nothing left to do.

But that doesn't mean that Northrop Frye himself was as suddenly freed from the grip of his traditional religious upbringing as he perhaps hoped, or imagined. He wrote to Helen, from Moncton, in 1932:

The Ministry is my "vocation." I have been "called" to it just as much as any blaspheming fool of an evangelist that ever bragged about what a sinner he was before he was converted. But that doesn't mean that I am fitted for it, necessarily. It doesn't mean that I am not deadly afraid of it and would rather do a hundred other things.

Above all it doesn't mean that my friends ever imagine I'll be a minister. "Minister," snorts the janitor at Gate House. "You'd make a damned good hypocrite, that's what you'd make!" My communist friend Norm Knight says, "My dear boy, you can't be a minister, you've got brains!" And so they go.

They are absolutely and devastatingly right, of course. I wonder what those writers who talk about . . . fate would say to a man who had two Fates, pulling in opposite directions. The trouble is, I can't figure out which one is God.

It was about that time, in a letter, that Helen confessed that she was in love with him. Another student, a man named Robert, had been teasing her, moving in on her perhaps, and asking her if she was in love with anybody. "Well," she wrote, "I did mention you, Norrie. Do you mind very much?"

You frighten me a little [he replied]. *Love may mean anything from a quiet friendship to an overwhelming passion. It may be anything from a purely sexual impulse to a declaration of honourable intentions based upon a close survey of the economic field. It acts like a tonic upon me to hear you say you love me, certainly. But it does make me nervous to be carrying such a warm, pulsating heart around in my pockets. I'm afraid it might drop out and break.*

One of the puzzles about the life of this undoubted genius is this: Given his absolutely radical take on the real meaning of the Bible and the Christian message, and his contempt for almost the entire traditional baggage and politics of the traditional organized churches, why did he go ahead with his "vocation" to the Ministry?

By the summer of 1933, Helen had gone to study in Britain, and he was in Saskatchewan. He got saddle sores riding the circuit as a student minister, and visiting farmhouses where he was incapable of the expected small talk.

Gull Lake, Saskatchewan, May 1934. There's nothing to say about the trip, pet, except that I made it . . . or most of it. If I were a mystic this past week . . . would register as the Dark Night of the Soul. . . . I can't figure out this damn country. . . . Twenty more Sundays. I don't quite know how I'll survive. . . . I am horribly homesick and thoroughly miserable. Yet I can't think I made a mistake in coming out here. Everything, horse, country life, standards of living, moral attitudes, conversation, interests . . . are so absolutely different from anything I've been accustomed to. If I thought I should have to stay out here all my life I would commit suicide without the slightest hesitation.

By the time he had done the apprenticeship in the field that being ordained required, he had decided firmly that teaching, not the Ministry, was his real vocation. He enrolled at Oxford, to round out his studies. And yet, before he left, he went ahead with the ordination, and became the Reverend Northrop Frye, brains or no brains.

Now it was 1936. In Europe fascism was growing like a diabolical weed. It had already spawned the Nazi party and would soon bring the greatest war in the history of the world, and the Holocaust: the massacre of the Jews of Europe. Frye's tutor at Oxford was the renowned literary scholar Edmund Blunden. Frye was shocked to find that Blunden, like the poets T.S. Eliot, W.B. Yeats, and a number of other intellectuals, seemed to think that fascism might contain a ray of hope for a confused world. Moreover, Blunden had trouble with Frye's ideas.

Blunden returned my Blake paper with the remark that it was pretty stiff going for him as he wasn't much accustomed to thinking in philosophical terms. I could have told him that there was a little girl in Toronto who could follow it all right . . .

He was twenty-four. Helen was in Canada.

Merton College, Oxford. 1936. There are very few moments, if any, when you are out of my mind. I think at least half of you must be inside me. I feel as though I had only to turn around three times to turn into Helen. Nobody can talk to me five minutes without hearing about you somehow, and without realizing that I am prouder of my attachment to you than anything else. I love you all day long. And if you would mind stepping across the Atlantic a minute, I would soon prove it.

It was during this time that his undergraduate lightning flash about Blake was beginning to mature as he found words for Blake's revolutionary images of liberty and love and the divinity within the human mind, not in some God-in-the-Sky whom Blake (a devout Christian) dismissed as an

Old Nobodaddy aloft
Who farted and belched and coughed.

As the spectre of fascism, with its sanctification of blood and authority grew stronger and stronger, so too did Frye's conviction that there was a vision of liberty in Blake that had to do with basic human needs and values. He, Northrop Frye, could bring these metaphors to the attention of the world, or at least to the world of scholars. It was a challenge to explore the creative experience as the starting point for a larger life and a better world.

I propose spending the rest of my life, apart from living with you, on various problems connected with religion and art. Now religion and art are the two most important phenomena, for they are basically the same thing. They constitute, in fact, the only reality of existence. Atheism is an impossible religious position for me, just as materialism is an impossible philosophical position. And I am unable to solve the problem of art by ignoring the first and distorting the second. Read Blake or go to Hell; that's my message for the modern world.

He came home to Helen. *The Toronto Daily Star*, August 24, 1937:

In Emmanuel College Chapel, Reverend Arthur Cragg, a classmate of the groom, peformed the marriage of Herman Northrop Frye and Helen G. Kemp. The matrimonial pair will honeymoon at the bride's parents' cottage, Gordon Bay, Muskoka, after which they will reside at the University Apartments, 6 St. Thomas Street, adjacent to Victoria College.

As World War II raged across Europe and through the Pacific, Frye, medically unfit for military service, threw himself into the book on Blake. He was a popular lecturer at Vic, often testing his ideas in the classroom where his students were sometimes shocked and often provoked to the point where they started digging into Blake themselves. The Blake book was still in the works. Northrop Frye's view of life began to converge so closely with that of the difficult and brilliant genius he was studying that, in chapter after chapter of the book he was still labouring on, it was increasingly difficult to discern whose voice the reader was hearing, Frye's or Blake's. The message was not one you would expect from a soft-spoken, apparently retiring United Church minister:

Tyranny requires a priesthood and a God. Religion has been called the Opiate of the People. But religion in its conventionally accepted and socially established form is far more dangerous than any opiate, whose effects are transitory.

The book was called *Fearful Symmetry*, from the poem beginning "Tyger, Tyger," quoted above. Frye finished it at last, in 1945. That date is a dividing line in Blake studies: before Frye and after Frye. Scholars, poets and students are still reading *Fearful Symmetry*, putting it down in astonishment, picking it up and starting all over again. From 1945 on, if there was ever any doubt that the world of literary criticism had a new giant to contend with, that doubt vanished. What scholars and lovers of literature found in *Fearful Symmetry* was an argument for the power of myths and metaphors that brutally tested the conventional scientific and materialistic view of the nature of reality.

Michael Dolzani:

Blake thinks almost purely in terms of myths and metaphors: the units that poets think in . . . a different way of thinking . . . a different mode of perception. They're native to all of us, because the deeper layers of our mind do think metaphorically, do think mythically. Our dreams are evidence of that. . . . The thing is to bring it up into daylight, and integrate that into consciousness. We live at about a tenth of the level of consciousness and being that we could . . . Blake . . . says that if the doors of perception were cleansed we would see much much more than we do now.

From now on, for the next quarter-century, when Frye wrote, the literary world read, and paid attention. His next major work would be an original theory of literary criticism published in 1957: *Anatomy of Criticism*. Writers and scholars talk of it as a book that changed their lives. There had not been a theory of literary criticism before Frye. He argued that criticism was not a matter of saying whether a work was good or not, but of identifying the myths and metaphors it contained, telling the reader where they came from and why they were powerful and what they were connected to, so that the work could be seen as part of a whole.

That was the radical idea. What Shakespeare, William Styron, Montaigne, Li Po, and the many authors of the books of the Bible (who often disagreed with each other), and Walt Kelly, Walt Disney and Stephen Spielberg were all doing was a part of one comprehensive world vision. Whether or not they knew it, they were all working out of the same body of myths whose great expression in the Western world begins with Greek mythology and the books of the Bible. You could not understand, Frye argued, what you were doing here if you didn't know about Greek myth and the great formative stories of the Christians and the Jews.

He took his own prescription to heart, adding Greek to the Latin he already knew from high school, and then going on to Hebrew and Sanskrit. He was at ease with French and could make his way in German, and pretty well in Italian and Spanish too. Armed with these tools he would penetrate deeper and deeper into the stories, myths and metaphors in which he was convinced were buried the meaning of the human experience.

Poet and novelist Margaret Atwood, who received one of her many honorary doctorates from Frye's hands, said,

Norrie . . . said essentially the comic book and the Jane Austen novel and the Greek myth have the same structure. What are we talking about? Human desire. What is one of the greatest human desires? To fly about without an airplane and to be all-powerful. Captain Marvel? Zeus? Take your pick.

And Michael Dolzani, again:

[Frye] did not read the Bible as history, because the Bible is not history. . . . Blake said that the Bible is the "Great Code" of art, and art is the great key to human behaviour. Then you get a sense of the patterns we all live out. Jung said that he began his career by asking himself What myth am I living? And that's the moment when we wake up; when we ask ourselves that question. . . . We do live out myths in our daily life. I mean long before Frye came around, Freud and Jung and the early depth psychologists were very articulate about how we're always playing out myths. The Oedipus Complex is only a stock example, but even if you don't like that one, [try] scapegoating. Anyone who was ever on a playground in an elementary school knows [about scapegoats]. Why do we pick out one kid and beat him up and bond as a group? That's mythical. It's a primitive sacrificial ritual that binds the group together.

The Canadian poet and playwright James Reaney adds, "The Nazis . . . took the whole thing [about the

scapegoat] and turned it into a Jew, and started slaugh-
tering them."

All this seems to convey the impression of a scholar
whose preoccupation is with evil. But in fact Frye's excitement with the work of Blake, and with the vision he felt he
had received about the almost identical qualities of the idea
of God and the idea of the human imagination, was joyful.
Sometimes the language he used to make his points was
quite playful, and young people, fascinated with his legit-
imization of sex, joy, play and wit, flocked to his lectures by
the hundreds, to hear things like this:

> *Blake suggests that eternal joy is a positive thing, an
> achievement in a world of gratified desire. [Now] a world
> where the lion is said to lie down with the lamb is a world
> of stuffed lions. Sexual love, however, is the door through
> which most of us enter the imaginative world. Mating
> and copulating may be "animal," but imaginative love is
> part of our* divine *birthright.*

Frye's was a long, productive and rewarding scholarly
life. He would give guest lectures in other universities, in
Canada and abroad, and his lectures would be made into
books. Unlike many senior academics, who find teaching a
chore and undergraduates a nuisance, Frye seemed to understand what every really great teacher knows deeply:
that the joy of bringing a young mind to the edge of discov-
ery is among the greatest joys that life has to offer. He never
stopped meeting with undergraduates, challenging them,
making them laugh, making them see life afresh. Impatient
with careless thinking he sometimes humiliated them when
they asked dull questions. Later he regretted his cruelty.

Music, which had informed his life as a gifted young pianist, was never absent from his study of all forms of art. He said that great writers know that if you get the sound right, the sense will take care of itself. He talked about the Order of Words. *Anatomy of Criticism* contains powerful arguments about the way in which certain structural combinations of verbs and nouns and adjectives are so embedded in the consciousness that they seem a response to inherited patterns in the brain. Rhythm and meter, waltz and mazurka, melody and rhyme, shape and colour: for Frye these were intimately connected, and partook of the experience of love.

Love brought him grief, too. Helen was stricken, and he had to contemplate this closest of all his imaginative accomplices deprived of her memory. When she died his old pal Kingsley Joblin conducted the funeral just a few metres from where he had stood agape with Norrie outside that famous Victoria College arch half a century earlier as Norrie curled the toes of the sophomores with his colourful obscenities. Joblin said that he asked Norrie to write a few words about Helen, but that the Old Professor could not bear to read them at the funeral; so the Old Clergyman read them in his stead:

> *The dark shadow of Alzheimer's disease fell across the last years of our life together. And I watched helplessly the gradual shrinking of her energies and personal resources. She was a generous and very pure spirit, no matter how amused or embarrassed she might be to hear herself so described. She died at 3:10 p.m. The medical attendant said 3:30. But I happen to know what time she left me.*

And that is why we called our documentary film "A Love Story."

Herman Northrop Frye died on January 23, 1991. He was seventy-eight years old. For some time his pioneering work had gone out of fashion as the hip scholars discovered something called deconstruction and forgot about myths and meaning in life and literature. But now he is coming back almost as if he had not gone. And when Frye scholars gather the outside observer might wonder whether the Old Professor would be happy to see how much they defer to his authority. If he listens closely he will find it is not deference; it is a spellbound attempt to unravel, to understand. For if Frye felt that his work was to make his strange visions clear to the world, he should be gratified to find that scholars are carrying on that work; not in abject agreement but in fascination and intrigue.

So: two last words on the life of this most famous of all the Canadian scholars: first from Professor Dolzani:

Literature is hypothetical, Frye said. All of these myths and metaphors are human creations. They are fictions. But . . . the moment of finding something whether in literature or in the Bible or any text, and saying, "That's for me: that is the guide for me, for my life and my quest": that is the moment you step from the fictions of literature into a more existential view of things. And that is a religious step: whether you believe in . . . God, or not.

And the very last word to the Old Professor himself, an obituary he left for us to find, in his notebooks, characteristically witty, but not really a joke.

The 20th century saw an amazing development of schol-
arship and criticism in the humanities, carried out by peo-
ple who were more intelligent, better trained, had more lan-
guages, had a better sense of proportion, and were infi-
nitely more accurate scholars and competent professional
men than I.

I had genius.

No one else in the field known to me had that.

◆   ◆   ◆

Northrop Frye: A Love Story was written and directed by
Daniel Zuckerbrot, with Terry Bartley as line producer
and Director of Photography Andrew Binnington. Assoc-
iate producer Roberto Verdechia. Sound, Ian Challis,
Margus Jukkum, Rod Kraft, Tom Bilenky. Editor, Michelle
Hozer. It was first broadcast on History Television on
March 29, 2000, and will be seen again in the spring of 2001.

Ribbon Finalist at the CAB (Canadian Association of
Broadcasters) Awards, 1999.

This program won a Bronze Plaque Award at the 48th
Columbus International Film & Video Festival (2000).

ADDITIONAL READING:

Northrop Frye: *A Natural Perspective, Anatomy of Criti-*
cism, The Double Vision, The Educated Imagination

John Ayre: *Northrop Frye: A Biography* (1989). Robert Den-
ham, ed., *A World in a Grain of Sand: Twenty-two Interviews*
with Northrop Frye (1991). David Cayley, *Northrop Frye in*
Conversation (1992)

◇ Part Eleven ◇

DISTANT SKIES
THE STORY OF WOP MAY

"They say you have angels on your shoulder; [well] Wop must have had a whole squadron of them."
—Marie Wright, pioneer ferry pilot and friend of Wop May.

It is a nickname that would be considered politically incorrect today, having been used to insult Italian immigrants to North America in times when that was considered acceptable. His real name was Wilfrid, his father having been a fan of Prime Minister Sir Wilfrid Laurier when the boy was born. When he was six his three-year-old cousin Mary came to visit. She couldn't say "Wilfrid"; it came out as "Woppie," stuck somehow, as such accidental nicknames often do, became "Wop" before long, and stayed there. In the old photos you can see it painted in block letters three feet high on the upper wing of the Curtis Jenny he was barnstorming in during the 1920's. But barnstorming was not what made him famous. For years he was known, not quite correctly, as "the man who helped shoot down the Red Baron."

Here is how the legend developed. Young Wilfrid and his brother Court had grown up thinking about aeroplanes and of learning to fly. It was an idea that was beginning to infect the whole continent; just beginning to change from a mythical dream into a real and present possibility. In 1903 Wilbur and Orville Wright had become world-famous overnight with the first-ever flight of a self-powered heavier-than-air machine. By means of another new technology called the motion picture the boys had seen images of that historic event. They now knew, for sure; that was for them. They made a pact that, together, they would fly. Somehow, some day.

The brothers had grown up around machines. They felt comfortable with them. Machines were not just to use, they were to take apart, to find out how they worked, to fix, to put back together again. The May family had found its way from England to Scotland to Ireland to Canada. Alexander May had a successful farm implements business in Carberry, Manitoba, when his son Wilfrid was born there in 1896. Cockshutt ploughs, reapers and steam-powered threshing machines, and — before long — the early gasoline-powered tractors with huge metal lugs on their wheels. Those rusting hulks can still be seen around small agricultural villages or out behind a barn or, even today, parked in the back lots of the present-day versions of implement businesses like Alexander May's.

Alexander had a well-stocked library: mostly military history and books about machines. The boys devoured those books. When the family moved to Edmonton, Alex May opened a service station, selling gasoline and tires and repairing these newfangled automobile things, which broke down a lot. By the time they were in their early teens the boys had developed a taste for speed and risk, and for working around gasoline engines where they came to love the smell of hot metal and oily rags.

They would race anything. There is a photo of young Wilfrid at the tiller of what appears to be an Aykroyd dinghy — in a race almost certainly. The Aykroyd was a fat, stable fourteen-foot clinker-built gaff-rigged catboat, designed and built on Toronto Island in the early part of the century. Thousands of kids across Canada learned to sail and to race in the handy little craft.

The first aeroplane Court and Wop actually saw came to Edmonton for demonstration flights in 1910. It was a Curtiss Pusher, not much of an advance over the Wright Flyer of seven years earlier. The elevators, movable horizontal surfaces that control the up or down attitude of the machine, were stuck out in front of the pilot on a sort of frame. The control wheel was very much like an old automobile wheel, big and ungainly. The heavy, not very powerful liquid-cooled engine, with a big radiator like a car, was behind the pilot and the propeller behind the engine, hence the name "Pusher."

On the Wright Flyer the wings were kept level or put into a bank by a set of wires that actually bent the shape of the flexible, cloth-covered bamboo frames that made up those wings. It may have been Curtiss who invented the movable winglets called ailerons that became the standard control surface before long, and the Curtiss Pusher the May brothers saw would probably have been so equipped. There may or may not have been a safety belt in Hugh Robinson's pusher when he had it shipped from town to town across the west that summer to do his demonstrations. The idea of strapping the pilot into his seat came only after somebody actually fell out.

At Victoria High School Wop met another student who was mad for aeroplanes. That boy's name was Roy

Brown. Their knowing each other would later have a big impact on Wop's life.

War had come to Europe. The boys heard that some Canadians who went over as foot-soldiers had managed to transfer to the Royal Flying Corps. There was no air force in Canada yet. They decided to try getting into the air by way of the infantry.

However, Court had suffered from poliomyelitis as a child, and the army would not take him. Polio was a common disease then, striking children more than adults and often called "infantile paralysis." Many died of it when their chest muscles failed. Others carried a paralysed leg or arm — or worse — for the rest of their lives. Court's paralysis left him with a serious limp, which ruled him out for active service and would tragically shorten his life. Wop joined the 202nd Infantry Battalion, known as "The Edmonton Sportsman's," and soon found himself on the way to England.

It took some time to get into the Flying Corps. Many young men saw air combat as a way to stay in the war but get out of the trenches. War in the air had glamour; war on the ground had mud and rats and almost certain death. So there was a waiting list. It was not until late in 1917 that Wop was accepted. By March of 1918 he graduated from 94 Training Squadron, at Acton. He had flown a total of 5 1/2 hours.

To put that in perspective: it would be unusual for a student pilot today to even take his first solo with less than ten hours. Fifteen is a likelier number, and you will be pretty impressive if you get your private licence with less than forty hours at the controls. In the two weeks after he left 94 squadron the young man would build up another 30-some hours, with gunnery and formation flying to prepare him for combat. But then, with no more time in the air than a newly minted private pilot of today, he was sent off to combat squadron number 209. Now promoted to Lieutenant, he was twenty-two.

The aircraft they trained on initially were not much like the fighters they would fly in combat. Some of those trainers were pushers, not much of an advance over that Curtiss, the first aeroplane that Wop and his brother had seen back in Edmonton. They were slow, underpowered and ungainly. Today they look just plain ugly and impossible. Once at the front lines the new fighter pilots were given the very latest machines, but even they were often awkward and, by today's standards, terrifying.

The machine Wop May flew in 209 squadron was considered the best yet: a British fighter called the Sopwith Camel. The Camel not only flew in France and Flanders, but were bought for the British Navy as well, and flew off the new aircraft carriers, as well as from improvised launching arrangements on cruisers and battleships. It was considered to be the summit of fighter design at the time. There were several versions, and Wop's was the top of the line. Powered by a British-built Bentley rotary engine of about 130 horsepower, it climbed well and could work effectively up to 12,000 feet. But it was difficult to fly. It often spun out of control in tight turns, and the problem was that *rotary* engine.

Most people even in the jet age know what a *radial* engine looks like, and a rotary looks like a radial but has one crucial difference. Radials powered the legendary DC 3, the De Havilland Beaver and most of the famous World War Two heavy bombers like the Flying Fortress B-17, the Liberator B-24, and the Mitchell B-25. The radial had five or seven or nine cylinders radiating out from the hub of the propeller like the petals of a flower. Some had two such "flowers" back to back, with as many as eighteen cylinders. The rotary also has the cylinders radiating out from the hub, exactly like a radial. But instead of the engine being fixed to the firewall (the flat plate forward of the cockpit), with the turning crankshaft sticking out ahead with a propeller bolted to it, in the rotary the engine was turned backwards, the crankshaft was bolted to the firewall, the propeller was actually fastened to the engine, *and the whole engine revolved*!

This meant that out at the front end of a wood and canvas aircraft that weighed (without armament) less than a thousand pounds, there would be three or four hundred pounds of metal rotating at 900 to 1200 revolutions per minute. A rotating solid object, like a flywheel or a planet — or a rotary engine — resists any attempt to change its attitude, to make its axis point in a different direction. Huge ocean liners were equipped with such big heavy wheels to help keep them from tossing about in storms and making the passengers ill. You can experience the effect by going to a toy store or a science store and buying a small gyroscope. Wind the string around the shaft and get the wheel spinning. Hold the wheel by the ends of the axle, so that it is spinning on a horizontal axis, as if it were a rotary engine with a propeller fixed to it. Now try to turn it, to left or to right. Depending on which direction you've got it spinning, it will not only resist your turning it, it will quite strongly either dip down or tilt up, in response to your attempts to turn it. That is what happened when a pilot tried to turn the Sopwith Camel. Pilots had to completely relearn how to turn in flight, if they had been trained in aircraft that did not have a rotary engine. Although the Sopwith Camel shot down more enemy aircraft than any other fighter in that war, more pilots died learning to fly in it than died in combat.

The rotary engine was lubricated by castor oil. The oil was not burned; helped by centrifugal force to spray out from the crankshaft to the ends of the rotating cylinders, it percolated through the engine and came out in the exhaust. At the end of every flight the fuselage of the aircraft would be glistening with a film of oil. There was always oil on your clothes and goggles, and on your face. If you hadn't been warned, or if in the heat of combat you forgot yourself and licked your lips, you could ingest quite a bit of it. Castor oil is a powerful emetic and laxative. It takes effect suddenly and explosively. Many a new Camel pilot, even though warned, would come back from a mission not only terrified by the experience, but with his flight suit sodden, inside and out, with the odorous results of swallowing castor oil. His plane's cockpit would have to be flushed out before anyone could fly it again.

But the pilots — those who survived their training — liked the eighteen-foot long machine, all the same. If you were a camel-driver you were good. It was faster than what they'd been used to (115 miles an hour), and was the first fighter to be equipped with two .303 Vickers machine guns. Unlike some of the earlier machines, you didn't have to aim the guns or even touch them. They were fixed to the fuselage and fired forward, through the propeller, with two firing buttons on the spade-grip of the joystick and a synchronizing mechanism that kept the bullets from hitting the prop. Some were equipped with guns firing straight down through the floor and were flown over enemy trenches to strafe the soldiers below.

So that was the plane which the brand-new fighter pilot, Wilfrid Reid May, nourished by what was probably an inappropriate level of confidence, would be flying into combat when he got to 209 squadron. The Flying Corps had a partying tradition. Pilots at the front used to joke about coming back from a mission and heading for the Officer's Mess, which meant the bar, and staying there so determinedly that the routine next morning would be "Get up; suit up; throw up; start up." Wop May got a head start with some sort of party en route to the squadron, and as a result arrived late and perhaps not in very good shape. The Major fired him from the squadron before he even got started. But the high school friendship with Roy Brown saved him, as it would save him more dramatically only a few days later.

Roy Brown was a Flight Commander. He ran into the disconsolate and hung-over lieutenant, interceded on his behalf with the Major, and got Wop re-instated. Then he took him under his wing.

Roy Brown counselled Wop May to stay out of the action during the first few sorties, and just watch the patterns of combat from a distance. They would be up against German pilots who had been fighting for months, some for years. It would be suicidal to tangle with them until he had observed war in the air from a close, but not engaged position, for at least a couple of missions. Indeed there was a possibility that the top German ace, the legendary Baron von Richthofen, the "Red Baron," would turn up; he was known to be flying in their sector. Richthofen had already tallied 80 kills. So stay out of it, was Roy Brown's advice.

Wop May was, however, and remained for the rest of his long career, impulsive, a risk-taker, a man who tended to be deaf to prudent warnings. The first two flights with 209 were uneventful. But on the third, the new boy, with zero hours of combat experience, suddenly saw an enemy aeroplane he thought he could handle. Into the fray he went. Before long he found himself with a red triplane on his tail. A Fokker triplane with black crosses on its wings that was firing machine-gun bullets at him.

May headed for the ground and zigged and zagged between trees and buildings, heading towards the river Somme. Roy Brown saw what was happening, and while he had no idea then that it was Richthofen on the tail of his inexperienced friend, he knew it was serious trouble. He dived after the Fokker, out of the sun, firing as soon as he got within range.

It has never been established exactly what happened next. Roy Brown got the official credit for downing the Red Baron that morning. The credit was also claimed by a group of Australian riflemen on the ground. There were at least half a dozen ground-based machine guns and hundreds of rifles firing up at the low-flying red triplane as it followed Wop May along the Somme. The chase was now across the lines, in Allied territory.

Baron Manfred Albrecht von Richthofen, pride of the Imperial German Air Force, had been urged to quit flying. He had done enough, they told him; he was more use to the war effort as a living hero than he would be dead. He had been shot down and survived twice, once in March and once in July 1917. The second time a head wound left him with agonizing headaches thereafter. And yet, he kept on flying and fighting, and his score kept mounting. But this time the Red Baron went down for good. Amazingly, after all that firepower they had thrown at him, from the ground and the air, he actually flew his plane to a landing that would have probably been successful had the ground not been rough enough to break off the landing gear. But he was mortally wounded. A British soldier ran up excitedly. Von Richthofen looked at him grimly, muttered something that included the word "Kaput," and closed his eyes forever.

They found only one bullet hole in the wrecked aircraft. The bullet that caused it had passed through Von Richtofen's body and fallen into his flight jacket. The bullet was lost; so who fired it is not known. Von Richthofen was twenty-five years old.

Those were still days of chivalry in the air war. The German ace was given a hero's funeral, full military honours, a 21-gun salute from the Australians. Wop May and another pilot took a set of photographs of the ceremony and dropped them over a German aerodrome. Richthofen himself was said to have lavishly entertained at least one downed and survived Allied pilot, sending him off to Prisoner of War Camp with champagne in his kit.

Wop became a skilled combat pilot in the last few months of the war. It takes three kills to earn the title "Ace"; May had thirteen before it was over. It was not fun. Here are actual excerpts from his log book.

May 14. I lost formation for about 10 minutes. Samie Taylor took my place. Bell took Samie's place and was hit by a direct hit by archie [anti-aircraft fire], *spun down. Fenton crashed & Harker crashed & Brettorious nearly crashed, none of the last were hurt. Bell I think has gone he was a friend of Stover's just came back off leave.*

May 15. Escort and H.O.P. escorted D.H.4's over met 2 Hun Scouts on a French Spad's tail, chased them off. Capt. Redgate got one, went in with D.H.4's tail. We chased them off and strafed with them. Capt Redgate and Brettorious and Wilson pushed off. Taylor and I stayed and scrapped with them for about 15 minutes he got one and I got one. Both my guns jammed and I came home. Taylor joined the formation they ran into a bunch of triplanes. Wilson and Brettorious were shot down, one was thrown out of his seat and the other spun to the ground. Capt. Redgate was wounded in the leg got home OK. 3 Bristol fighters also brought down.

The final entry reads "Taylor and I are all that's left in flight A." After that he stopped keeping a log. What was the point if you were going to die tomorrow?

But then came that day in November when the great guns went silent. Wop took the Sopwith Camel up for a last flight. He had the Distinguished Flying Cross now; he was a decorated hero. He went home with his medals and an odd kind of fame: five minutes of running for his life had written him into the history books. Back in Alberta his career would write a lot more aviation history: less glamorous, perhaps, but far more significant.

Court was waiting for him. They were going to open a flying business, remember? Court had lined up a Toronto-built Curtiss Canuck, the Canadian version of the Jenny, the standard trainer in American Army Air Corps training bases, had posted a bond for it and leased it from the city of Edmonton for $25.00 a month. There are still a few of these aircraft around. They don't look their age. In Edmonton a retired airline pilot named Jack Johnson still flies a rebuilt Canuck/Jenny out of the same field that Wop May used over eighty years ago.

"It's pretty slow," Johnson says, a bit ruefully. "I wouldn't say on the ragged edge of a stall but sometimes you're close to it. They spin nice and fly real nice on a nice smooth day. But on a gusty day they aren't too much fun."

So this was the machine they hoped to turn into a business. It did not work out very well, at first. There was some barnstorming, of course. You flew your clattering machine to a fairground and made a deal with the promoters to attract visitors to the fair by putting on stunts. Then you flew a few loops and rolls, and perhaps you got somebody to stand on the top of the wing holding on with a strap, and perhaps you took people up for a ride over the city for a couple of minutes, at fifty cents a pop. There was only one passenger seat in the Jenny.

Wop flew the mayor of Edmonton over the ball park, in the passenger seat of the Jenny, from which His Honour threw out the opening ball of the season. He would fly low over the city so that people would look up and see the big EDMONTON painted on the fuselage. If they were curious enough to find their way out to the airfield, they would see "MAY AIRPLANES LTD." painted on the tail. But the business was not coming in, and indeed they did not have a lot to offer, with one little passenger seat and almost no freight-carrying capacity. Wop became friends with the American barnstormers. But while that was fun it was not the business he and Court had in mind. They wanted passengers and freight and enough money coming in to buy a serious machine. In 1927 Wop founded the Edmonton Flying Club, and was Chief Pilot and Manager.

He got a contract to ferry two big Junkers JL6 aircraft from New York to Edmonton, for Imperial Oil, and hired a friend named George Gorman to fly the second machine. Six years before Lindbergh would fly the Atlantic, these two flew the Junkers six thousand kilometres from New York in the dead of winter, and made some news and a bit of money. But the flying business was so far proving unprofitable. And then a disaster struck: Court's leg gave way on a flight of stairs. He had a terrible fall and died from his injuries. That was it, for Wop. He couldn't take it any more. He was lonely, and when he met Vi Bode, a woman as mad for horses as he was for aeroplanes, he felt that at last there might be some sunshine somewhere in his life. And there was. They got married. Now he had to have a job. He found one as a machinist for the National Cash Register Company in Dayton, Ohio. It was 1924 and he was twenty-eight years old.

In that factory he had an accident worse than anything that had happened to him in the war. He was working a lathe when a fragment of metal flew into his right eye and partially blinded him. When he came back to Canada a year later he had to cheat on his aviation medical tests. The doctor would say, "Cover one eye and read the chart." He would raise his right hand and cover his right eye. Then the doctor would say, "the other one now," and Wop would raise his left hand and cover the right eye again. Sometimes he just memorized the chart. Pilots who have not tried flying with only one good eye will tell you — and it seems logical — that since depth perception depends on your having two eyes, it would be really tough to judge height and distance with only one. But that is not so; such judgments in flying are concerned with distances that are too great for the binocular function to be much good, and angle judgment is much more important. If you have only one eye, you have to develop a flexible neck for looking out the bad side. Wop seems never to have had any trouble, at least not with the flying. But the eye would cause him enormous grief a few years later.

By the late 1920's Canadians had begun to realize what a boon the aeroplane was in a land where communities were so widely separated, and where there was so much exploration and prospecting going on hundreds of miles away from any kind of settlement. Wop began to get work flying prospectors and supplies into the North. A few years later his experience in those vast barren lands would earn him another reputation as a hero.

It was 1929. Six hundred miles north of Edmonton, the settlement at Little Red River had been devastated by diphtheria, and there was a desperate search for a way to get anti-toxin serum to the tiny community. The Alberta Deputy Minister of Health, Dr. Malcolm Bow, asked Wop if it would be possible to fly the serum there. It was thirty below zero and the whole area was deep in snow. The only machine available was Wop's Avro Avian. There was no protection from the weather. The Avian was an open cockpit cloth-covered biplane on wheels, not skis. But Wop's son Denny May, now the custodian of the family history, says that Dr. Bow told him that characteristically Wop did not hesitate for a moment: "Of course! Let's go."

They wrapped the five hundred units of anti-toxin in woolen rugs around a little charcoal burner on the floor of the Avian to keep them from freezing, and off they went, Wop and his friend and fellow-pilot Vic Horner.

When the news reached Edmonton that the boys had made it and were on their way home, a welcoming party gathered. The whole city seemed to realize that something both heroic and historic had just happened, and it was an Edmonton boy who had made it happen. People began to gather at the airfield, but the little plane was long overdue, and anxious murmurs began to ripple through the thousands of people now gathered to welcome it home. Retired pilot Doug Matheson was there.

"I can still see that old train," he said, "chuffing down from Calder, down to the downtown area with this plume of smoke. Then suddenly out of the smoke came this little Avro Avian, and dropped down into the field and taxied in. The crowd all gathered around and shouldered them and carried them into town."

Wop's wife Vi was the first. When she unwound the silk scarf covering his face, the skin on his lips was frozen to it. You can see the raw patches in the photograph where bits of skin came away from his lips. The story of the flight made it into newspapers around the world.

This time Wop's fame brought him opportunity. A new company, Commercial Airways, had decided to buy a state-of-the-art Lockheed Vega (the same machine that the famed aviator Wiley Post was flying when he and comedian Will Rogers were killed in Alaska). Cy Becker, at Commercial, enticed Wop by asking him to go to Los Angeles and pick up the Vega, and then to fly it for Commercial.

In California the legendary Howard Hughes, with the famous *Frankenstein* director James Whale, was making a monumental 135-minute War In The Air film called *Hell's Angels*. The combat sequences were loosely based on the Red Baron story. When Hughes heard that the heroic pilot of Little Red River was in town — *and was the same guy the Red Baron had been chasing on that fateful April day in 1918!* — he asked Wop to come over and consult about combat flying. Wop and Vic actually flew some scenes in the movie. But a little bit of the movie business was enough for Wop. He and Vic fired up the Vega and headed north.

Soon, working with Becker, they established a base at Fort McMurray which was then on the north edge of the Frontier. Commercial bid against Western Canada Airways for the airmail contract, and won it, and now there was a steady revenue stream, reliable aeroplanes with enclosed cockpits and substantial cargo capacity. With the mail as the bread-and-butter of the business, and Cy Becker looking after the office, Wop was flying all the time now, the sound of his engine penetrating parts of the planet where no such sound had ever been heard. He joked that he was the first to bring ice cream north of the Arctic Circle. Prospecting was still an important part of the business, although the accountants would probably not have agreed. Denny May says of his father:

> *He grubstaked, I think, every prospector in the north. He probably outfitted them, gave them a tent and food, flew them into their site. They'd park the aircraft. They'd set up camp for the night on the shore and they'd sit around talking . . . it's absolutely spectacular country. He would pick them up at the end of the season. They [paid him with] shares in their gold mine, none of which ever panned out. I have an envelope full of shares that are tot-ally [worthless] . . . If you . . . broke down you can't just run to the nearest airport . . . you land on a lake and you fix your aircraft, you put it back together and you carry on.*

Stories abound of the ingenuity of downed pilots in that era, like rebuilding a busted propeller out of dogsled runners and boiled leather straps; escaping after the plane went through the ice through a zipper in the cloth roof, improvising a crane and block and tackle out of tree trunks and spare rope to haul the drowned plane up out of its watery grave and reviving it; draining the oil at night into a pail to keep you warm in your tent, and then, about midnight, it's your body heat that starts to return the favour; keeping the oil fluid so you can pour it back into the subzero engine in the morning before you hang your tent over the cowling, light up a glow pot which you hope won't ignite the fuel line, and warm the frigid cylinders up so you can start it up again.

When Canadian Airways bought out Commercial, in 1931, Wop went to Canadian as well. It was about that time that the RCMP assigned him to try to find the Mad Trapper, a murderer on the run, on snowshoes, who had killed a Mountie. Wop's mechanic Jack Bowen took photos during the chase. In the few hours of decent flying weather they could get, up the Eagle River in a wet, snowy May, they followed the elusive fugitive's tracks from the air and finally found him. Wop directed the police to the scene. From the air he and Jack Bowen observed the final gunfight between Johnson and the police, and landed at the scene to take the body back to Aklavik (along with another man who was wounded in the gun fight). When it was over, a photograph of the dead killer was printed in every newspaper in the country and once again Wop May became a household name.

But it was the depth of the depression all the same. Life in Fort McMurray was tough. Denny was born in

1935, so there was an added responsibility. Work was undependable. There was a bright moment when Wop was awarded the Order of the British Empire. But then there came a dark moment, the darkest that can happen to a pilot for whom flying aeroplanes is what life was meant for, as it seems to have been for Wilfrid Reid May. They took away his licence to fly.

It would not happen today. The Transport Canada officials responsible for assessing a pilot's ability to fly do not proceed simply by arbitrary rules: they test you. If you can do it, you get your licence renewed. If not, down you go. Of course if you have a heart condition that predictably could strike any time, then you don't get a licence. But if it is a physical disability, such as an impaired limb, you go for a test flight and if you can pass the stringent but fair exercises you are instructed to fly, you get your licence. Since the 1950's more than 700 Canadian pilots with monocular vision have had their licences renewed.

Wop did not. The damaged eye had gone bad and had to be removed. There was no more faking the vision test in the medical. He only had one eye. That did not meet the standards. The standards were made by an international commission and controlled by the RCAF in those days. Our Civil Aviation Branch hadn't been formed yet (though it would be launched only months later). Perhaps Canada was still in a slightly colonial state of mind, still doing its best to respond to standards that were set by the Important Countries, by some commission, distant, bureaucratic.

The present writer, learning to fly in 1966 with an above-the-knee-amputation, was told quite simply by the Civil Aviation inspectors, "Show us. If you can fly it, you get the licence," and became a commercial pilot, and an instructor. Had Wop May's eye troubles happened today, to such a demonstrably skilled, able, successful pilot, an inspector would simply have put him through his paces, rigorously. Then (as would almost surely have been the case with Wop May) when he flew as certainly and deftly as he had always flown, he would have his licence back the same day. But in 1936 they took his paper away; he was grounded.

His goddaughter and close friend Marie Wright, the ferry pilot, says, "It's like telling a person to stop breathing, tell him, a man like Wop May, tell him you're grounded? I mean, all pilots know they're going to be grounded at one point in their lives. But it's never going to happen to you. It's always the other fella."

Wop and Vi left the North and moved back to Edmonton where they adopted a second child, Joyce. Wop got a desk job. At least he would have more time for Vi and the kids. But imagine the blow to the spirit, of having to give up the air, when you were a pilot who had practically *invented* bush flying in Northern Canada, had flown that incredible adventure in the gunsights of the Red Baron, had advised Howard Hughes, flown the first great Mercy Flight, found the Mad Trapper. . . . It could scar the soul of a lesser man, and it probably scarred Wop May's soul too; but there was a family to raise and a life to be lived, and he got on with it.

When World War II broke out, it was decided that Canada was the place to train pilots from the Commonwealth countries. Young men and women arrived from all over the world, from Britain, Australia, New Zealand, South Africa, the Free French, the Polish kids in exile, and quite a few Americans in the 16 months of that war before the United States came into it — American boys who wanted part of the action. Edmonton became a major training centre. Soon the runways were crowded with De Havilland Tiger Moth primary trainers, and the lumbering Avro Ansons for training bomber pilots, observers and navigators. When the question arose as to whom to put in charge of the Edmonton training establishment, Wop May was the obvious choice.

Imagine the cachet that would go with it, for a young pilot who could say — as a lot of them probably said (pilots having been known to exaggerate occasionally) — *I was trained under the man who shot down the Red Baron.* But May's concern was to put in place a training regime that would equip those kids *not* to get shot down, to bring them back alive. And he did what he was asked to do, always around flying, but not flying any more. Later, Canadian Pacific would hire him to help expand their overseas markets. And he was good at that. While his ports of call were once Snowdrift and Rat River and Aklavik, now they would be Hong Kong, Bangkok, Tokyo. But someone else was flying the planes; Wop was a passenger, an administrator, and still as always a man who pushed himself and expected others to push themselves too.

But one day in 1952 he said to Denny, who was seventeen then, "Look, I need a holiday;" and off they went to Utah to explore the Timpanogos Caves, near Provo, just a few miles northeast of Utah Lake. Denny May recalls the day they went there.

We headed off down there and started hiking the trail. And it was quite a steep trail up to the cave. About halfway up he said, "I can't go any further." He said, "I'll walk back to the car and wait for you there." I started up the trail, and he called me back and he said, "Take my picture to show people I got this far." And I didn't think anything of that so I took his picture, and then I headed back up the trail. And came back about half an hour later, walking on the trail, and very close to the top of the trail there was Daddy, lying dead on the trail, a fellow guarding him . . .

The funeral was huge. Standing room only. The people of Edmonton loved Wop May. They had not forgotten what he did. Max Ward, another great pioneer, would later name three successive airliners after him. One of them, a 310 Airbus, C-GKWD, now in Canadian Airlines colours, is a personnel transport for the RCAF, which seems appropriate. He is, of course, in Canada's Aviation Hall of Fame.

But a pilot, now, looking back on the story of Wilfrid Reid May, has to think to himself: How devastating was that day when he was forty, only forty years old, and they said he could never fly again? This was a man who had pushed the limits of possibility in the air.

He had lived moments which, once lived, cannot be eradicated from the soul. Every pilot who has done it seriously for any length of time has had those moments. You are at seven thousand feet, say, at night. The weather is closing in ahead. It could be clear if you go higher, and you can check your compass against the stars. Or you could go down, beneath the clouds. Perhaps there are five or six hundred feet of clearance above the ground, although it will be turbulent down there, and very, very dark. Up here, at least, there is starlight, and even in the thin clouds there is a faint luminescence from those stars.

You go up. Eight, nine thousand. At 9,500 you're well above the clouds, but you go on to 10,000 anyway. There is old Polaris, the North Star, hanging out there where it is supposed to be, exactly seven bowl-widths off the dipper bowl. And your compass checked against that star and the known deviation says you are almost exactly on the right heading. As you check your watch, you judge that at this height the wind will have veered about five degrees more, because you know about winds. You kick in another five degrees to starboard, no maybe that is too much, let's do *two* degrees . . . and the old cylinders are still thunking away, the way they are supposed to do.

You are alone. And yet the whole universe and everyone who ever lived in it is there with you, including all those who worked out the metallurgy, the chemistry of fuels, the maps, the aerodynamics of propellers, the tensile strength of cables, they are all there with you. There is a sense of celebration of the human adventure in reaching out. The engine may be producing sixty decibels, who knows, but you are in utter silence with the stars.

You check your watch. *If* you have guessed right at that veering of the wind, and *if* all your other guesses — not *guesses* really, you have done this many times — if the forces of the sky have held still for you the way they mostly do, then in exactly nine minutes you will be overhead Fort Charles. Right now you could start down gently, hold your course, maybe come out right overhead, on time, that would be elegant. But it is very fine up here, in the starlight, the still air, no bumps, the clouds a milky cushion just below your wings.

You stay at ten thousand for five minutes, eight minutes, eight-minutes-thirty, nine minutes. You bank left (you always bank left, not right, why is that?) and pull the throttle back, and start a slow, circling descent. Lots of fuel, all the gauges saying what they're supposed to say. Seven thousand feet, five thousand. It is warming up to the point where moisture in the cloud is beginning to make a little ice on your cold wings. Never mind, you will be out of it shortly. Three thousand, slowly circling to the left, throttle right back, carburettor heat ON so you don't make any ice in *there!*, hold it just above the stall so it's sort of whooshing softly down, scarcely flying at all, a leaf falling gently. One thousand feet. Should be seeing some thinning in the cloud now, uhmm, ahh, what is the height above sea level right here? I should remember, oh yeah. A little power on now, slow your descent, seven hundred feet, shoot! Should be seeing something now, have to do sumpn soon if I don't! . . .

Suddenly dark wisps the size of elephants stream by as the cloud breaks up. The black beneath is *very* black, no light penetrating from above, but we are out in the clear, and where the hell is Fort Charles, it *should be right there*, keep the wings almost level now, slow circle to the left, scan . . . the horizon . . . which you cannot see, only an impenetrable black soup.

And then, three-quarters of the way through that 360 degree turn, about three miles off to your left, a little cluster of lights. There can be only one cluster of lights, out here, in the middle of the distant barren. So the sky has met the ground, and you know that you have made your voyage, and your compact with the Gods, and with your passengers for tomorrow's journey home.

When you have spent just one night like that, even just one, and then they tell you that you will never spend another, it must leave a wound that will shorten your life.

Wilfrid Reid May, DFC. 1896–1952.

Canadian Pilots Licence number 49, June 1919.

◆　◆　◆

Distant Skies, the television biography of Wop May, was written and directed by Tom Radford and produced by Carrie Madu. The Director of Photography was Dwayne Dorland, sound by Carey Opper and Larry Macdonald, and editing by Doug Forbes. The program was first broadcast on February 23, 2000, and will be rebroadcast on History Television in the spring of 2001.

ADDITIONAL READING:

Sheila Reid, *Wings of a Hero: Canadian Pioneer Flying Ace Wilfrid Wop May* (1997)

◇ Part Twelve ◇

ALEXANDER MACKENZIE
FROM CANADA BY LAND

Vancouver is a sprawling city of some four million people if you count all the municipalities and suburbs that go to make it up. For an eastern inland city dweller used to a regular grid of streets and some reliable indicators of where north and south are to be found, this hilly, meandering collection of spectacular buildings with majestic mountains reflected off the acres of glass-walled buildings and the various incursions of the Pacific Ocean right into the downtown area, it can be a disorienting experience for the first few days. But the city seems solid, at ease with its ocean and its mountains. Despite the adventurous modern architecture it almost seems to have been there forever, so well does it reflect and connect with its breathtaking landscapes. Bridges are an important part of it, and thinking about Vancouver always brings to mind the crossing of water, by way of soaring arches and the demonstration of the engineer's craft.

For most eastern Canadians the first visit to Vancouver, whether by air, train or car, is an eye-opener. The part of the journey that crosses the mountain ranges, for those who have never seen real mountains, is unforgettable. From Montreal by air it is a little more than five hours. The lucky traveller who has clear skies below will have moved from urban congestion over eastern woodlands, the largest freshwater lakes in the world, an apparently dead flat prairie that seems to have no limits in any direction, and then those mountains, followed by the world's largest ocean.

Eastern Canadians tend to think they live in the centre of the universe, but that centre tends to shift its position after a trip through the Rockies, and that can mean a radical change in their attitude towards the rest of the country. "That's mine?" people have been heard to say. "That's all part of Canada? I own that?"

The native peoples who have lived on the west coast for at least three thousand years are not inclined to respond positively to that rhetorical question. Quite apart from their having been on the land and fishing the waters for more than two millennia, they traditionally say that people do not own land at all, but have the use of it by the beneficence of the Great Spirit who made it, and expects his human tenants to look after it lovingly. And there are still some Indians in British Columbia who express regret that they were so helpful to the first Europeans to arrive on these shores, by water or by land, men with guns and metal who destroyed a way of life.

The first European settlement at Fort Taylor was established in 1827, and then New Westminster in 1859. The railroad would be the major influence on the development of cities here. Port Moody was established as the western terminus of the Canadian Pacific Railroad, in 1883. But CPR chief William Van Horne was soon persuaded that there was a better harbour twenty miles west, and Vancouver replaced Port Moody in 1886. Until the railroad, most of the newcomers had arrived by sea.

The first European visitors of whom we have any records began sailing up this picturesque coast in the late 1700's. The British explorer James Cook anchored off Vancouver Island in 1778, just months before he was killed in a dispute with local people in the Sandwich Islands. Captain George Vancouver had sailed with Cook and helped him chart part of the northwest coast. He decided to come back and continue that work, and met the Spanish explorers Galiano and Valdes off Point Grey in 1792. Those charts fascinated the British and the settlers in Eastern Canada, particularly the business pioneers who had long realized that this huge land mass held resources that would make them all rich. But although the French, British and Spanish had already explored hundreds of thousands of square miles, had found and crossed the Mississippi River and the deserts of the southwest, no European had yet crossed the continent by land north of Mexico.

It was the fur trade that spurred the first crossing. The French had pioneered it, pushing up the Ottawa River and into and beyond the Great Lakes. French explorers had found the headwaters of the Mississippi and left French place names all over what is now the Canadian and American West. Some of them believed that if they could get to the Western Sea they would be staring at the east coast of Asia. One explorer even took oriental silk robes with him in his birch bark canoes so that he would be able to dress appropriately when he met the Emperor of China. Bit by bit the traders had pushed west and north, some of them mapping meticulously as they went. But there were still vast areas of *terra incognita*, and while the Rocky Mountains seemed an immense barrier to the Pacific, they were also a challenge and an invitation.

A young Scottish fur trader picked up the gauntlet. His name was Alexander Mackenzie. He was born on the stony island of Lewis in the outer Hebrides, in 1764. The Mackenzie clan owned the island then, and Alexander's branch of the family were closely related to the clan chieftain, Lord Seaforth. It was a troubled time in the Highlands of Scotland. Scottish Nationalists, determined to protect the Gaelic culture from the expansive English, had rebelled against the King. The rebellion was brutally crushed in a slaughter culminating at the terrible battle of Culloden in 1746, where the young Mackenzie's father Kenneth had fought on the side of the King of England. There followed a crushing of the thousand-year-old Gaelic nation, a crushing that today would probably be called Ethnic Cleansing. The old tribal ways, where land was shared on a tribal basis among the members of a clan, and disputes were settled with the sword, were over. It was the entrepreneurial class in the ascendancy now. And the Mackenzie family was part of that class. They lived in reasonable prosperity in the port of Stornaway, and the young Alexander was given an excellent private education. But in 1774, when the economy had been worsening for a while, and his wife Isabella had died, Kenneth Mackenzie took the young Alexander with him and set out for the New World.

He had left a Scotland that was still wounded from warfare and social upheaval, and he was not to find much peace on the Eastern Seaboard, where the American Revolution was brewing. Mackenzie, of course, enlisted in the

British Army, and sent young Alexander up to Montreal, which seemed safer than Philadelphia or New York. Montreal was the hub of the fur trade. As the deepest inland port, it was the logical place for the traders to return from inland with their piles of beaver skins, and for the trade goods to offload from ships from Europe; to be put into wagons or canoes and moved inland for the new settlers and as trade goods for the furs. Young Mackenzie smelled opportunity here, and a couple of years after America declared its independence, he declared his as well and moved into a job at the Scottish fur traders, Gregory and MacLeod. It was those men and their French predecessors who had laid out the routes to the west. When Mackenzie decided to try for the Pacific, about two thirds of the distance was already mapped and established as a known route. Although the fur traders would pass through native communities, and often enlisted the natives to travel with them as helpers and interpreters — and sexual partners — the settled communities were few and far between, and the men had to live off the land as they went. Fish were plentiful. They would paddle or carry their canoes twelve or fourteen hours a day, often trailing a fishing line as they went.

Game was plentiful as well, most of the time, but the weapons were still fairly primitive and you had to be a patient man to be a successful hunter. The rifle had not yet been invented. A musket was loaded from the muzzle of the barrel, each load consisting of, first, a carefully measured quantity of black gunpowder (which had to be carried in a waterproof container, often a cow's horn with a close-fitting metal lid). The powder was packed down into the smooth barrel with a ramrod, carefully, as a too vigorous push could detonate the explosive mixture and turn the ramrod into a projectile. Next came the wadding of paper or bits of rag, followed by the bullet, a single round ball or a spoonful of small buckshot, depending on the game. Buckshot for birds, a single solid lead ball for deer. When Mackenzie set out on his historic journeys the musket of choice was probably a heavy British product called a Brown Bess. It fired a very large ball, and if your aim was reasonably good you could bring down anything in the woods you were lucky to get really close to. The musket was pretty useless at a range of more than thirty or forty feet, and a single shot was all you would have a chance for, because loading the weapon took at least two minutes and one shot would scare away all the game for miles around. Trapping was more reliable, unless you had experienced native archers with you. A man skilled with the bow could hunt silently, shoot a deer a hundred feet away, and get off five or six arrows a minute.

Curiously, the native peoples loved the musket despite its cumbersomeness and inaccuracy. Perhaps it symbolized the strange power of the newcomers. Perhaps there was a quality of mystery to it. In any case, it was one of the most seductive trade goods the Europeans had to offer. It was said that a musket would fetch a pile of skins as tall as the musket itself. By the end of the eighteenth century the native peoples of North America had far more firearms per capita than the whites.

It was the boat-building skills of the native peoples that made all this exploration possible. Archaeologists say that the birch bark canoe may have evolved to virtually the form it has today as long as three thousand years ago. Certainly by the time the Europeans arrived it was a piece of sophisticated design and construction that would not be improved upon for more than a century. And some canoe builders will tell you today that the architecture of those hulls made a better shape to be paddled through the water than anything that would be built since, until the evolution of computer-assisted design.

Even the large freight canoes were light enough to be carried by two or four men. If you crashed into a rock, you could usually make repairs overnight with materials you found growing close by. The oily, waterproof bark of the silver birch, tough stringy spruce roots for stitching the sheets of bark together, spruce gum boiled with fat and charcoal to make a tarry waterproof seal for the seams, and lightweight, springy, easily bent strips of white cedar to replace broken ribs or stringers. If you lost or broke your paddle, a good craftsman could take his razor-sharp axe and carve a serviceable paddle out of a piece of dry spruce in a couple of hours. As late as the 1950's this writer worked with an Irish immigrant named Alex Culhane who still worked in the bush, well into his eighties, and would still use his axe to make a paddle at least once a year, "Jist to keep in practice," and perhaps to show off what was after all a remarkable skill.

Of course you had to have water. Canada has such an abundance of surface water that it really is possible to paddle and carry your canoes from Montreal to the Pacific Ocean. In 1967 a group of hardy young Canadians decided to mark Canada's hundredth birthday by testing that possibility again. They built a large freight canoe, and re-traced the same journey that Alexander Mackenzie had first made in 1793. The longest portage they had to make was just a few kilometres.

Shawn Patterson, the curator of the museum at Old Fort William at Thunder Bay, Ontario, told us that,

If you . . . throw two darts anywhere on the map of Canada, you could put a canoe in at one place and paddle to the other and you would never have to carry that canoe more than thirteen miles. That's the longest portage across the country. . . . From your Montreal shipyard you can take those [trade] goods all the way up to Great Slave Lake, all the way through the Rocky Mountains to the Pacific Ocean, and you would never have to walk more than thir-teen miles.

Eighty percent of the trade goods we are talking about were textiles. Steel axes, knives, muskets, ammunition and copper pots were prized, of course, and would revolu-tionize the lives of the native peoples, who had no met-als technology. The great totem poles, which we think of as the hallmark of the northwest native culture, the Salish, Haida, Kwakiutl and others, came into existence only after the arrival of steel tools in the 19th century. But in terms of quantity it was wool from the Oxfordshire mills, Indian cotton woven in southern England, and even Cant-onese silk, that were the really hot items in those trading camps and at the forts. Now, instead of having to kill large animals and process the skins, the native peoples could trap the plentiful beaver and exchange them for colourful and easily handled fabrics that saved an immense amount of labour. The native peoples began to make themselves a large variety of colourful clothing which their own technology had not yet made possible. Textiles, like metals technology, had a considerable effect on the life and culture of the native peoples, not always to their benefit in the long run.

But the killer trade item was not textiles or guns, it was rum. Fifty years after Mackenzie's explorations, a young naval Captain named John Franklin made an astounding fifty-five-hundred-mile trek from the shores of Hudson Bay to the Arctic Ocean, via Great Slave Lake, and back. He recorded in his journals heartbreaking accounts of native communities that had been demoralized and almost destroyed by the cruel and cynical trade in rum that so many of the fur traders were exploiting.

But that is another story.

The bright young Scotsman, unlike many of his high-handed predecessors, went out of his way to get to know the native peoples, to be courteous and respectful to them, and to patiently win their confidence. Had he not done that, we would not be reading about him today. Mackenzie recognized that he had a great deal to learn from them and seemed to understand that their traditions and memories would be a vital resource for any one trying to find his way across the continent.

And finding your way in the days before the invention of reliable portable clocks was hard. Why clocks? An instrument called a sextant could reliably establish your latitude — how far north of the equator you were — by measuring the angular height of the sun above the horizon at noon. You had to know the date, and you could tell when it was noon when the sun was at its highest, or was due south if you had noted the position of the North Star the night before. The North Star itself would give you your latitude on a clear night.

But to know your longitude — to tell how far east or west you had travelled, you needed to know what time it was at your starting point, or at any fixed point you wanted to measure this distance from. If, for example, you saw the sun at its highest point overhead, noon wherever you were just then, and your reliable portable timepiece, which you had set at Montreal when you departed, informed you that it was two p.m. in that port city, you would know that you were exactly 30 degrees of latitude west of your starting point. The sun's apparent position travels west at exactly 15 degrees every hour. Thirty degrees is something in the order of 1,200 miles in the Canadian prairies, and that 1,200 miles you could refine to a precision of less than one mile once you checked your latitude.

The timepiece that would make this possible had finally, in fact, been invented. The Royal Society in London had offered a large cash prize to anyone who could demonstrate a genuinely reliable chronometer that would keep accurate time at sea or travelling by horseback, whatever motion it was subjected to. A genius named Johnson, after decades of painstaking labour, had finally produced one. Mackenzie did not know this, yet. All he had was a timepiece that was very accurate as long as it stood still, but it gained or lost badly whenever it was moved, so it had to be reset by the sun every day. This gave him the local time, but there was no way to know what time it was in the London suburb of Greenwich, where the zero longitude line lies now, by international convention. There was no such convention then and even had there been Mackenzie, with his unreliable instruments, would still have had to do his best by dead reckoning. This meant primarily estimating the exact distance traversed every day, an uncertain affair. His not having certain knowledge of his longitude would give Alexander Mackenzie some very bad days, indeed, as he tried to find his way by land to the Pacific.

In 1780 Lake Athabasca was the end of the mapped world, so to speak. It was called the Lake of the Hills then. An American fur trader named Peter Pond had found his way there in that year. He spent the winter on the lake, collecting from the Chipewyans twice as many furs as his canoes could carry. Muskrat was still a desired fur then, and the area was so rich in muskrat that a Chipewyan was said to be able to take a hundred a day. That could bring him the equivalent of a thousand dollars in today's currency. John Rigney, a guide who works that territory today, told us that taking muskrat two hundred years ago was "like picking carrots in your garden."

Peter Pond had put together some oral geographical information he got from the Chipewyan and Cree peoples he met, and had come up with a kind of a map of the as yet unexplored territory to the northwest. Pond had read Captain Cook's account of his voyage up the northwest coast and had been struck by Cook's description of an inlet that he believed to be the mouth of a great river. If he could just find the headwaters of that river, Pond thought!

By now Mackenzie's company, Gregory and McLeod, had gone into partnership with the much larger Northwest Company. The management of the newly merged companies decided to appoint Pond as the manager of the Athabasca trading centre. Peter Pond had been implicated in the murder of a couple of men who had died in a dispute when the two companies were at each other's throats, before the merger. It was only a rumour, but it affected management's assessment of Pond's eccentric behaviour, so they decided to appoint the twenty-three-year-old Mackenzie to replace him. It was a recipe for conflict, but instead of quarreling the two men seem to have taken to each other. Mackenzie was impressed with Pond's energy, experience and optimism. Pond shared his dream of a river route to the ocean. He had concluded, quite mistakenly, that the river flowing west from Great Slave Lake was the very inlet that Captain Cook had written about.

Listening to Pond, Mackenzie conceived an ambition that would drive him relentlessly until he realized it. This bright young lad from Lewis, kinsman to the Chief of the Clan Mackenzie, decided that he would be the first to chart a route by land all the way to the Pacific. It became his obsession. With the diplomatic and psychological skills for which he was already well known in the Company, he persuaded Pond that he was the one to carry out the dream that Pond had been nursing for so long.

He was in charge now, so he left Pond to run the trading centre, and in June of 1789, still only twenty-four years old, he left Lake Athabasca through the confused delta where the Peace comes in from the west and the Slave flows north to Great Slave Lake. That delta is kind of a mess. John Rigney says, "The delta changes from year to year, from season to season. In a century a river channel can disappear and a new one open up." There is no way today to chart exactly where Mackenzie went, because the route he followed then has disappeared with the constantly changing sands and currents of the delta.

He had to make a crucial decision now. To turn west would have taken him towards the Pacific, but of course he had no way of knowing that. Because the northbound river was flowing out of Lake Athabasca, and Captain Cook's inlet was a "river mouth," he followed the river northward and was, in fact, on his way not to the Pacific but to the Arctic Ocean.

He had one big freight canoe and three smaller ones, and a group of voyageurs and native guides. The interpreter was a Chipewyan leader, Nestabeck, whom Mackenzie called "The English Chief." They turned west in Great Slave Lake and sure enough found an outlet. This must be it! The Dene people called it *Deh Cho*, the Great River.

Here is Mackenzie's diary entry for Sunday, July 5th, 1789:

> *At three quarters past seven o'clock we perceived several smokes which we made for with all great speed. We soon saw the Natives run about in great confusion, some making for the woods, and others to their canoes. Our hunters landed before us and spoke to the people who had not run away.*

Another Dene man whom Mackenzie persuaded to come with him seemed to believe he would never see home again. Mackenzie wrote:

He cut a lock of his hair, separated it into three parts, one of which he fastened to the hair of the crown of his wife's head, blowing on it three times as hard as he could and repeating some words. The other two he fastened to with the same ceremony to the heads of his children.

The present-day Dene chief Greg Nyali finds the story of Mackenzie perplexing in more than one way.

He was one of the first European people to come into contact with our people, the Dene. I guess at that time our people didn't know what Mackenzie was up to . . . or even in fact who he was. I think they were a little bit startled by the fact that he was of quite lighter complexion from our people. . . . From what I understand . . . they probably thought he was pretty sick and needed a little bit of help.

And they gave him that help. Chief Nyali, with only a trace of humour, says that turned out to have been a bad idea.

Our people must have helped him . . . [by] providing such things as whitefish and coney (rabbit). Moose were in abundance way back then and we even had bison. [But] I think . . . if our people might have seen into the future, and . . . really see what type of impact meeting Mackenzie and helping him out . . . I think that our people would have thought twice. I think that if they had seen all of the oppression and destruction as a result of it, I think they probably would have took him as an enemy and they probably

should have killed him. And then we probably wouldn't
have all the problems that we have today.

But they did not see into the future. Nor would it have
done them any good to kill Mackenzie; if it had not been
him, it would have been someone else before long. Mackenzie, in fact, while some historians say he would use
any means he could to secure the services of the native
people, seems on the whole to have treated them with
respect and to have earned their admiration. The Dene
women were especially helpful. They hauled the freight,
put up the tents, brought in the firewood, skinned the
game, cooked the meat, and made the moccasins. The
men were the guides. And within 100 kms, this new river,
this great hope for the Pacific route, turned north, paral-
leling the Rocky Mountains.

Now they were crossing into Inuit territory, the enemies of the Dene. His guides began pleading to turn back.

The information that they gave us respecting the river
seems to me so very fabulous. They would wish to make
us believe that we would be several Winters getting to the
Sea, and that we should all be old men by the time we
would return. That we would encounter many monsters,
which exist only in their own imaginations.

Curator Shawn Patterson says, "The Dene guides
became more and more anxious . . . that they are going
to meet with an end similar to the slaughter that Samuel
Hearne describes, with the Inuit butchering everyone in
the camp. . . . It's quite impressive to think that they continue . . . There are local people telling them that they're
going into a very dangerous place. And they continue."

In fact the Inuit encampments they came to were deserted.

Our conductor says they are gone to where they fish for whales, and kill reindeer.

They had reached the delta of the Great River, where billions of litres of freshwater flow into the ocean. The delta was rising and falling with the rhythm of the tides. It was the Arctic Ocean. And after all this hardship and the overcoming of obstacles, it was the wrong ocean; not the dreamed-of Pacific. He knew now that there would be no easy route. He would have to cross the Rockies.

It turned to be a much longer journey than he had expected. When he came back to Lake Athabasca just in time to beat the freeze-up, he met Philip Turnor, a survey-or from the Hudson's Bay Company. Turnor actually had one of those new-fangled, dead-accurate chronometers with which he could find the exact longitude. He was able to demonstrate that Mackenzie had probably been 700 miles short of the position that his dead reckoning had produced. This was disappointing but it did not cool Mac-kenzie's obsession. He called that northern river that had led him astray the River of Disappointment. He would not be disappointed again, he said. Mackenzie decided he needed to know more about navigation and he needed a chronometer like Turnor's. He went to London. He sought out the best navigators in London and acquired the latest instruments. The dream had taken over his life. He would make it to the Pacific by land, or die in the attempt.

Four years later, in May 1793, he set out once more, this time taking the Peace River westward, even though he was going up river, against the current. West. The Peace split in two. His guides told him to take the southern branch. As he followed the sinuous path of the flood plain, on what was what we now call the Parsnip River, he could see the land rising ahead of him.

June 11th, 1793. The lake is about two miles in length, East by South, and from three to five hundred yards wide. We landed and unloaded where we found a beaten path leading over a low ridge of land to another small lake. We embarked on this lake which is of the same course and about the same size as that which we had just left and from whence we passed into a small river that was so full of fallen wood, as to employ some time and require some exertion to force a passage.

But soon there was another river, a major river. It flowed west. He had crossed the height of land. He did not know that this river flowed into the Ocean he sought, but the hopeful thing was that it flowed west, southwest in fact. It was the river we now know as the Fraser. The guides told him that it was dangerous water, and that he would be better from now on to take an overland route called the Grease Trail, which the Carrier people had used for generations to trade with the coast.

These people describe the distance . . . as very short to the Western Ocean, and, according to my own idea, it cannot be above five or six degrees.

This would mean some two hundred miles at that latitude.

Sunday, 23rd June, 1793. I was very much surprised by the following question from one of the Indians. "What,"

*demanded he, "can be the reason that you are so particu-
lar and anxious in your inquiries of us respecting a knowledge of this country? Do not you white men know everything in the world?"*

*I replied that we certainly were acquainted with the
principal circumstances of every part of the world; that I
knew where the sea is, and where I myself then was, but
that I did not exactly understand what obstacles might
interrupt me in getting to it . . . Thus fortunately I preserved the impression in their minds, of the superiority of
white people over themselves.*

It is probable that by now a fur trade route was no
longer Mackenzie's concern; he was simply possessed by
the goal; the ocean; by whatever route and means. They
followed that Grease Trail, west across the lava flow to a
high plateau and a pass that bears Mackenzie's name today.

*Before us appeared a stupendous mountain, whose snow-
clad summit was lost in the clouds. The Indians informed
us that it was at no great distance. We continued . . . We
arrived at the bottom where there is a conflux of two rivers
that issue from the mountains. They are both very rapid
and continue so until they unite their currents, forming
a stream of about twelve yards in breadth. The water of
this river is the colour of asses' milk.*

Now there was unmistakable evidence that they were
getting somewhere. They encountered people who spoke
a language none of the interpreters had ever heard. They
communicated by signs. The new people received the
strangers courteously. Mackenzie asked for the loan of a

canoe. They provided one and a young chief offered to come with them down the river. Now he was in what could only be an inlet of the sea. It was not over yet.

21st July, 1793. I began to fear that I should fail . . . our provisions were at a very low ebb. . . Ten half-starved men in a leaky vessel and on a barbarous coast. Under the land we met with three canoes with fifteen men in them. They manifested no kind of mistrust or fear of us . . . They then examined everything we had in our canoe with an air of indifference and disdain.

These disdainful men were fur traders from the coast, native fur traders. By an extraordinary coincidence just a few weeks earlier they had seen another vessel, they told Mackenzie's guides. It was, they said, very large and carried sails, and much grander than this "leaky vessel on a barbarous coast." Mackenzie had just missed what would have been a dramatic encounter with another famous explorer. These natives had seen Captain George Vancouver who, that same summer of 1793, had made a second voyage up the inlet he had first discovered a few years earlier.

One of them made me understand, with an air of insolence, that a large canoe had lately been in this bay, with people in her like me, and that one of them whom he called "Macubah" had fired on him and his friends . . . he wanted to see everything we had, particularly my instruments. While I was taking a meridian two canoes of a larger size, and well-manned, appeared. . . . My people were panic struck and asked if it was my determination to remain there to be sacrificed. My reply was . . . that I would not stir until I had accomplished my object.

"Macubah," of course, is a pretty good approximation of "Vancouver."

The new arrivals proved friendly after all. They were also fascinated by the instruments. Having taken his sights and determined his latitude at last, Mackenzie knew his mission was complete. The inlet was in fact, an arm of the Pacific Ocean. He was twenty-eightyears old.

I now mixed up some vermilion in melted grease, and inscribed in large characters on the southeast face of the rock on which we had slept last night, this brief memorial — Alexander Mackenzie from Canada by land, the twenty-second of July, Seventeen Ninety Three. I took five altitudes. The mean of these observations is equal to 128 degrees, 2 minutes, west of Greenwich.

Well, he was off by about 40 km. But he had made it. The vermilion and grease are long gone but you can still see the rock, marked with a plaque. It is a good-sized boulder, with a fairly flat sloping face on which Mackenzie painted his famous words "From Canada by Land."

The ambition had been satisfied. Perhaps he was tired. He said that he was thinking of staying on in trade in Canada, perhaps starting a great new company. But he went to England, got married, was made a knight, and somehow never came back to the land of his sometime obsession.

He died in Scotland in 1820, at the age of fifty-six The rock is his monument, a national monument to a great adventure and a great spirit.

◆　◆　◆

From Canada by Land, the Alexander Mackenzie television biography, was a Canada/Scotland co-production written by David Halliday and Finlay Macleod. It was produced by Brian Dooley and Sam Maynard, directed by David Halliday, with Dwayne Dorland as Director of Photography, sound by Larry Macdonald and John Blerot, and editing by Alex Broad. It was first telecast on History Television on February 28, 1999, and will be rebroadcast in the spring of 2001.

ADDITIONAL READING:

Dava Sobel: *Longitude, the True Story of a Lone Genius who Solved the Greatest Scientific Problem of His Time*

Derek Howse: *Greenwich Time and the Longitude*

W. Kaye Lamb, editor: *The Journals and Letters of Alexander Mackenzie*

There is an ALEXANDER MACKENZIE VOYAGEUR ROUTE web site for a heritage trail following the route of explorer Alexander Mackenzie at:

http://www.amvr.org/

Part Thirteen

SAM HUGHES
The Enigma

Of all the really puzzling figures in this country's recent history — people about whom we have extensive records and know a great deal, yet still find them difficult to understand — not many are as baffling as this boy from Darlington. He became a famous and troublesome politician, a controversial military leader, and a man whose record still has our most prominent historians almost at verbal fisticuffs over the balance of good and evil in his heritage. We know that he was genuinely crazy in the last years of his career as a cabinet minister (although he would continue to sit in the House of Commons for another three years). But whether those who say he was mad from the start are right, or those who say he was simply outspoken, determined, vain and maddeningly successful — that is part of the riddle.

If you stop people on the street in any Canadian city today and ask them who Sir Sam Hughes was, unless you are on Parliament Hill and maybe even then, you will draw blank stares. During the first two decades of the 20th century, Sam Hughes was a household name, but often as not that name was spoken with contempt if not with hatred.

The many photographs we have, and the magnificent oil portrait at the War Museum in Ottawa, all show a powerfully handsome face on a proudly erect body, an aristocratic bearing, a penetrating brown-eyed gaze, a determined jaw, the mouth characteristically downturned. The lower lip is often pushed forward defiantly or perhaps just confidently. Scores of raucous political cartoons of the period from about 1910 to the end of World War One show dark bushy eyebrows, a cruelly caricatured square jaw and a trap-door mouth.

It seems that he was not someone to whom painter, cartoonist, or even the camera could be indifferent. Who was he, and where did he come from?

His gravestone says Sam, not Samuel, and gives no middle name. He was born into a family of Irish immigrants in a part of rural Ontario that is only a few hours by car from Toronto today, but then was on the edge of the wilderness. In the mid-nineteenth century Canada was a hoped-for salvation for thousands of Irish people who fled grinding poverty and the cruel indifference of their British rulers. From 1848 to 1852 what pitiful viability their world offered was devastated by a potato blight that led to a famine that killed tens of thousands. While the British and Anglo-Irish landlords continued to export milk and butter to England, few ever lifted a hand to help their starving tenant farmers. Canada's rich heritage of Irish names and mythology, especially in Ontario and Quebec, stems from that period, and it was just at the end of the peak immigration spurred by the famine that young Sam saw the light of day at Solina, near Darlington.

Like other farm kids he was used by his struggling father as cheap and controllable labour. But the five a.m. daily call to shovel out the stables or the cowbarns, or head for the hayfields or the plough still left the brilliant, tough and wiry youngster with the energy to get himself enough education so that, by the age of sixteen, he was teaching on a temporary permit in a local primary school.

Within a few years he had earned a regular teaching certificate. Then, still a young man, Sam wrote and published two school textbooks. He got himself appointed as an Ontario school inspector. *Mens sana in corpore sano*, "a healthy mind in a healthy body," was one of the favourite slogans of educators in those days, and Sam Hughes exemplified that motto superbly. He played outstanding lacrosse, was a champion long-distance runner, and a tough and enthusiastic wrestler.

He had an appetite for fame that would endanger his later career. He loved to win and to be seen to win, and he loved the very idea of glory on the field of combat. He had fed on tales of soldiering and adventure from his early years, and he revelled in his prowess on the playing field, as if it were a rehearsal for the battlefield. His appetite for victory and recognition drove him hard. He tried his hand as an inventor, and got a patent for a railway-car ventilation system. He quit teaching at the age of thirty-two and moved to Lindsay, Ontario, where he bought a newspaper, *The Victoria Warder*. Here too he succeeded. As an influential local editor/proprietor he played to the prejudices and values of his readers, and built himself a reputation along with his very satisfying subscription list.

Lindsay was Orange country. The Orange Lodge, based upon Irish Protestantism, loyalty to the King and a hatred of Catholicism, has dwindled almost to invisibility in Canada (though not in Northern Ireland). As recently as the 1960's many Ontario communities still held their July 12th Orangemen's parades, with the British Flag, banners for each local chapter, and grown men wearing outlandish bowler hats. In Hughes' young days it was shiny top hats. The men and the boys marched to loud band music that was meant to let Catholics know they had better keep discreetly in their places if they didn't want trouble. That trouble frequently meant violence.

The Ontario Orangemen hated the French Canadians, too. In *The Warder* Sam Hughes would write:

The unfortunate French-Canadians are very little better than brutes. The poor creatures have for ages been kept in darkness, ignorance and superstition till now; they are dulled and blinded as to be insensible to the ordinary feelings of humanity.

It was, of course, the priests who put them there; every Orangemen knew that. So it is not surprising that at least one Canadian historian accuses Hughes of being one of those responsible (in this land of extraordinary tolerance) for making religion a source of serious division. Author Jack Granatstein says that Hughes helped make Canadian politics "in the 1890s in particular, revolve around religion. What are the rights of Catholics [to publicly supported sectarian schooling]? What are the rights of French-speaking Catholics to be? People like Sam Hughes are . . . making those strains real, turning them into fissures in our public life."

But another distinguished historian, Professor Desmond Morton, who directs the McGill Centre for the Study of Canada, argues that in this regard Hughes was not far from the mainstream liberal tradition in Canada. To support his view, Morton looks ahead to the time when Hughes was in government in Ottawa, as Minister of Militia, roughly the equivalent of today's Minister of National Defence.

Professor Morton says that Hughes

believed, like many Canadians, that Church and State were separate, so that when he found . . . that Quebec militia units participated proudly and actively in religious ceremonies he put a stop to it. When . . . Archbishop Bégin [was made] Cardinal, the militia vied for the honour of welcoming him home with guards of honour, Hughes put a stop to it. Why should some Romish potentate have Her Majesty's Soldiers — even if they were the militia of Lévis — on parade. This was stupid on his part, but . . . many liberal Canadians might think he was right.

Professors Morton and Granatstein differ even more sharply on the question of Sam Hughes' mental stability. For Granatstein Hughes was "certifiably mad . . . probably schizophrenic, probably should have been institutionalized. . . ."

For Professor Morton, "he was that fatal phenomenon; an honest politician who did what he set out do. Thank God we haven't had very many."

Professor Ronald Haycock, at the Royal Military College in Kingston, Ontario, agreeing that Hughes was "wrong-headed and wrong — a lot!" adds that "there is more about this very complicated man that deserves analysis."

So let us try to do some of that.

The old-fashioned view of war as heroic and glorious is not in vogue these days. Machine guns and poison gas in the so-called Great War made it possible for tens of thousands of hapless kids to be killed before breakfast. Aerial bombing put an end to the old principle that it was the brave military who got killed in a war; now whole civilian populations can be wiped out in a single raid. But it was not simply the geometric multiplication of the numbers of the dead that changed the world's view of war; it was also media. Before the American Civil War that began in 1860 there had been no photography on the battlefield. But now the citizens at home could begin to see the horrors of war. For about a century the propaganda offices kept the worst of it from them while the war was actually in progress. But at the end of World War One, the Great War, the photographs of thousands of rotting corpses — men and horses — of the stinking, mud-soaked horror of the slaughter began to lay the ground for a new view of war. Television would be the medium that would make that view so strong that it would bring a major war — Vietnam — to an end.

But in the 1890's when Canada was asked to raise troops to go off to fight for the Empire in South Africa, most Canadians thought that was grand and noble. They turned out in the streets not to mourn but to celebrate. Commanders hoped to be given cavalry, for a glorious troop of lancers on horseback would strike fear into the boldest adversary. This stupid attitude would send thousands of riders and their mounts to almost instant death under the relentless fire of German machine guns in August 1914, before the lofty British High Command finally caught on. But when this country sent troops out to South Africa, the cavalry myth was still in force, as was the notion that war was glorious.

Sam Hughes was by then a Member of Parliament. He was completely ingrained with that romantic view of war. And, like the Israeli view of its army today (which does not much include the glory part any more), and indeed like the attitude of that first Greek democracy 2,500 years ago, he saw militia service as a noble and appropriate extension of citizenship itself.

Jack Granatstein says, "Hughes was a great believer in the idea that every Canadian was a natural soldier. Just give a Canadian a rifle and he was immediately an expert marksman. Make someone a Lieutenant and he would automatically become a Field Marshall, just by virtue of the innate skill that resided in every Canadian."

The mirror of that was Sam Hughes' view of the professional soldiers. Men who joined up for a career were not to be trusted, he said. They had abandoned the civic responsibilities of civilian life in order to live off the state and wear a uniform and swagger around whether there was a war or not. "Layabouts," he said. "Parasites. A drain on the state when you didn't really need them."

Professor Haycock says that Hughes saw the Militia as a kind of social and moral force that would permeate the whole fabric of the country and help build a healthy society. It seems that he also thought that a Canada strengthened by its Militia would help save the British

Empire, which suffered not from being an Empire, but from the English who controlled it. They lacked the decency and courage and other social and moral qualities that Sam Hughes believed were part of the real imperialist way, and were to be found in Canada more than anywhere else in the world. Canadians were superior human beings; it was as simple as that.

So the new MP was not your average rookie. He was forty years old. He had been running a very political newspaper for seven years. He knew everybody in his Ontario community. He had made a mark in the militia. He had thought about things, a lot; he had what almost amounts to a theory of society and a theory of politics. His energy was legendary. He was an indefatigable worker, with a playful side and — at least at the beginning — the ability to laugh at himself. This, unfortunately, he would soon lose.

But as he arrived in Ottawa he felt himself poised to take a position of power. He was very much interested in power. He understood that the Militia could help his political career, and soon learned that politics could advance his position in there too.

When the South African War broke out, late in the 1890's, Hughes was quick to ring the bells of national pride, and the honourable citizen role of the Militia. He stood up in Parliament and said that it simply would not do to let the Australians send a larger contingent to South Africa than Canada was sending: Canada must take the lead among the Dominions. It was an impressive speech and it worked, though not as completely as he had intended.

Hughes had hoped that the Militia in its gratitude for his intervention would give him a command in the war, which the Imperial forces were bound to win, no doubt about that, everybody knew. But perhaps he overstepped the bounds. His aggressiveness in Parliament, and around Militia headquarters, began to irritate people. And already some were inclined to see him as too eccentric, unpredictable, troublesome. He had no experience in combat or training for command in the field. The Militia chiefs, supported by the Government, refused to give him a command. He went off to Africa anyway, as a junior officer. Once there, when the hostilities got hotter and there were not enough British officers to go around, he was put at the head of a scouting platoon south of the Orange River.

Before long, letters describing his heroic adventures began to appear in the press. In one, his most famous, he took a detachment of cavalry out against a town called Uppington, which was held by an enemy garrison far bigger than his own little troop. We have the story only from Hughes himself. He wrote that he and six others galloped ahead of the wagons, impatient for the fray, and rode hard as they approached the enemy to drive up as much dust as possible so that Uppington would think the attackers to be greater in number than this gallant handful of seven men.

According to Hughes it worked. The Boer garrison surrendered, but because he did not have enough men to effectively guard his captives it seems they slipped away in the night and disappeared into the grasslands. But he had taken Uppington. Or had he?

Jack Granatstein is not sure. "To the best of my knowledge he plays no major role [in the Boer War] except in his own mind. And his own mind was such that he could convince himself that he had done great things."

Professor Granatstein is careful not to accuse Sam Hughes of lying: his portrait of Hughes is that of a man who was not only unstable, but capable of believing his own fabrications. He also made a lot of enemies.

Desmond Morton says, "He broke all kinds of gentlemanly and military behaviour by writing frank and insulting comments about his superior officers in the British Army, and sending them to the Capetown newspapers. This is not done . . . and it was for that specifically that he was sent home."

At home the people of Canada knew nothing about this. They had read only the glory stories. And when Hughes came home he was a hero, and poised for another run at Parliament. Then a curious thing happened.

Hughes was a Conservative. The Liberals, under Sir Wilfrid Laurier, were in power. Hughes was the opposition Militia critic, and seen as an asset by the government, as he was a bit of a loose cannon in the eyes of his own colleagues. And with his particular brand of partisan cunning, Laurier named Hughes to a parliamentary committee looking into the possibility of a Canadian-made rifle for the Canadian army, which until then had always used British weapons.

Laurier's own Minister of Militia had found it difficult to get his men enough small arms in the Boer campaign. A British industrialist, Sir Charles Ross, proposed building a weapons factory in Canada, to build a rifle named for himself, the Ross Rifle.

The Ross Rifle would end up shooting down Sam Hughes himself. It was not he who had accepted Sir Charles Ross' proposal, but he would become the rifle's staunch advocate at a time when Canadian soldiers in the field were cursing it and throwing it away even during battle. Hughes would keep on saying that it was the most accurate firearm ever made. That would earn him the undying contempt of thousands of the poor mud-soaked foot sloggers who had to fight with it and try to keep it from jamming on the imprecisely machined British-made ammunition they had been given. But that happened a few years later.

In 1911 the government of Sir Wilfrid Laurier was defeated over Free Trade. When the Conservative leader Robert Borden began to put together a cabinet, the experienced militiaman and much celebrated African Wars veteran seemed the logical choice for that ministry. But there were already enemies within the party itself, who warned the new Prime Minister about Hughes' eccentricities and, as Borden wrote in a letter summoning Hughes to a showdown in Ottawa, his "erratic temperament and immense vanity."

It seems that Hughes contritely admitted his faults, promised solemnly to mend his ways, shook hands on the commitment, and was made Minister of Militia. Then within a few years we were at war again, and it was Hughes' responsibility to raise the armies Canada had undertaken to send to Europe.

As a Dominion of the British Empire, Canada still considered the military support of Britain to be a responsibility and had kept a mobilization plan in force. But Hughes said that all he would need to raise an army was determination, energy and patriotism, and a direct call to his old comrades-in-arms. He sent out a direct appeal, in the form of personal telegrams, to all the heads of militia units across the country, asking for volunteers. He even swallowed his contempt for the Quebecers and designed recruiting posters that he hoped would appeal to their sense of being members of a special fighting unit.

Then he decided to build a big new army base at Valcartier, Quebec, on an unused tract of land north of Quebec City. There the expected recruits would be assembled and trained for combat before shipping out to England. The order to build went out on August 7th. By early September the four hundred workmen on the job had installed water mains, sewers, tent platforms, administrative buildings, and even a special rail link to Quebec City. Hughes' critics, who had scorned the extravagance of his recruiting and training initiatives, were effectively silenced as the twenty thousand men Hughes had asked for grew to twenty-five and then almost thirty thousand, as the Valcartier Base materialized almost by magic.

Hughes was in his element. He would drive up in front of the parading recruits and make patriotic speeches to them from the back of his car. He took the Prime Minister with him once, and Borden led the men in cheers for the Militia Minister. Hughes would parade the training grounds like a Field Marshall, upbrading slackers, heaping praise on the diligent, demoting an officer here and creating one there, as if the Canadian Army were his personal fiefdom. And it is likely that in his heart he believed it to be so. If the men laughed at him behind his back when he came out on the range to show them how to shoot or to fight with the bayonet, or to demonstrate his own favourite wrestling holds for man-to-man combat, they didn't let Sam Hughes know they were laughing. And it is likely that he very soon began to believe in his own legend, the single-handed creator of a great fighting force.

The legend persists. Even his great-grandson Samuel G.S. Hughes will tell you today that when the Canadians arrived in Britain, and the British wanted to distribute them in the British Army under British Command, Sam Hughes went straight to Lord Kitchener, the Commander-in-Chief, and said firmly that the Canadians would serve together, in Canadian units under Canadian commanders, or he would ship them home. Professional historians say that they can find no evidence for this very attractive legend, but it keeps on getting repeated.

And there are professional historians, such as Jack Granatstein, who decry Valcartier and dismiss it as only part of the legend. "Sam Hughes screwed up," Professor Granatstein insists. "There had been a mobilization plan in place that called for the rational calm way of mobilizing a Canadian Expeditionary Force . . . Hughes threw it out . . . He 'miraculously' created a camp that didn't have to be created, mixed up historic regiments. . . . It was, I think, totally disorganized chaos."

But Valcartier was a huge public relations success. It made Canadians proud, and it made Hughes, once again, a national hero. And yet it was done by a man who had completely ignored the vital separation of the civilian government from the military machine it creates in order to carry out the political intentions of that government. For Sam Hughes, it seems, there really was no distinction. It was all for Canada, his great Canada. And not only was he the man who created the army, he now decided he would lead that army into battle; glory was only an ocean away.

Now this was all fiction. While he knew that he did not have the confidence of the government or the senior officers (even though he appointed those officers), and must have recognized that he did not have the experience to lead an army at war, yet he went ahead and announced that he was going to do just that. He put out a story about an assassination attempt — against himself — that was false and later seen to be only another publicity stunt. When the first troops shipped out from Halifax he went down to see them off, made a long patriotic speech at dockside with a patriotic song at the end of it, did not seem to notice or mind that they laughed at him, and went off to New York to catch a fast ship that would get him to Britain in time to welcome the lads when they landed.

Once there, he put out a story that he had received secret German strategic information from a beautiful woman on board his ship who was actually an espionage agent of some mysterious origin, and that he had personally taken this information to the King, George the Fifth.

It was all made up. Fantasy and reality may have been so closely intertwined in the Hughes narrative of himself that they could never be separated. And the fantasy led him into experiments in weaponry.

Perhaps the most bizarre of these, though not in the long run as damaging to his reputation as the Ross Rifle, was the shovel shield. A secretary, it is said, suggested that if the shovels the infantrymen were issued to dig trenches with had a small hole in the blade, they could be stood on the ground convex side to the enemy while the soldier fired his rifle through the hole and lay behind the shovel, protected from enemy fire.

They did not work, either as a shovel (a shovel with a hole in it?) or as a shield. But Hughes ordered fifty tons of those idiotic things, the taxpayers paid for them, and they were eventually all sold at a loss for scrap.

And yet even Sam Hughes' most severe critics agree that he was a seasoned politician, a diligent and often brilliant student of military matters, and a leader capable of daring decisions. Jack Granatstein, who never met Hughes but still seems angry at him eighty years after his death, said that when Hughes' son Garnet, an officer in the British Columbia Militia, recommended to his father that Arthur Currie be made commander, a great service was done to Canada. "Hughes listens to his son," Professor Granatstein tells us, "and appoints Arthur Currie as one of the brigadiers in the first Canadian contingent that goes overseas, and Currie turns into the most skilled soldier of the Canadians in the First World War, and arguably the most skilled general this country has ever produced."

But many of his appointments were less felicitous. When Hughes tried to redirect the haemorrhage of Canadian dollars that were leaving the country to buy munitions in the USA, he appointed friends and at least one relative to the Shell Committee, and they weren't appointed for their competence. "Buffoons and fools," says Professor Granatstein. "Corrupt friends. To run our war effort! I don't think Hughes himself was corrupt, but he didn't pay much attention to what his friends were doing."

Even after one of those friends was revealed to be on the take, Hughes defended him. Sir Joseph Flavelle would call Hughes "a degenerate, without moral sense," and then Flavelle himself would be accused of profiteering from the wartime sale of bacon to the armed forces, and although an inquiry exonerated him, his reputation was badly damaged. So perhaps it was a time when Canadians suspected a degree of corruption amongst their politicians — Sir John A. Macdonald having been exposed in his corrupt dealings with the Canadian Pacific Railway with scarcely a scar to his enormous popularity.

It was also an era when Canadians received honours from the British Crown. Flavelle himself would be given a baronetcy, the last hereditary title awarded to a Canadian. And Hughes undoubtedly began to agitate with the Prime Minister for a Knighthood. It was normal to reward political loyalty in that way. A Prime Minister of one of the Dominions had simply to send his annual list to London, and with relatively few exceptions the honours would be agreed to. Prime Ministers themselves were routinely knighted. But the process was troublesome. Sir Wilfrid Laurier, delighted to receive his own knighthood, nonetheless found preparing the annual honours list troubling. He probably knew the saying of the great French minister Talleyrand, that bestowing an honour created a hundred enemies and one ingrate. The subject was much in debate by the time Borden became Prime Minister, and by 1935 knighthoods for Canadians were abolished.

But this was 1915, and maybe Borden thought it might calm Hughes down, and so his name went on the list and he became Sir Sam. It seems not to have calmed him down; in Professor Granatstein's view it "tended to increase the madness."

Now the Great War was getting worse. Terrible tales of slaughter in the mud were making their way homeward. The casualty lists were appalling. In four years Canada would lose more than 60,000 men, and thousands more were wounded in body and in spirit. And it began to be said that one of the reasons for our losses was the Ross Rifle, which Sam Hughes continued to champion. It was Canadian. It was made here, and it was, undoubtedly, very accurate. But part of its accuracy was due to its weight, almost ten pounds, which kept it steady in your hands but was a terrible burden for a soldier who was already carrying a heavy kit into the field. And another part of its accuracy was its very precise machining, which demanded perfectly made ammunition if it were not to jam. The British munitions industry was turning out bullets by the tens of millions; the standards of precision the Ross needed did not apply to the British Lee-Enfield rifle; and the Ross was jamming, and — worse — sometimes "blowing back." Thousands of soldiers just threw it away and picked up Lee-Enfields from fallen British comrades or German weapons from fallen enemy soldiers.

At the battle of Ypres, where we lost six thousand men in just a few days, a third of the Canadian troops threw down their Ross Rifles.

Sir Sam Hughes had not developed the Ross. But he kept insisting on its excellence, against all the evidence, and thousands of Canadian soldiers (this writer's father included) came to loathe his very name.

When General Alderson, the commander of the Canadian Expeditionary force, persuaded the government to let him switch to the British Lee-Enfield, Hughes accused Alderson of cowardice and sent a copy of the accusation to Lord Kitchener. Kitchener was shocked, the King was angry, and the Duke of Connaught called for "that conceited lunatic" to be court-martialled. In fact by now, despite his very real accomplishments, almost nobody could be found to have a good word for him, and his whole organization came under increasing scrutiny. His personal appointees — and he had three or four senior military men in England each of whom thought *he* had exclusive power delegated to him by Hughes — began to quarrel. The Canadian High Commissioner in London, Sir George Perley, who despised Hughes and thought him totally vain and incompetent, took over as Minister of the Overseas Forces.

By this time Hughes really was losing his bearings. He wrote a letter to his own Prime Minister, the man upon whom he depended utterly for his position in government, accusing him of lying and of conspiracy. Borden had no choice. He fired Hughes. This time the public, on the whole, approved. The halo of heroism had been shot to ribbons by the Ross. A soldier serving in the Canadian Field Artillery wrote home, "The Mad Mullah of Canada is deposed . . . I do not like to kick a man when he is down, but I would break nine toes in kicking Sir Sam in the stomach or the face or anywhere else."

Perhaps the worst thing Hughes did, in the end, was to try to destroy his own best General, Sir Arthur Currie, by accusing him of wasting Canadian lives at Mons, the last battle of the war, which ended only with the armistice on November 11th, 1918. Perhaps it was because Currie had refused to promote Garnet Hughes, Sam's son, who had recommended Currie in the first place. That story will be told in a later volume of *The Canadians, Biographies of a Nation*. It is a sordid story, and Hughes' actions helped fuel a scandal that nearly killed a great, great general. There was, as it turns out, no evidence to support Hughes accusations. Perhaps he knew that. Perhaps it was just the last lashing out of a failed hero, a deeply disappointed man whose stability of mind, never one of his great strengths, had deserted him utterly. This man of enormous capacity and drive, of energy and invention and courage, and a deep passionate love of his country, was finished; a shell; going through the motions.

He stayed on in Parliament for almost three more years. When he knew he was dying they arranged a private train to take him back to Lindsay. He had long ago planned a huge funeral, and in the event twenty thousand people would turn out for the procession. But it was on that train, heading back to Lindsay, that the last words are recorded that seem to speak for the man. Once he was installed in his chair, and the train had pulled out of the Ottawa station, the engineer came back to the car and asked the frail old man, "Sir Sam, what speed should I go?"

"Go like hell," said Hughes.

◆ ◆ ◆

The Enigma of Sam Hughes was written and directed by Daniel Zuckerbrot, with line producer Terry Bartley and associate producer Roberto Verdecchia. Director of Photography, Andrew Binnington. Sound: Ian Challis, Margus Jukkum, Myroslav Bodnarlik. It was first telecast on February 2, 2000, and will be seen again on History Television in the spring of 2001.

ADDITIONAL READING:

R. G. Haycock, *Sam Hughes: The Public Career of a Controversial Canadian*, 1987

◇ Part Fourteen ◇

GREY OWL
The Fraudulent Environmentalist

On a soggy April day in 1938 two Canada Parks rangers in Prince Albert National Park, about 200 km north of Saskatoon, trudged through the heavy snow around the edge of Lake Ajawaan dragging a sled long enough to carry a human body. They had not heard for several days from the resident of a lonely cabin on that lake, who worked for the Parks Department. They knew he had been sick, and they were worried. While he was a real pain in the neck, this contract employee, with his heavy drinking and erratic behaviour, was also probably the most famous Canadian in the world, and unquestionably the most famous North American Indian.

Those rangers had read the sensational reports about his recent appearance at Buckingham Palace where he had shocked the protocol officers but kept King George VI and his family (including the nine-year-old future Queen Elizabeth) spellbound with his tales of the Canadian wilderness. He had talked to the young princesses passionately about his woodcraft and of the beavers whom he had befriended and written very successful books about. And he had — as he did everywhere he went — made a passionate plea for the protection of the wilderness and its inhabitants; for this man was a pioneer conservationist who had changed attitudes towards wilderness, on both sides of the Atlantic.

The rangers found his cabin a stinking mess, bottles everywhere, including a cache of dozens of bottles of extract of vanilla, which some people used to drink when the liquor stores wouldn't serve them any more. The man in the bed was racked with coughing and almost too weak to move. They bundled him up warmly and put him on the sled, and took the shivering wreck back to hospital in Prince Albert. Three days later, on April 13th he was dead.

And it was only then that those Park Rangers and indeed the rest of a very shocked world — for Grey Owl was known worldwide — would discover that he was not an Indian at all, he was not even a Canadian. He was an impostor, a very successful impostor. His son John used to call him Archie Baloney. His real name was Archie Belaney. He was a superb woodsman, a fine writer, and an accomplished naturalist. He was also a drunk and a bigamist.

Archie Belaney was the son of an unsuccessful, alcoholic Englishman who had gone to America to make his fortune, failed, and returned bankrupt to his seaside home town of Hastings (where William of Normandy had conquered the English and killed their King, Harold, eight hundred years earlier).

George Belaney had married a seventeen-year-old American girl, and brought her with him, pregnant, when he slunk back to the Sussex summer resort town. Archie was born in 1888 at a house that still stands: number 32 St. James Road, Hastings. Neither of the parents wanted the boy. They soon turned him over to George's unmarried sisters, and then disappeared.

It is not surprising that the imaginative young boy asked a lot of questions about who his parents were. The aunts were trying to raise him as a young English gent, and put him off with vague answers. Somehow the idea of his father's being in America stuck, and later he would tell his friends that his dad was travelling with Buffalo Bill Cody's Wild West Show.

That might have had a touch of credibility to it, because Buffalo Bill had, in fact, brought his show to Hastings when Archie was about fifteen. The boy had been devouring books about Indians and the American Frontier, and suddenly there was a whole troupe of honest-to-god Indians in eagle-feather headdresses riding bareback pinto ponies and shouting war cries. Archie began to dream a dream.

For a while it did not very much impede his education. He was a very bright boy, tall, good-looking in an angular way with a strong, straight nose and deep-set brooding eyes. He loved to read and began to do a little writing. He studied the piano and played more than passably. The aunts wanted him to study medicine, but Archie pleaded with them to let him go to Canada. He did not tell them that he wanted to become an Indian. The aunts, however, were not about to send him off across the Atlantic, and it is not clear whether his subsequent erratic behaviour was just the way he was, or whether he was trying to make his continued presence in Hastings uncomfortable for the maiden ladies. In any case the turning point came one summer day when he lowered a package of fireworks, with a lit fuse, down the chimney of his boss's office, where he had a summer job at the lumber works. When the fireworks exploded in the office grate the job was abruptly terminated, and apparently that was when the sisters decided that Canada might be worth a try, after all.

He got off the boat in Halifax in the spring of 1906, not quite eighteen years old. The first record we have of his finding a job is in the kitchen at the then new Temagami Inn in Northern Ontario. Before long he was volunteering to help the guides and trappers, and learning to handle a canoe. The dream was taking concrete shape.

It received considerable impetus two years later when he fell in love with Angele Egwuna, an Ojibwa girl. The Ojibwa had become one of the largest of the Algonkian-speaking peoples in North America by that time, having spread out widely from their original territorial centre near the present-day Sault Ste. Marie (they were earlier called *Les Saulteaux,* by the French). Further south they were called Chippewa, and to the west sometimes Bungi. Angele spoke Ojibwa fluently and offered to teach it to Archie. She was also an accomplished trapper and canoeist, and taught him what she knew about those disciplines as well. Perhaps jokingly Archie said that he would make a white woman out of Angele, or perhaps he thought that was what *she* wanted. But she said, No, she would make an Indian out of him. And it may have been at that point that the dream he had been harbouring, in some shapeless, undirected way, suddenly came into focus. They married, he moved in with her traditional Ojibwa family. They soon had a daughter, Agnes. Archie grew his hair long, tied behind in a long tail, and took an Ojibwa name.

Scholars translate the name, *Washa Quon Asin*, as White Beaked Owl. It is easy to see where the white might have come from, and the Belaney nose was indeed an impressive beak. Archie like, to tell white people later that the name meant "He Who Walks By Night," and then, after a while, he just settled on Grey Owl, the name by which he became famous around the world.

If he felt the least bit indebted to Angele for having transformed him into something approaching the heroic figure he had been aspiring to since childhood, he did not show it very well. Within three years he simply walked out on his wife and child, and headed west.

Biscotasing, Ontario, has a population of less than fifty now, but before World War I it was a busy little town, and Archie Belaney settled into the life of the trappers and rivermen, and tried to let on that he was an Indian. He became close to an Ojibwa named Alex Espaniel and his family, who more or less adopted him and continued his education in the ways of the wild, and let him prac- tise the language. Alex's daughter Jane would remain a friend for most of Belaney's life. She told her grandson Armand Ruffo, a poet who wrote a book called *The Mystery of Archie Belaney*, that the tall Englishman's masquerade hadn't fooled them, but in their adoptive way they "just let him go on . . . didn't pay him any mind." If the man wanted to be native, then they would help him be native.

"Native people have always adopted non-natives into their tribe," Armand Ruffo says, "into their communty . . . it wasn't anything out of the ordinary."

Gradually the English voice was edged and sculpted into the sounds of the voices of Biscotasing, the skin darkened, perhaps with some chemical help, the hair too. Archie called himself Grey Owl from time to time, but didn't insist on it with his Bisco friends. Like them he drank a lot; that was what you did in Bisco. He worked as a fire ranger in the summertime, or on the railroad, and did a bit of trapping in the winter. He moved in wth Marie Gerard, a Métis woman. They had a son, John. And then, just as he had with Angele at Temagami, he walked out on them and disappeared.

It was 1915. The War that was going to be over by Christmas, 1914, had settled down to the horrible carnage that was to continue for four slaughterous years in the mud-filled trenches of Belgium and France. Archie told the enlisting officers that he was an Indian and a crack shot. They put him in a uniform and trained him and sent him off to the Western Front as a sniper. It didn't last very long. He was wounded in the foot — some said later he did it to himself when he discovered just how dreadful trench life really was — and they shipped him back to convalesce in a military hospital in England.

By chance that hospital was on the east coast, at a Sussex town called Hastings. One day he ran into Ivy Holmes in the street. Ivy was a dancer, the daughter of friends of Archie's aunts. They renewed their friendship. Before long it had become something rather more than that, and they got married. Archie did not mention to anyone that he had a wife named Angele in Temagami and a daughter named Agnes, and a four-year relationship with a

Métis woman in Biscotasing. He told Ivy Holmes that he would go back to Canada and prepare a home for her and send for her. And indeed he did go back to Canada, but that was the last he saw of Ivy, or she of him.

It was 1917. Marie Gerard had died of tuberculosis. Their son John was living with another family, and would grow up as Johnny Jero. Archie never even went to see him. This was the boy who would later call his father "Archie Baloney." Archie stayed on in Bisco, picking up odd jobs here and there, trapping, drinking with the trappers, and learning to throw knives. That skill fascinated him, and would later get him into trouble. For now it was part of "the Indian thing," as he saw it. The Ojibwa and Cree of Bisco didn't find his "Indian thing" very endearing, especially when he started doing what he declared to be an authentic war dance. He did not know how to play the drums; the music must have been something he heard in the Buffalo Bill show or just made up. It was all wrong, offensive even. But they were tolerant people and "didn't pay him any mind."

The police did, though. Some time in 1925 he was seen throwing knives at passing trains, drunk and erratic, and they issued a warrant for his arrest, and once again Archie disappeared.

It does not, until now, seem to be shaping up as the story of a visionary conservationist who would, even after the imposture was exposed when he died, still be blessed by millions of people for his contribution to the industrialized world's awareness of the dangers of the disappearing wilderness. He just seemed, to the people among whom he lived, another drunken trapper who liked to play at being an Indian.

He went back to Temagami and moved in with Angele again, and in 1926 they had another daughter. Well, Angele had the daughter; Archie had vanished again when he discovered the pregnancy. This time he left for good. In 1925 the Ontario Government had banned trapping to non-natives. Archie was too well known to the Ontario Lands and Forests officials to try pulling his I Am An Indian stunt on them, and trapping was the one economically viable skill he had. He moved over to the Quebec side of Lake Temagami.

There was a lovely girl working as a waitress in the local hotel. Her name was Gertrude Bernard. They called her Pony, nineteen years old and strikingly good looking. She was Iroquois but had lost touch with her people's culture and was trying to make a life for herself in the white world. A pair of wealthy American tourists had been struck with her grace and beauty and natural intelligence, and had offered to finance her education at an expensive boarding school in Toronto. She had jumped at the chance.

But fate and Archie Belaney intervened. Perhaps his story up to now makes this man seem very unattractive. But a photograph of him in his forties, just a few years later reveals a tall, seriously handsome man with a kind of nobility in his face, especially when he was acting the part of Grey Owl. That part would soon completely take over his life. From his other adventures we know that women were quickly attracted to him. When we see him in the many films he would later star in for the Parks Department we can sense the charisma. When he utters the poetry, the mystic connection with the great trees and the wild things that he communicated so powerfully, then it is not possible to think that he was cynical about *that*.

When Pony first saw him he was wearing a red sash and a tall fedora pulled down over his eyes, just so, and a silk scarf. And on his hip he wore a silver-plated revolver. He was a *presence*. She had no reason to doubt that he was what he said he was: a trapper, part native. He found out she was Iroquois and told her that he would bring her back to the great wisdom and treasures of her Indian heritage. He gave her a name to go with it. Gertrude Bernard became Anahareo, and was so smitten with this soft-spoken veteran of the traplines and the woods and rivers that she gave up her chance at an education, and stayed that winter in Temagami.

In the archives of the National Film Board of Canada there is film we were able to use in the documentary, of Pony talking about her famous lover long after his death. In her sixties she was still a wonderfully attractive woman, and although she had been hurt and disappointed, there was a wistfulness about her when she spoke about the man.

"He told me that his mother was Apache and his father a Scotsman, and that they lived in Mexico. If I had ever suspected . . . his being an Englishman, I would have tumbled to a lot of things."

But instead she tumbled into his bed, and if Archie Belaney ever really loved any of the women he was involved with, those who have studied the mystery of this brilliant impostor's life agree it was Anahareo. He abandoned the other women he'd lived with; Anahareo would change his life forever.

She had never been on a trapline. She pleaded with him to take her out trapping, and struggled with the awkward, unfamiliar snowshoes, and was eager and excited as a teenager, which she still almost was, until she saw him kill a beaver.

It disgusted her. The animals would be caught by the leg in a powerful spring trap with sharp pointed jaws. The trapper would take a hatchet out of his belt and club it to death, pry open the trap and set it again and move on to the next one. She couldn't take it. Somehow she persuaded him to let her bring home two helpless kits whose parents he had killed, and she raised them in the cabin that winter. Soon Archie began to see beaver in a different way. They named the kits McGinnis and Mc-Ginty. It was a kind of love affair. In one of the early films he made for the Parks Department he talks about that time in a tone that seems to us today a touch theatrical, a little over-earnest and contrived, but at the time seems to have mesmerized his viewers:

I began to have a faint distaste for my bloody occupation. These beasts had feelings and could express themselves very well. They could talk. They had affection. They knew what it was to be happy, to be lonely. Why, they were like little people! And they must all be like that! To kill such creatures seemed monstrous. I would do no more of it.

How would they live then? As a wounded veteran he had a small army pension, but that was his only regular income. They set up a tent and charged people ten cents to see him play with the beavers. He wrote proudly to his aunts in Hastings about "my wife Anahareo" and said she was the daughter of a chief. The aunts were now in touch with Kitty Belaney, Archie's mother. After a silence and absence of some 35 years, mother and son began to correspond.

Kitty Belaney was enchanted with the letters she received from her son. Perhaps the idea of writing had always been in his mind since his schooldays. He kept notes and journals and a record of times and temperatures, and descriptions of people they met and animals and landscape and the quality of the water. Those descriptions he sent off to his mother were so lyrical that she forwarded them to the hugely popular British monthly, *Country Life Magazine*, asking wouldn't they like to publish them? Better than that, the editors commissioned an article. He sent them an essay called "The Men of the Last Frontier." The editors loved it.

Archie knew his readership, of course. He had grown up on *Country Life*. He correctly guessed that there was a romantic curiosity about Indians in the English countryside, and he decided he would be their Indian, an Indian with a message. It would revolve around the beaver, with whom he had so suddenly and revolutionarily identified. He would use the beaver as the symbol of this new vision he had of himself as the saviour of the wilderness. He told his editors that he had spoken "nothing but Indian" for 15 years, that he had been adopted by the Ojibwa, and soon he was saying that he wrote solely as an Indian, whatever that meant.

McGinty and McGinnis, the two kits whom Anahareo
had rescued on a whim, had become the focal point of
their lives. And suddenly, they disappeared. Trappers had
been seen in the area, and perhaps that is what happened
to them. Or perhaps they had reached the wander year
that all young beaver come to. But they were gone. Signing
himself Grey Owl, he wrote:

> *At last we knew that they were gone forever into the dark-*
> *ness from whence they came. And they left behind them*
> *no sign, no trace. And the aged trees whose great droop-*
> *ing crowns loomed high above our heads, omniscient in*
> *the wisdom of the ages, seemed to brood and whisper and*
> *look down upon our useless vigil in a mighty and com-*
> *passionate comprehension. For they were of the wild, as*
> *we were, the wild to which, in our desolation, we turned*
> *for a solace and a refuge, that ageless wilderness that had*
> *ever been and would, somewhere, always be, long after*
> *we had followed our little lost companions and were*
> *gone.*

He actually spoke this way in public. People drank
it in. They felt illuminated, even blessed. If the words
sounded much more like a well-educated Englishman
who was intimately acquainted with the King James Bible
than like a native Canadian who had "spoken nothing but
Indian" most of his life, no one remarked upon it, at least
not out loud. The editors at *Country Life,* having observed
the transition, may have been amused. For many whose
concept of the native Canadian still bore traces of the
French philosopher Jean-Jacques Rousseau and his notion
of the Noble Savage, it was probably comforting to feel

that under the buckskin jacket and the long hair dyed black he was "just like us."

It was now that the Parks Department got interested. They had started producing short films to promote their work, and here was the perfect spokesman. They gave him and Anahareo a cabin in Riding Mountain National Park. Five hundred metres above the Manitoba Plains, on a rolling escarpment of mixed forest and grasslands rich in lakes and swamplands, the park has plenty of beaver and about sixty other mammals, including bison and black bear. The Cree and Assiniboine peoples had first hunted there about 1,200 years ago. It had just been established as a National Park in 1929, and the Parks Department wanted to bring in tourists from all over the world to camp and explore its miles of wilderness hiking and riding trails. Grey Owl would draw them in. He was paid as a ranger, but his real job was starring in their films. Those films were sent to Canadian embassies all over the world.

There had to be beaver, of course. The new pair were called Jelly Roll and Rawhide. Grey Owl called Jelly Roll "King of the Beaver" until she got pregnant, and then it became "Queen of the Beaver." She and Rawhide would be seen by international audiences sitting up to drink milk, nuzzling Grey Owl and his "Iroquois Princess," mewing and paddling about, climbing in and out of the canoe, stealing scenes from their human friends.

Grey Owl was becoming famous.

Country Life now commissioned a book. Archie gave it the same title as that first essay, *The Men of the Last Frontier*. *The Times Literary Supplement*, as hard a marker as you can find in the world of book reviewing, said that it would be difficult to recall another record of the Great North that was so brilliantly and lovingly handled. *The Canadian Historical Review* said it was "extaordinarily vivid."

It was 1931. The Great Depression had the world in its grip, but Archie and Anahareo were doing just fine. He was invited to go lecturing with the films. That boosted the sales of the book. He discovered that he really loved writing. The next year the Parks Department moved him up to Prince Albert National Park, to Lake Ajawaan, and built him a special cabin with an entrance for the beaver who came and went like members of the family. There was plenty of money for booze now, and they both got into it with gusto. Margaret Connibear, who lived in the vicinity, remembers hearing a woman who had a cabin near them talk about some of the goings-on.

She was out in the summer kitchen and she could hear shots being fired out in the woods. It wasn't hunting season. This was strange, so she decided to go and investigate. She was about four foot ten, I think. Anyway, she went tromping out to the bush to find out what these shots were about, and came across . . . Pony, who was Anahareo, sitting on a tree stump with a rifle taking pot shots at Grey Owl's heels, chasing him, shooting just behind his heels, chasing him from tree to tree . . . And they were both drunk as skunks. She must have been a wonderful shot!

A daughter, Dawn, was born in Prince Albert. Grey Owl and Anahareo went back to the lake, and Dawn was left in Prince Albert with a foster family named Winters. But it was not like the rude abandonment that the other three children, John and Agnes and Flora, had suffered. Dawn's foster sister Margaret Winters later got to know Archie very well when he hired her to type his manuscripts, and she remembers him fairly kindly.

He always said he wanted Dawn to be brought up . . . to be like me. I was the only girl. He saw her whenever he could, and being at our place, anytime he was in Prince Albert he knew he could be with her. And Anahareo used to take her to Wascasu where he could see her there, and even up to the cabin, so he was in contact with her as much as he could, living where he did. It was no place for a child.

But the fights were becoming bitter now. Maybe the drunken pot shots were a game, but it was a dangerous game. Anahareo was an active young woman; sitting around for days when he did nothing but drink and write made her restless and resentful. "She wanted more in life than being connected to a pen," says his biographer Don Smith, of the University of Calgary. When Archie announced a speaking tour of England where he would dress as an Indian chief and unequivocally declare himself to be an Indian, she was embarrassed and angry. In her words, in that archival film:

I said, why not go as the woodsman that he was? He says, "They expect me to be an Indian. I'd stand on my head if I knew that people would listen. And besides, if the lecture was a flop I'd at least have given them a show for their money."

When Dawn was a year old, Anahareo left Archie. Armand Ruffo says that Grey Owl wrote to a friend "'We are finally broken up, as Anahareo tried to choke me for forty minutes,' or something like that."

Nursing his wounds he went off to England. They had heard about him, and read his pieces in *Country Life*. His book, *Pilgrims of the Wild*, an account of his conversion by Anahareo, was in all the libraries. His Indian act was an outstanding success. The industrial towns of northern England were desperately bleak in the middle of the Depression, and when this beautifully dressed, beautifully spoken, desperately handsome Noble Savage stepped out on the stage with a maple leaf in his hand and said, "I bring you a green leaf," there was a breath of hope in it from the new world. He would show the films of Jelly Roll and Rawhide, and himself and Anahareo as they had been, and people would forget the cold nights and the locked mills and the breadlines and the fear.

Grey Owl was now Canada's greatest celebrity, perhaps the greatest we had ever had. The publishers were ready for another book. So back he went to Ajawaan and an empty cabin. That would be the title of the next book, he decided: *Tales from an Empty Cabin*. Margaret Winters and her brother moved into a neighbouring cabin where she typed up the pages from Archie's terrible handwriting. He would stay up all night with the night-loving beaver as company, and a bottle. In the morning Margaret would tiptoe in and pick up the scattered barely legible pages. The writing would be worse towards the end of the session as the lamp burned lower and the bottle got emptier. Margaret said that perhaps Archie had been left-handed as a child, and had been forced to change to the right.

The vision was authentic though, clouded as it may have been by loneliness and drink and the masquerade. A genuine ecology pioneer, he lobbied the Parks Department to hire native Canadians as game wardens, because they would understand. He fought the development that he saw poised to contaminate and maybe destroy the wilderness that he now so deeply identified with. In a way he was his own wilderness. All around him they were measuring progress in terms of trees cut down and dams built, while he was angrily calling upon them to preserve, to treasure, to cherish. Trees spoke to him, he said. He is not the only one to have said that.

Lonely without Anahareo, he married yet again, and then again, without bothering to divorce either of his other two wives. In Ottawa he had met yet another woman, a French Canadian named Yvonne Perrier. He told her the story about the Apache mother and the Scottish father, but this time he had to be careful because there were legal records in two countries of the marriage of a man named Archibald Belaney. He invented a family of some distinction, the McNeils of Barra. He took his oath on the marriage licence that his name was Archie McNeil, and under that name he married Yvonne Perrier.

Whatever the triplicate word is for bigamist, he had become that. But it did not seem to help; his life was unravelling now, in many ways. His latest film had been shot in northern Quebec, and the producers had told the Department that he came to work drunk every morning; so they began to think it was time to bring that contract to an end.

Other things were coming to an end. His health was failing under the enormous stress, part of it from the constant watchfulness required to keep up the imposture. He was too far into Grey Owl now to tell the truth. He must have known how risky it was to be drunk so much of the time. He could not confide in Yvonne. He had created a fictional rocket that was travelling so fast now there was no way to jump off.

A year after his return from England a very curious thing happened. A reporter for the *North Bay Nugget* found Angele, and Angele spilled the beans about who Grey Owl really was. The reporter took the story to his editor, and they talked it out; the scoop of the decade, it would get the *Nugget* into every major paper on the continent, in Britain too, hell, all over the world. And they made a very strange decision. They suppressed it. They so admired what Grey Owl was saying to the world about the need to save the wilderness that they decided to protect him and his message by silence. Was it a good journalistic decision? Perhaps not; it would certainly not happen today. But the moral fibre of those two journalists is impressive. In any case, when Archie planned another British tour, for 1937, he was still safe. Or, the imposture was safe; he was in terrible shape.

Like other showmen he pulled it together brilliantly. Pushing the limits he decided to put Hastings on the itinerary, perhaps to see if anyone twigged. That is what Armand Ruffo says the motivation was. And he wanted to show off to the aunts, whom he could trust. In the event another woman, a friend from his youth, decided that

Grey Owl looked an awful lot like the Archie Belaney she had gone to school with. She asked the aunts about it. They told her everything. She agreed to keep the secret.

He himself went to see the aunts on the morning of December 15th, 1937, and took tea with them, and perhaps he even played on the old piano. They promised their discretion. They came to the White Rock Pavilion to hear him speak (that was where the other woman had recognized him). Then he bade them farewell and never saw them again.

Buckingham Palace was the high point of that last tour. The King had asked especially that the great Indian visionary come and meet his daughters. Protocol demanded that the guests be in place before the Royal Personages entered the room, but Grey Owl was feeling his oats and insisted that he come in last. Apparently the King agreed. Yvonne was introduced as the Mohawk Princess Silver Moon.

He may have begun, as he often did, by saying, "On my buckskin shirt I wear a beadwork pattern of the maple leaf, Canada's national emblem, and the emblem of a beaver, my patron beast." For three hours he held them, rapt, with his tales and his soaring rhetoric. He told them, as he told us all and we still remember, "You belong to nature; it does not belong to you." At the end of his presentation, although he had been firmly instructed to bow and to wait until Their Majesties had left, he ignored the instructions, bowed for applause, stepped quickly forward, and then stunned the stiff and correct Palace officials there present by actually touching the Royal Person. Grey

Owl put his hand affectionately on the shoulder of George VI, King of England, Scotland and Ireland, and of the Dominions Beyond the Seas, Emperor of India, and said, "I guess I'll be seeing you, brother!" Then he swept out of the room leaving everyone speechless.

Even knowing as we now do about the drunkenness and the bigamy, the violence, the abandoning of children, the lies and the masquerade, it is hard not to be charmed by the balls of it, the chutzpah, the effrontery. There is a Grey Owl Society in Hastings today, and perhaps the *North Bay Nugget's* men had not really needed to be so protective. In Hastings and anywhere else where Grey Owl is still read or otherwise remembered, it is mostly as a prophet of the wilderness and not as a fraud. Colin and Betty Taylor, who are the curators of that Grey Owl Society in Hastings, talk over each other, interrupting in their enthusiasm as they tell the Buckingham Palace story on camera.

"'I'll be seeing you!' He was a pretty easy-going fellow. I don't think he was overawed by anybody. He was pretty sure of his ground. He probably had a good stiff drink before he went to the palace."

Probably. In those last weeks, he was living on whisky and two raw eggs a day. He survived the brilliant British tour long enough to follow it up with another, in North America, where the publicity from England helped him play to huge audiences. That went on until early April. When they arrived back in Saskatchewan they were both totally worn out. Yvonne was admitted to hospital for exhaustion. Archie insisted on going back to the cabin.

Then there was silence. The rangers began to worry.

"Archie Belaney is dead," Robert Duncan wrote, at the end of his film. "But the legend and the spirit of Grey Owl live on."

The legend does indeed live on. Fraud he may have been, but it is beyond question that without Grey Owl we would be far less ready, today, to understand and respond to that authentically North American native message he left with the King: "You belong to nature; it does not belong to you."

◆　◆　◆

This episode of *The Canadians* was written and directed by Robert Duncan, with co-producers Barbara Shearer and Jonathan Desbarats. Cameras: Keith Taylor, Bill Clegg, Scott Imler, Bill Casey, Peter Walker, John Collins, Tony Zapata, Alan Ramsey; Sound: Bob McKenzie, Francois Proulx, Margus Jukkum, Bruce Cameron, Keith Henderson, Greg Van Asperan, Bill Bass. Editor, Paul Fafard. It was first broadcast on October 18, 1998 and will be seen again on History Television in the spring of 2001.

ADDITIONAL READING:

Grey Owl: *The Men of the Last Frontier* (1931); *Pilgrims of the Wild* (1934); *The Adventures of Sajo and her Beaver People* (1935); *Tales of an Empty Cabin* (1936)

Lovat Dickson: *Wilderness Man* (1973)

◇ Part Fifteen ◇

BOBBIE ROSENFELD
THE NATURAL ATHLETE

There were fifty thousand people in the stadium in Amsterdam that day, for the women's 800 metres. They knew they were in for a dramatic race. The Canadian women had already done spectacularly well in the 100 metres, and were thought to be very strong contenders for the relay. Their star 800-metre runner, Jean Thompson, was looking very good to the insiders, but then so was the American Betty Robinson, the sixteen-year-old who had taken the Gold from the Canadians a couple of days earlier, after a very controversial decision by the judges. The Japanese runner Kito was a third strong contender. The Canadian Jean Thompson was said to have injured herself, but she was still in the race so the injury could not really be serious.

It was going to be an outstanding race, all right. But not one of those fifty thousand people could have anticipated the heroic act that would transform the race into something more than a contest, and provide a display of athletic generosity virtually unheard-of in the annals of competitive sport.

It was 1928 and the first time women had been allowed to compete in track and field at the Olympics. De Coubertin, the old-school chair of the International Olympics Committee, had said that if women were to be at the Games at all, it should be just to place the laurels on the brows of the men who had won. But de Coubertin had retired. The twentieth century was taking hold. The rules had been changed, and Canada had sent a women's team. There were only six of them, compared to forty-nine male athletes, but those six women made history.

The women were Ethel Catherwood, Ethel Smith, Jane Bell, Myrtle Bell, Jean Thompson, and a funny, rangy, outspoken long-nosed Jewish kid from Barrie, Ontario, an immigrant girl of twenty-four named Rosenfeld. Her real name was Fannie, but after she had bobbed her hair when that became fashionable just a few years earlier, the flapper thing, they started to call her Bobbie and Bobbie stuck.

It was true that Jean Thompson had hurt herself. It was not serious enough to keep her out of the 800; she and the coach and the other girls knew she could run all right, and had the stuff to win. But they were worried about her morale and her confidence, and so was Jean. The spiritual and mental state of an athlete are at least as important as her physical condition, and Jean's teammates felt she needed a little extra moral support for this very demanding race. Some of them went to Bobbie Rosenfeld, who had won silver in the 100 metres against that sixteen-year-old from the States, and they said to her, "Look, it's not your distance, 800 metres, you're a sprinter, we know that. But look, you are so good at everything and it would be a boost for Jean Thompson's morale and confidence if you would enter the 800 with her, just run beside her till the final when she would do her characteristic pulling ahead thing and try to go for a medal." Bobbie was a good sport and a real team member, and of course she agreed.

In addition to the coaches and athletes, there was a solid contingent of Canadian fans at the games that summer. Post-war prosperity was at an all-time high. Except for a few gloomy economists, to whom no right thinking people paid any attention, nobody was worried at all that the financial bubble might be getting too big to last. People had money to spend and lots of them had come to the games. They were already pointing with justifiable pride at young Percy Williams from Vancouver, about to go home with not one but two Gold Medals, and the label The Fastest Man in the World (see *Part One*).

Percy Williams would be in the stand to watch the Women's 800 metres that July day in 1928, along with his coach Bob Granger. The women's team had sent him flowers when he won his second Gold; he wanted to be there to watch them and to cheer them on to a win as well.

The race started for the two Canadian women more or less as they had strategized. Jean Thompson moved into the fifth position early on, where she could run comfortably until her tactical sense told her it was time to put on the steam as they moved into the final 100 metres or so. Bobbie Rosenfeld kept a couple places back, close enough to be able to call out an encouraging word, not so close as to throw Jean off her stride; Bobbie wasn't there to win anything, just to be moral support for Jean. Jean stayed solidly in fourth place, running easily, greatly reassured by Bobbie's being right behind her. It didn't mean anything in a practical sense, but the moral effect was palpable.

Now it was time, the last two hundred metres. Jean sucked in her breath and gauged her position and where everyone else was running. Then she made her break to pull ahead. At exactly the same moment the Japanese runner, Kito, broke as well. Suddenly they bumped into each other, and Jean veered off into another lane.

Nobody was hurt. But Bobbie Rosenfeld could tell from, well, from what? From the rhythms of the other runner's limbs? From posture? From how *she* would have felt about being thrown off her stride? She sensed that Jean was fading slightly. She pulled up from sixth to fifth, a close fifth, right beside Jean, inches behind, and she hissed, "Keep going! You can do it."

And Jean Thompson recovered her morale, and her stride, and kept going.

Teammate Jane Bell, watching from the sidelines, knew that she was witness to a heroic act of giving. She said afterwards that Bobbie could easily have beaten Jean Thompson that day. But it was Jean's race, not Bobbie's; Bobbie had gone in to give her moral support, and that is what she did.

And even if she was thinking, I could pull ahead of Jean now, Jane Bell thought afterwards, *even if she was thinking Hell I could* win *this thing, I could get that gold that Betty Robinson stole from me in the 100 metres . . . even if she was thinking that . . .* she stayed back!

She stayed back, right at Jean Thompson's shoulder, at her ear. She kept saying, "Keep going. You can do it." And Jean kept going, she made fourth, a good fourth place, and Bobbie came in fifth. But it wasn't only Jane Bell who said to herself, Bobbie Rosenfeld could have won that race. People are still saying it, seven decades later. Nobody had seen anything like it before, and a lot of eyes filled with tears at the generosity of it.

Bobbie Rosenfeld was born in Russia in 1904, a time when being Jewish in that country was even worse than being Jewish in most countries at the turn of the century. Russian Jews were in constant danger of harassment, destruction of their property, and even loss of life as vandals and thugs started pogroms in the Jewish quarters at the drop of a hat, with no interference from the police and often tacit encouragement from officials. Bobbie's father went ahead to Canada and sent for his wife and the two little girls, Gertie and Fanny, as soon as he could, and over they came, little Fanny seasick all the way, and worse, with an almost fatal dose of smallpox.

They settled in Barrie, Ontario. Ontario was a pretty anti-Semitic place to live in those days, in fact. There was nothing like the overt violence of Russia, but Jews were expected to "know their place." Many professions were either closed to them or difficult to enter. There was a quota at the medical school of the University of Toronto, limiting the number of Jewish students coming in each year, but it was never referred to openly. As late as the early years after World War II, despite the transforming lessons of Nazi Germany, Jewish kids were still insulted in the streets, and young Jews wanting to get into the teaching profession would have a tough time if they had no friends in influential positions.

Max Rosenfeld opened a shop with one door on the streetside and another in the lane at the back. The sign at the front said "Antiques Sold Here," and the one at the back said "Junk Bought Here." Despite the fact that Jews, and especially immigrant Jews from Russia, were unfamiliar to most of the pretty conservative inhabitants of the small Lake Simcoe town, the business thrived and the kids made friends at school and life was a lot better than it had been back in Russia.

Fanny was not yet known as Bobbie; that would come later. Her sister Ethel Berman tells how her interest in track and field came about more or less by accident.

My sister Gertie and Bobbie went to a fairground and took their lunch, and they lost their lunch. And there was a race on and the prize was a box lunch. So Bobbie took my sister Gertie and they entered the race. And Bobbie won and dragged my sister across; so she came second. And they had two box lunches.

And young Fanny Rosenfeld realized that she was pretty fast on her feet, and that she *really liked winning.* So for the next few years she went in every race she could, and almost always won. The year she entered First Form (what we now call Grade Nine) of high school, the word got around that she was as fast as a boy. So somebody decided to put *that* silly rumour to bed. The Simcoe County Archivist Bruce Beacock tells the story with a real sense of relish.

As she became a little older and she pretty much exhausted the competition among the girls, it was not unusual for her to run against boys. And there's a famous story where the year she entered Barrie Collegiate she ran against the three top male sprinters. They graciously gave her a three-yard head start, which turned out to be a bit of a mistake because she extended the head start a little bit by the time she won the race. So, I think after a while, the male ego being what it is, she had trouble getting competition against male runners as well.

The whole school applauded when she beat those three boys. She was on the way to a new career that would be flooded with applause.

"She loved applause," Ron Hotchkiss says. Hotchkiss is a member of a pretty small specialist profession: he is a sports historian. And he believes that Bobbie Rosenfeld was perhaps the greatest athlete Canada ever produced; not the greatest woman athlete of the half-century, which she was formally declared to be in 1950, but simply . . . The Greatest.

She loved applause. She was a performer. She took strength and satisfaction from the response of the crowd. Hotchkiss says that sports helped move the outsider inside. What he means is that, for all the relative peace and prosperity of her early years in Barrie, the girl felt very strongly that she was . . . different. She was a woman in a world where women didn't do much more than marry and have kids or teach school or work in a shop. And she was a Jew and an immigrant. And she wanted to really be part of this Canadian world. Sports would make that happen.

And, adds her sister Ethel, "She was one of those people for whom, well, to win is great, but *to compete is imperative.*"

Well, there would be a lot more competition in Toronto, already a real city in 1920 when Bobbie turned sixteen and bobbed her hair in the flapper style and earned the nickname that everyone called her from then on. More competition, bigger audiences, more fun, and somehow the teenager persuaded her parents to let her go to Toronto.

She had already become interested in baseball. Before long she would move into track and field, including the shot put and the javelin. She was an outstanding lacrosse player by then. And hockey. She played for the City of Toronto's women's team, and they won the Championship two years in a row. Years later she would tell Foster Hewitt, in a radio interview, that it was a pretty rough kind of hockey.

"We played outdoors, of course, on the cushions (rinks) at Trinity Park and places like that. And we were really rugged. I remember one game, it was about 15 below zero [Fahrenheit: the equivalent of $-26°$ Celsius], and none of us realized how cold it was until I shot the puck and it hit the goalpost, and the doggone puck splintered in about 29,000 pieces."

After a while she joined the Young Women's Hebrew Association (YWHA) and played basketball with them until 1926. She would take up lawn tennis at about that time, and after less than a year at it she entered the Toronto Lawn Tennis City Championships and won the singles.

But in a way it was baseball that brought her back into serious track and field competition. In 1926 she was playing shortstop in one of those commercially sponsored little teams that were just beginning to be a popular way for small businesses to get a little publicity, Hind and Docked it was called. The manager of the team, Elwood Hughes, arranged for them to play an exhibition game in a Northern Ontario town, and as a publicity stunt put on an exhibition track meet. On the other team was the city champion sprinter Rosa Grosse. So he put up a prize for a "Hundred Yard Invitational," all comers welcome, try to beat Rosa Grosse. They would run it off before the ball game, bring a lot more spectators in, who would then stay and watch his girls play ball and see the company name on their uniforms.

He entered his outstanding shortstop, Bobbie Rosenfeld, in the Invitational, in her baseball uniform, with, as Bobbie would say, "the pup-tent bloomers." Bobbie not only beat Rosa Grosse, who was a close second, but she also came within 2/5 of a second of the women's world record for the 100 yards.

Then the famous University of Chicago team came to the CNE, and Toronto put up four girls against Chicago: Myrtle Cook, Grace Conacher, Rosa Grosse and, of course, Bobbie. The Canadians beat Chicago in the relay, and in the 100-yard dash Rosa and Bobbie were first and second.

Now the papers really began to pay attention to this incredible all-rounder. For some of the sports writers it appeared a bit unseemly that she should be so good at so many things. They began to urge her, in print, to specialize. And if there was to be a specialty, that 2/5 of a second off the 100-yard dash World's Record seemed to point to what it should be. But all the same, she was so good at baseball, for example, that people would come down to the old Sunnyside Stadium (where the Boulevard Club is now, on Lakeshore Boulevard), just to watch Bobbie Rosenfeld play baseball. Two miles east there would be men's pro ball teams playing in the old Maple Leaf Stadium, down by the ferry to the Toronto Island Airport, but there would be 1,500 to 2,000 people out at Sunnyside watching Bobbie; she was outdrawing the pros.

However, she got to thinking about that close approach to a World's Record, what it might mean. And so although she didn't give up on the hockey and the basketball — or indeed the javelin or the shot put — she really settled down to polishing the run. The starts needed work. There were really no coaches for women's track in those days, so she had to solve her problems on her own, but it would help to be in some kind of team, to have pals who were running too, trying out different rhythms and strategies and exercises. So when her boss at Paterson's Candy, realizing he had a budding star working for him, proposed forming Paterson's Athletic Club, she readily agreed to be part of it. Soon they were giving her time off to practice — and to compete — and Mr. Paterson's company name was getting a lot of ink because Bobbie just kept on winning and winning and winning.

According to sports activist Phyllis Berck, Bobbie became "as famous in her day as any pro athlete today, and as good a team player as she was an individual competitor."

And greater fame was yet to come. But the city knew Bobbie Rosenfeld now, and wasn't Mr. Paterson pleased. For Paterson's Athletic Club the long-faced girl from Barrie took five firsts for Ontario in that first year, and a trophy as best all-round woman athlete of the year. And Papa Rosenfeld would come down from Barrie to watch her run or play hockey, and when the crowd leapt to its feet to cheer for Bobbie he would shout, Ethel recalls with a grin, "Dot's mein goil!"

They ran on cinder tracks in those days. Today the tracks are all synthetics, and as far as we know the only cinder track left in Canada is at Varsity Stadium, the soon-to-disappear University of Toronto's historic sports ground. Bruce Kidd, the first Canadian to break the four-minute mile, laughingly calls it "the fastest cinder track in the world," as he talks, with wonder on his face, about the Rosenfeld versatility and style. Like Hotchkiss and Berck he sees her as being in a class by herself, unique in her capacity not just to play but to be better than anyone else in sight at all those different sports.

And the next cinder track that would beckon would be the one they were planning for Amsterdam, in the summer of 1928. The first Olympics for women runners. So the Canadian officials had to hustle to put together a women's team, and all the hopefuls who could somehow rustle up the train fare went off to Halifax to show their stuff. The judges hit their stopwatches and checked out the styles and the endurance and picked six women. Ethel Catherwood and Ethel Smith; Jane Bell and Jean Thompson (she of the 800 metres, at the start of this story); Myrtle Cook, and of course Bobbie Rosenfeld, who, in those Halifax trials, set a couple of Canadian records and a world's record as well.

Remember that although there was no television then, and radio had not yet found a way to make sports the big item it would later become, everybody read the paper, and Bobbie's face was always in the paper. People stopped her in the street to tell her how great she was. And so when the papers said that she was off to Amsterdam, while there would have been a good crowd of well-wishers to see off the women's team, our first, whoever they were, the fact that Bobbie was on it meant that thousands turned out at Union Station.

The Canadian men's team, forty-nine of them, were given rooms in a shabby little hotel, and the women in a rooming house. Those six girls went running in the streets, chasing streetcars. The mailboxes were on the backs of streetcars in Amsterdam then, and it was more fun to post your postcards on the run than it was to decorously wait for the tram to stop. And while they were seriously training and qualifying, they were going to have fun too. A popular tourist's way to see Amsterdam then was by horse and carriage. Bobbie, who still spoke Yiddish well enough to get along, found a Yiddish-speaking cabbie. She talked him into letting her take the reins and the whip while he sat back with the rest of the girls as Bobbie drove them up and down the canals and over the bridges of the famous old city.

She was entered in the 100 metres, the shot put, and the four-person relay. But there was a scheduling conflict that forced her out of the shot put; so the first event was the 100 metres. Her serious competition was a sixteen-year-old American girl named Betty Robinson. Myrtle Cook and Ethel Smith also made it to the 100-metre finals, which Bobbie won to become the official Canadian entrant for the Olympics.

Bobbie was not as fast out of the blocks as Robinson, but she paced herself well against the flying little American, and began to pull ahead in the final as she liked to do. Her teammates all believed she had won. It looked to them as though Robinson had touched the tape with her arms, which was a disqualifier. But the judges gave the race to Robinson. When the coach started over to the judges' stand with a written protest, the head of the Amateur Athletic Union of Canada, who was also an Olympic Committee official, Dr. A.S. Lamb, put a stop to it. Decorum demanded respect for the judges' decision, he declared; there would be no protest.

The athletes and historians interviewed in the documentary still sound angry at the injustice of that decision, and the failure of the Canadian officials to protest it. The photograph of the two young women hitting the tape is not perfectly clear. Are Robinson's arms touching the tape? Or just above it? The Canadian historians still say it should have gone to Bobbie Rosenfeld, but Betty Robinson, remembering her Gold with satisfaction seventy years later, said simply, "No. I won it. I was the fastest." Bobbie said at the time that it was too bad, because if she had won Gold they would have given her a synagogue when she got back to Toronto; now all she would get was a pew. That was typical of her humour.

There was one more race to run. Myrtle Cook and Ethel Smith and Bobbie had run the relay together at the Canadian National Exhibition in Toronto, the CNE; here at the Amsterdam Olympics they would get a new fourth member, Jane Bell. Myrtle wanted to be the finisher, and

Jane said she always liked chasing someone, could she run third? That left first and second, and since Bobbie was clearly the fastest she would go first, to set a lead and discourage the other teams, and that left Ethel in second place.

Historian Ron Hotchkiss tells the story with so much excitement you would think he had been there, even though it took place more than twenty years before he was even born.

The gun goes off and there was no false start and away they went. When Bobbie handed the baton to Ethel Smith, she had given the Canadians a good two-yard lead. Smith puts up the baton and extends the lead somewhat and hands it over to Jane Bell, and Jane Bell takes it and runs around the curve as she did so well and perhaps probably of the four runners she ran the best leg of the relay, but she got the baton to Myrtle just before Myrtle stepped out of the passing zone, and Myrtle grabbed the baton and sped away with Betty Robinson close on her heels. But Cook crossed the line ahead of the United States, and jumped up and down, the other runners you can see the videotape of them jumping up and down as they ran to Myrtle to embrace one another.

And Bobbie's sister Ethel Berman says, "When we heard how well she did in the relay, well of course we all needed bigger bra sizes."

And then there was that amazing act of generosity and spirit in the 800 metres; by the time they got on the boat for Montreal the Canadians were national heroes and Bobbie Rosenfeld was a living legend. The Canadian women had racked up a total of 26 points, well ahead of the Americans, and of those 26 points Bobbie Rosenfeld had 13.

Toronto went mad. Ron Hotchkiss says that there were two hundred thousand people waiting to meet the women when they got off the train at Union Station, and another hundred thousand at Sunnyside Stadium for the speeches and presentations. Crowds lined Lakeshore Boulevard all along the route to the stadium. People ran into the road to touch the athletes as they went by, slowing down the parade. When Ethel Catherwood complained about the slowdown, Bobbie, who was uncharacteristically silent, said that it was all right with her, it could last forever as far as she was concerned.

There were fireworks and speeches and the Jewish Community gave Bobbie a car. Her father built a special cabinet for all her medals and trophies, and her mother polished them "as if they were her best silver," says Ethel Berman.

But if it looked as though a lifetime of triumph lay before Bobbie Rosenfeld, tragically it was not to be. She had noticed some pain in her ankles, even before she got home from Amsterdam. For a while she probably thought it was from all that running, but it was not. Deep inside her system nature had played her a nasty trick. White blood cells, which are one of the great defences against injury and disease, had started to act perversely. They invaded the tissues around the joints in her ankles and feet in a way that caused an enzymatic reaction, in which a kind of detergent began to demolish the cartilage that cushions bone from bone. When they had finished with the cartilage, they began to eat away at the bones themselves.

And then the doctors said they would have to amputate a foot. The foot of the most spectacular female athlete the country had ever seen. The foot of a runner. Bobbie Rosenfeld was twenty-five years old.

She refused the amputation; she could not believe she wouldn't heal. She had always beat the competition, she wasn't going to give in to this one. The pain was tremendous. The medical profession did not then have the immense armamentarium of benign analgesics, anti-inflammatories or cortisone, and if she was going to keep that foot it would mean bed rest, continuous bed rest, and ice packs; and that would go on for nine months. Her mother looked after her throughout the whole anguished time.

With her indomitable spirit she was soon up again and out in the world on crutches. Her old hockey teammates invited her to come down and watch a game. When it became clear that the team was losing, Bobbie went back to the dressing room to see them all before the last period, and decided that there were worse things than the pain in her ankles. She dressed, put on a pair of skates, left her crutches in the dressing room, and went out on the ice and scored the winning goal.

Once again nobody had ever seen anything like it, and sports physician Ed Keystone, looking back on that day, says it "is what I call nothing short of a miracle."

But Bobbie Rosenfeld's days as a sprinter were done. She made a try at baseball, but she couldn't do it. She saw the dream of the next Olympics, 1932 in Los Angeles, fade like a cloud in a brilliant sky. As an athlete she was done. What had been a time in the sun that could be called nothing less than incandescent, was now a huge black hole. *National Post* Columnist Robert Fulford, who had joined the staff of the *Globe and Mail* a few years later, when Bobbie was doing a sports column there, and came to think of her as a big, loud, emphatic woman, says now that there was a melancholy about her too, a constant. "It never left the room. It was her partner."

But it did not stop Bobbie Rosenfeld. She put together the Toronto Pals, a girls' hockey team, coached them and got them to Madison Square Gardens in New York to play against the New York Wolverettes. She was still signing autographs, they still recognized her in the street, and for some reason she began to sign herself "Just a Natural: Bobbie." And her old friends say that was appropriate. Because Bobbie Rosenfeld was a natural athlete.

She moved to Montreal for a while and wrote a column for the *Montreal Gazette*, and then the *Globe and Mail* called her back to Toronto. For this writer, growing up on that newspaper, her column "Sports Reel," with her photo in curled hair and heavy lipstick, seems, in memory, to have always been there.

In the year 2000 it is not easy to conceive of a time when the idea of a famous female athlete was, well, strange. But sportswriters, historians, athletic officials and professionals looking back on those last few years of the 1920's give Bobbie Rosenfeld a substantial part of the credit for bringing women into the foreground in sports, for showing the world that women can compete just as well as men. And perhaps — although the Toronto that this writer remembers as a child was still carelessly anti-Semitic — perhaps she really did make an important dent in that shameful part of our growing up as a nation. Because everybody loved Bobbie Rosenfeld. And there was no doubt that Bobbie Rosenfeld was a Jew. And it is not really possible to be a commited anti-Semite when you are in love with a Jewish girl.

In 1950, when they named her Woman Athlete of the Half-Century, there were some who thought it should have been simply Athlete of the Half-Century. And most of the people who contributed to this fine film biography by Martin Harbury talk as though she should have been Athlete of the Century too. Bruce Beacock, in Barrie (now a city), where they still feel they *own* Bobbie Rosenfeld, says flatly, "I would challenge anybody to look objectively at the facts, and talk to people who were active at the time, to look at the number of sports she played, and played well, and *dominated* . . . and tell me that there has ever been an athlete in her class. Anywhere."

If people fell in love with her, did she fall in love? This is not entirely clear. Her sister talks of a boyfriend, another Olympic athlete, whom Bobbie might have married if he had been Jewish, but she would not marry out of the faith while her mother lived. Others talk about her living with a woman companion.

But in the end she was alone. One day when she had not answered her phone for more than twenty-four hours her sister Ethel called the Super at the apartment building, and the Super came back to the phone to say that Bobbie's newspaper was still outside the door.

She had died in her sleep. She was sixty-five. Today, Jane Bell, who ran that third position in the relay at Amsterdam seventy-two years ago, said at the time that a part of herself had died too. They were no longer a team. Bobbie had been the glue that held the team together. The Natural Athlete.

◆　◆　◆

The Natural Athlete was written and directed by Martin Harbury, with Carrie Madu as line producer. Michael Savoie was Director of Photography, sound by Hugo Bugg, and editing by Peter Shatalow. The program was first telecast on January 26, 2000, and will be seen again on History Television in the spring of 2001.

◇ Part Sixteen ◇

TOM THOMSON
THE REAL MYSTERY

On a chilly spring day in 1913 a man stepped off the train at a tiny station called Joe Lake carrying a backpack, a small wooden case and a fishing rod. It was his first visit to a part of Ontario that would not only change his life, but also affect ever after the way in which Canadians see their own country.

Almost three hundred kilometres north of Toronto there is a largely uninhabited tract of land nearly 8,000 square kilometres in area. Its rolling topography ranges across the southern limits of the Canadian Shield between Georgian Bay and the Ottawa River. It is mostly Precambrian granite — some of the oldest rock in the world — granite that was polished in some places, pitted and scarred in others, when the ice sheet that once covered it receded about ten thousand years ago. It is called Algonquin Provincial Park.

There are some 2,500 lakes in the park, many of them linked by rivers, which give paddlers 1,500 kilometres of canoeing and portaging. Hunting is forbidden. Logging is controlled in 90 per cent of the Park, although in the 21st century that control has become far too lenient for most conservationists.

From the time of its founding in 1893 until the end of World War II, it was almost pure wilderness, though by no means in a pristine state of nature. Logging operations had left it with thin, poor soil, and a harsh climate, and many forest fires gave the Park a varied and changing second growth forest: red and white pine, spruces, birch and poplar. Wolves patrol throughout. Canoe trippers around their campfire at night will, if they are lucky, be treated to the spectral symphony of a wolf howl that is picked up by another voice from another direction and then another, until sometimes the whole sky seems to resonate with the long, eerie wails.

Deer and bear are common. Driving the road that cuts through the southern sector, providing a route from Huntsville to Ottawa, travellers can stop and watch moose calmly grazing by the roadside, apparently confident that they will not be shot.

By 1945 the few Fire Rangers' towers and their accompanying cabins were decaying, as the fire patrol had gone airborne out of a float-plane base on Smoke Lake, in the southern sector of the park. The Park was served by rail until about 1960. There was a hotel and a store at Joe Lake, a few kilometres inside the east boundary, and another at Smoke Lake about ten kilometres further along. There are a few commercially operated summer camps for children. One of them, Camp Ahmek on Canoe Lake, has been host to a number of boys who later became prominent in Canadian public life. Our Prime Minister for close to fifteen years, the late Pierre Trudeau, was seen by millions of Canadians in a television biography that was rebroadcast after his death in 2000, paddling with the distinctive Ahmek Stroke, the upper hand never rising above the chin line, pushing straight ahead on the stroke, the boat heeled sharply to the paddling side, the gunwale only a couple of inches above the water.

On a couple of the roadside lakes there are a few cottages now, mostly with fixed-time leases from the province. Apart from that it is a wilderness that has given Canada some of its most defining images. A painter named Tom Thomson brought those images into focus more than anyone else — first for other painters, then for the world.

There are two mysteries about Tom Thomson. In the summer of 1917 his body was found in Canoe Lake with his feet trussed in copper fishing line and a wound on his head. Inexplicably, the coroner called it drowning. But people have not stopped speculating about what really happened.

The mystery of his death, however, is overshadowed by the mystery of his life. Until the last five years of that life he seemed unremarkable, a journeyman commercial artist and engraver, whose work was skilled but undistinguished. Yet in those last five years, between the ages of thirty-five and forty, it was suddenly clear to his fellow artists that they were in the company of genius. And then he was gone, leaving us with a vision of our land that has legendary power.

Tom's British grandparents immigrated to Canada in the 1830's, and eventually moved to a 150-acre farm near Claremont, Ontario. The farmhouse today looks much as it did when Tom's father John Thomson was born in it in 1840, and when Tom himself was born in it in 1877.

Joan Murray, an art historian and Director Emerita of the Robert McLaughlin Gallery, is writing the Tom

Thomson Entry for the new edition of the *Canadian Encyclopaedia*, and has published a book entitled *Tom Thomson's Trees*. She has been fascinated for years with the Tom Thomson story.

When Thomson was only a few months old he and his family moved to the Leith area. His father was rather a character. Apparently he carried money from the sale of the house in Claremont, with him in a sack. And when he saw a farm that he thought appropriate, he stopped the carriage, got out with his sack of money, and bought the farm for cash.

That old farm is still there. The house still stands on a rise just north of Owen Sound, on the shores of Georgian Bay. The present-day picture we see of that house in the documentary is easily recognizable as the house in the family photos from the late nineteenth century.

Tom's childhood there was a happy one. There is a treasury of early photographs in the documentary. As a boy he had a smooth, round, almost angelic face but with a touch of curiosity and humour peeping out. The eyes in those photos are almost always contemplating the lens, and they are powerful, almost spiritual eyes. There is a lock of hair hanging down over the right side of his forehead.

He was the sixth of nine children, all of them talented to some degree, and almost all of them musical. Tom himself played cornet and violin, and his favourite, the mandolin. His father liked to sketch, and Tom soon began to do puzzle caricatures, meaning that they were designed to get people to guess who they represented.

Although he had weak lungs from childhood, he developed a profound love of the out-of-doors, and in this he was strongly encouraged, Joan Murray told us, by a distinguished relative.

There was one great man in the family, Dr. William Brodie, that's Tom's cousin. A true, truly great biologist of the period. Before Dr. Brodie died he was . . . head of the biological section at The Royal Ontario Museum. He died in 1909, and he was the most distinguished biologist of his day . . . a true scientist and a wonderful man. He used to take the children on Saturday morning walks which extended for miles, and he would name the plants, and speak of philosophy and speak of poetry. . . . Our Tom Thomson . . . collected specimens for Dr. Brodie.

For a while Tom even considered becoming a professional naturalist. He gave his parents a drawing he called *Nature's Peace.* He wrote on it: "Be glad of life because it gives you the chance to love, to work and to play, and to look up at the stars. Spend as much time as possible, with body and with spirit, in God's out-of-doors."

In 1899 at the age of 22 he volunteered for the expeditionary force going off to South Africa to fight in the Boer War. His lungs were not up to the training and although he tried three times to enlist he never made it. He tried apprenticing as a machinist at the Kennedy Foundry in Owen Sound, but was often late, did not get along with the boss, and was fired after less than a year. According to Joan Murray, despite the apparently vigorous cultural life at home, Tom's school days had been as unsuccessful as his industrial apprenticeship.

He actually never completed grade school. He never went to high school. [He went to] a little business college in Chatham . . . Canada Business College . . . and Thomson was good at penmanship. . . . His brother George [who had also gone there] went ahead to Seattle and started his own business college, and [Tom] went there too.

Brothers Henry and Ralph were also in Seattle when Tom arrived in 1901. His first job was elevator operator at the Hotel Diller. Then he did design work for George's business school, a poster, a newspaper advertisement and a business card. These he took around to commercial art firms in Seattle as samples of his work, and began to get some assignments. Evenings he and George would go to the theatre or to a concert, or visit friends with the mandolin for an evening of homemade music. The Seattle photographs show an almost overwhelmingly handsome young man, his nose now much sharper than in the boyhood photographs, the eyes still dark and compelling, the lock of hair over the forehead almost a trademark. Sometime in 1903 or 1904 he met Alice Lambert, a woman eight or nine years his junior. Joan Murray tells what happened next.

He decided to marry her and he proposed . . . outside the boarding house, and he said the words [and] she was so nervous — it's the stuff of movies — she was so nervous she giggled. Now Tom Thomson had a very thin shell. . . . He was shocked. . . . He turned on his heel, went back to the boarding house where he roomed, packed his bag and left Seattle. And he never wrote her or spoke to her again.

Joan Murray showed us her copy of a book by Alice Elinor Lambert, who became a successful writer. Two of her novels are still available via the Internet. In *Women Are Like That* (1934) she wrote of a fictional character:

> *For one disturbing year she had been desperately in love with a tall dark boy named Tom, a commercial artist who in the summer used to take her on streetcar rides to Alki Point. . . . He had gone East. The girl, unversed as she was in the art of pursuit, had let him go, powerless to hold him, or call him back. . . . Years later, when she learned that he had been drowned while on a sketching trip in the North, a section of her heart had sealed up, never again to open.*

When he came back to Toronto in 1905 the tall dark boy went to work as a senior designer for Legge Brothers. He was twenty-eight. From time to time he jumped on the train on a Friday afternoon and went to visit his parents in Owen Sound. He began seriously sketching in the out-of-doors too, particularly up the shallow reaches of the Humber River just west of the city.

> *That's when he decided to become an artist* (Joan Murray recounts). *He had no thought of it earlier. . . He went to school at night and he learned to draw . . . in a painting class by a wonderful teacher named Cruikshank . . . One of his early works . . . is just like an amateur sketch, but . . . Cruikshank . . . the great man, spoke to him and said, "Did you do that?" and Thomson said he did. And Cruikshank said, "Well, you better keep on."*

That was 1906. A.Y. Jackson, one of the founders of the Group of Seven, said that Cruikshank was "a cantankerous old snorter" when Tom was studying with him at the Ontario College of Art.

A painting of a man with a pair of horses, the man's back to us, survives from that period. While it is competent it is completely without interest and foreshadows nothing of what was to come. Soon he moved over to Grip Limited, a design firm whose name survived into the late twentieth century as part of Rapid Grip and Batten. They were typesetters, an industry that vanished overnight a decade ago, when the computer age made obsolete the setting of type by pouring hot lead into molds.

At Grip Limited Tom met a group of artists who would change his life, as he would theirs. Arthur Lismer was at Grip then, and so were Frederik Horsman Varley, Franklin Carmichael, Franz Johnson, and J.E.H. Mac-Donald, four of the seven painters who would form the famous Group of Seven in 1920. He appears to have lost some of the impatience and erratic behaviour that had often brought him trouble in earlier jobs. He seemed to feel at home here. The artists at Grip liked him immediately, and later talked of him as a quiet man, easy company. They praised his landscape painting too, and encouraged him to keep on working at it. Lismer and Varley made some playful pen-and-ink sketches of their new friend, which survive. They encouraged him to take a look at the wilderness north of Toronto, as a stimulus for the landscape painting. And so he boarded that train in July 1912, for the Canoe Lake Station, just above the dam at the north end of Canoe Lake.

Eighty-eight years later the director of our biographical documentary invited Toronto artist John Fraser to go to Canoe Lake, to see that landscape today through the eyes of the Tom Thomson of 1912. John Fraser is a versatile artist who works on computer images more than with paint these days. He has an impressive ability to paint like other painters, and on an afternoon in the autumn of 2000, he set up an easel on the shore of Canoe Lake and demonstrated the Thomson technique and style. John Fraser knows the lake well, and is a skilled paddler, like the man whose work he was reproducing with uncanny verisimilitude.

He said, as he painted for the camera,

Tom's work has a very strong sense of the subject, a very strong sense of the environment he's in moving through him and onto the canvas. It was a moving, active process. It was definitely . . . the painting was a verb, it was not a noun. He tended to work on a birch panel. It would be pre-oiled . . . so that the paint would ride really nicely over the surface. . . .The colours I'm working with here are the same ones that he would have had back then. And this is a conventional oil palette. Some of the colours we have today didn't exist back then. I have enough paint on the brush where the paint is actually delivering itself. I'm really not letting the brush influence. As much as I can I'm just trying to keep enough paint on the brush that the paint will just sort of onload itself on the existing wet paint underneath, and that's what keeps it fairly alive.

As Fraser works, what appears to be a Tom Thomson painting takes shape on the panel in front of him.

He worked overhand, a good distance from the painting. He didn't get caught up in details. He . . . was involved with the colour, the play of the light. I'm now going to go with the burnt umber and the ultramarine blue which was the classic way in which the Group of Seven and Tom Thomson . . . made black. They never used black [from the tube], black was absolutely a no-no. The colours themselves were not mixed too heavily together, they were sort of loosely folded *together so that the original quality of the colour would be able to come through. . . . The idea is to have a folding together of the complementary colours so that they work together and [convey] a sort of light and a shadow at the same time.*

Tom was seen by his artist friends at Grip Limited as a kind of natural, according to Dennis Reid, Chief Curator of the Art Gallery of Ontario:

He was understood by his contemporaries to be somebody who was essentially untrained and who responded in a very natural way to the Canadian landscape . . . somebody who essentially sprang from the soil. . . . And they saw this as being the essence of genuineness. So he was authentic. . . .

Joan Murray adds:

They all liked Thomson and they lent him the studio on the weekend, Grip premises . . . because he had no place to paint. And everyone took a hand in teaching him. . . . Varley apparently took the brush from his hand to help him show certain areas in a painting.

That painting may have been a canvas based on sketches he made that first wilderness summer of 1912. He had gone from Algonquin Park along the Spanish River to the Mississagi Forest Reserve between July and September, with a painter named William Broadhead.

When he came back one of the sketches, *Northern Lake,* so impressed his artist friends that they persuaded him to work it up into a full-size canvas. The Province of Ontario bought the work for $250. As Tom was earning 75¢ an hour at Grip Limited, that was the equivalent of about two months' salary.

In the fall of 1913 Lawren Harris, a painter who became famous both for stark paintings of the north country and for homey views of Toronto streets, was developing studio and living quarters for artists to share in, The Studio Building, at 25 Severn Street. Their sponsor was Dr. James MacCallum, who would also become Tom's sponsor. The Studio Building was soon full, and Tom set up a combination studio and living space in what had been a construction shack. In the fall of 1914, Dennis Reid says, the other artists were beginning to look on Tom's work as something *they* could learn from.

> *They all went up to Algonquin Park and there was very much a sense of Tom introducing them to the Park. They were all there together. [A.Y.] Jackson wrote back to Dr. MacCallum, who was patron to all of them . . . "Tom's making great strides." . . . I think each one of them felt that they had a hand in directing him along, in bringing him out. So it's an unusual relationship . . . they felt like the parents in a certain sense, but then they somehow ended up feeling like progeny.*

Now he would go to the Park every year. Another "Northern" painting, *Northern River,* one of his most famous, its foreground laced with the naked branches of swamp spruce, sold for $500 in 1914. His confidence was soaring. James Marsh, who wrote about Thomson for the *Canadian Encyclopaedia*, said, "His work now had the smash and stab of passion without thought." The big canvases are the traditional form that makes a painter's name. But Dennis Reid says he is convinced that the sketches were more important than those forty canvases.

I mean there are aspects of The West Wind, *that great icon, that are clearly unresolved. So I don't think he was . . . right there . . . in terms of his canvases. But his oil sketches, he was entirely comfortable with them as a vehicle. There was a strong sense of development in them, every time he went out. I think people sense that when they confront them. I think people also sense that these were very direct responses to a moment, to a place, a time. And so there is a sense of actuality, a sense of being there that is magical . . .*

Important though they were, he often gave them away or sold them for a few dollars. If he liked a motif in one, he would take it into the studio and develop a canvas from it; he was responding to that tradition. It is possible that he himself did not recognize the power of those birch panels.

There are emotionally powerful photographs of him from those days in the Park, not painting but paddling or fishing or showing off his catch. Nearing forty his always good-looking face had become intensely handsome. There is a serenity in the strong eyes when they gaze at you, and in the comfortable angles of the body as he stands on the river bank contemplating something we cannot see. The strong forelock is still hanging down like a slash over the right side of the forehead. He is usually clean-shaven, sometime smoking a pipe.

He was perfectly at home in the canoe. The theory was circulated later that he had fallen out of his canoe while standing up to haul in a fish, which got him all tangled up in the copper fishing line. It is an absurd idea, as any paddler knows who has half Tom Thomson's skill and experience. Perhaps somebody was trying to justify the "Death by Drowning" verdict from the Coroner, but it rings false. Thomson was in his canoe for months at a time. When he was paddling, it almost looked as if the small craft were an extension of his tall, capable frame.

In Europe and America, in the years leading up to the Great War, there had been a yeasty ferment of painterly innovation. Tom Thomson was only fleetingly interested. The cubists, the post-impressionists, and the non-objectivists, were redefining the art world, it seemed, almost every year. Tom was redefining the world inside his head and out there in the wilderness. While he may have lost an opportunity to grow and prosper artistically from the stimulus of these European and American movements, critics now say that it was that very freedom from any of the demands of artistic fashion that allowed him to develop the style that now speaks to most Canadians as if it were *the* Canadian style.

Joan Murray said, "He seemed to see around the edges of the land . . . the land kind of extends beyond the painting."

When war broke out in the summer of 1914 Tom tried again to enlist and again was refused. A.Y. Jackson and Fred Varley would go overseas as War Artists; Tom would head back up to the Park with his knapsack, fishing rod and paint kit. The tree that served as the model for *Jack Pine* is pointed out today as an almost bare-branched wreck, still there on the shores of Canoe Lake. Whether or not it is the actual tree, visitors still come to stare at it. The spirit of Tom Thomson is palpable on that lake. There is a cairn to his memory at the north end, on a point thrusting out into the water, with an inscription by his friend Jim MacDonald:

> *He lived humbly but passionately with the wild and it revealed itself to him. It sent him out from the woods only to show these revelations through his art, and it took him to itself at last.*

This writer met a professional guide on Canoe Lake in the summer of 1949 who quite seriously told about portaging into the Oxtongue River, just south of Canoe Lake, from a day's fishing in Drummer Lake, two or three miles west of the river. He said he was carrying his canoe at night with a storm lantern hanging from a thwart to light his way. He saw a man carrying a grey canoe coming towards him on his way into Drummer, and stepped aside to let the man pass. At that moment, Hopkins swore, the man and the grey canoe vanished. "I know who it was," Hoppy Hopkins said. Somewhat spooked by that story, a few weeks later, when I was paddling up the lake at five o'clock in the morning, I was terrified for a moment to see out of the corner of my eye a man paddling beside me, matching me stroke for stroke, in absolute silence. For a moment *I knew who it was, too.* But then I realized it was my moonshadow on the wall of fog rolling out of the bay that bisects Camp Ahmek, where I was working at the time. I used that story to open my novel *Ahmek*, in which Tom Thomson plays a major role. Almost everyone I ever met on Canoe Lake had some kind of story about Tom Thomson. Mark Robinson, who had been the Park's Chief Ranger when Tom was painting there, almost ninety when I knew him, loved to tell the boys at Ahmek about the time Tom asked him where he could find "a buncha birches, shaped just so," that he wanted to paint and did not want to invent. The boys sniggered a bit about Old Mark and his Buncha Birches, but they were excited all the same to have met a man who actually knew Tom Thomson.

Much of the power of that *presence* on Canoe Lake flows from the belief that Tom Thomson was murdered, and the mystery attached to that murder since he was so liked and admired. There was talk about a ferocious argument the night before he vanished, an argument about the war with a German named Martin Bletcher. There was talk about a fight with another man, Shannon Fraser, over money, or perhaps over a woman.

Here are the bare bones of the story. He had been seeing a woman named Winnifred Trainor whose family had a nearby cottage. Winnifred is said to have said there was a reason they should get married, and Joan Murray, among others, has speculated that Winnifred may have been pregnant. At about this time, on July 8, 1917, Tom went off alone on a fishing trip. The next day Martin

Bletcher told neighbours that he had seen an overturned canoe on the lake, and when found two days later it was identified as the Thomson canoe. It was a week before they found the body, the feet tangled in fishing line, the head badly bruised.

Joan Murray tells another story about Thomson's last night, which he had spent at a hotel called Mowat Lodge.

We may imagine that Thomson had a few drinks. And his friends did. And somehow he approached one of the friends he'd lent money to. . . . And he must have appeared threatening to this man because apparently this man punched him and Thomson fell backwards and hit his head on the grate.

The Coroner's report said later that he had a four-inch bruise on his right temple. So that man panicked. His name was Shannon Fraser. He was the postmaster of Algonquin Park and he was the owner of the Mowat Lodge, which was the hotel where Thomson stayed during inclement weather. And that man panicked and asked his wife to help him. Her name was Annie. They packed the canoe apparently with Thomson's body. They tied fishing line around his wrists and feet, and put him overboard in Canoe Lake. And that is Annie's story. She told a girl-friend named Daphne Crombie. And Annie told this story a second time on her death-bed, made a death-bed confession to a friend.

Our documentary crew found and filmed the cross that marks where Tom Thomson was buried in the small cemetery on the west side of Canoe Lake. After a few months the family had the coffin disinterred and shipped home. There was a rumour that the coffin contained stones, not a body. Dennis Reid shares the puzzlement that every student of the Thomson story feels.

In fact what happened, it is just all speculation. Other than the fact that he certainly seems to have died suddenly and at the hands of another. The family had the body disinterred from the grave at Algonquin Park in which it was first placed, and brought back to . . . Leith and buried there. A curious Justice of the Peace, Judge Little, took it upon himself to probe the grave at Algonquin Park, and found remains in the grave still. Because of his connections he was able to take them to the forensic clinic in Toronto here and they were examined and it was determined that the head was probably a Cree.

That skull, as shown in the documentary, also appears to have a fracture in the temple. What had killed this native Canadian, if indeed he was a Cree? And how did he end up in Tom Thomson's grave? The family have refused to have the body exhumed from the family plot for forensic tests. The mystery may never be resolved.

And the mystery about the late surfacing of the brilliant and innovative painter, whose artist friends found suddenly that instead of teaching him they were learning from him? It is not an unheard-of change of direction. Every great artist has been an apprentice who almost always outshone his or her teachers. The great Artemisia Gentileschi, heroine of *The Obstacle Course*, Germaine Greer's pioneering work on women painters, was a student of her very successful portrait-painting father. By the time she was a young adult all of Rome was seeking her out for portraits, instead of commissioning the father who had taught her. Rembrandt had his teachers and examplars, and so did De Kooning and Lucian Freud. What is different in the case of Tom Thomson is that the great ability took so long to surface — perhaps it was just hiding there, waiting for the teachers he should have had twenty-five years earlier. There were about five hundred of the little birch panel sketches when he died, but only forty canvases. While a canvas sold in 1914 for $500, you would be lucky to get it today for a million dollars. The sketches, on the rare occasion when one is sold, are valued at well over $100,000.

J.E.H. MacDonald wrote once that "Tom was never very proud of his painting, but he was very cocky about his fishing." But, "Without Tom the North Country seems a desolation of brush and rock." A.Y. Jackson wrote; "My debt to him is almost that of a new world."

That seems to be what most feel who study this man's legacy, that he helped us to see our land with new eyes. He brought to Canadians a vision of our own skies and lakes, our rocks and trees, a vision that had little to do with the heritage of another culture. It was not the European visitor, sophisticated and wise in the ways of paint on canvas. It was not the powerful vision of the West Coast native sculptors with their magical merging of the animal and the human, or of the Eastern woodland native painters with their brilliant mythic panels. It was the view of the newcomers to Canada, the children of immigrants still feeling a bit fresh and amazed at the vastness and still fascinated with the pure unmediated *surfaces* of a land that their First Nations' predecessors had long since transformed into a vision that goes far below the surface into deep spiritual meanings.

◆   ◆   ◆

The Mystery of Tom Thomson will be broadcast for the first time on February 21, 2001. It was written and directed by Daniel Zuckerbrot, with Andrew Binnington as Director of Photography and Ian Challis on sound. The editor was Allan Gibb, and Associate Producer Roberto Verdecchia.

ADDITIONAL READING:

Harold Town and David B. Silcox: *Tom Thomson*.

Joan Murray: *Tom Thomson's Trees*, McArthur & Company

COVER PHOTO CREDITS

1. Bible Bill at Desk (William Aberhart). — Glenbow Archives, Calgary (NA-4454-3)
2. Grey Owl w/ Baby Beaver. — Glenbow Archives, Calgary (NA-4868-211)
3. Pauline w/Feather Boa. — Courtesy of The Brant County Museum & Archives
5. Sam Hughes. — Courtesy of The National Archives of Canada (PA20240)
6. Thomson Portrait. — Courtesy of The National Archives of Canada (PA121719)
7. Wop in Stunt Plane. — Courtesy of Denny May
8. Northrop Frye. — Courtesy of Tom Sandler
9. Ben Dunkelman. — Courtesy of Yael Dunkelman collection.
10. Pauline /SM. — William Ready Division of Archives and Research Collections McMaster University Library, Hamilton, Ontario